Palgrave Studies in Religion, Politics, and Policy

Series Editor
Mark J. Rozell
Schar School of Policy and Government
George Mason University
Arlington, VA, USA

This series originated under the co-editorship of the late Ted Jelen and Mark J. Rozell. A generation ago, many social scientists regarded religion as an anachronism, whose social, economic, and political importance would inevitably wane and disappear in the face of the inexorable forces of modernity. Of course, nothing of the sort has occurred; indeed, the public role of religion is resurgent in US domestic politics, in other nations, and in the international arena. Today, religion is widely acknowledged to be a key variable in candidate nominations, platforms, and elections; it is recognized as a major influence on domestic and foreign policies. National religious movements as diverse as the Christian Right in the United States and the Taliban in Afghanistan are important factors in the internal politics of particular nations. Moreover, such transnational religious actors as Al-Qaida, Falun Gong, and the Vatican have had important effects on the politics and policies of nations around the world. Palgrave Studies in Religion, Politics, and Policy serves a growing niche in the discipline of political science. This subfield has proliferated rapidly during the past two decades, and has generated an enormous amount of scholarly studies and journalistic coverage. Five years ago, the journal Politics and Religion was created; in addition, works relating to religion and politics have been the subject of many articles in more general academic journals. The number of books and monographs on religion and politics has increased tremendously. In the past, many social scientists dismissed religion as a key variable in politics and government. This series casts a broad net over the subfield, providing opportunities for scholars at all levels to publish their works with Palgrave. The series publishes monographs in all subfields of political science, including American Politics, Public Policy, Public Law, Comparative Politics, International Relations, and Political Theory. The principal focus of the series is the public role of religion. "Religion" is construed broadly to include public opinion, religious institutions, and the legal frameworks under which religious politics are practiced. The "dependent variable" in which we are interested is politics, defined broadly to include analyses of the public sources and consequences of religious belief and behavior. These would include matters of public policy, as well as variations in the practice of political life. We welcome a diverse range of methodological perspectives, provided that the approaches taken are intellectually rigorous. The series does not deal with works of theology, in that arguments about the validity or utility of religious beliefs are not a part of the series focus. Similarly, the authors of works about the private or personal consequences of religious belief and behavior, such as personal happiness, mental health, or family dysfunction, should seek other outlets for their writings. Although historical perspectives can often illuminate our understanding of modern political phenomena, our focus in the Religion, Politics, and Policy series is on the relationship between the sacred and the political in contemporary societies.

More information about this series at
http://www.palgrave.com/gp/series/14594

Sabrina P. Ramet
Editor

Orthodox Churches and Politics in Southeastern Europe

Nationalism, Conservativism, and Intolerance

Editor
Sabrina P. Ramet
Department of Sociology
and Political Science
Norwegian University of Science
and Technology
Trondheim, Norway

Palgrave Studies in Religion, Politics, and Policy
ISBN 978-3-030-24138-4   ISBN 978-3-030-24139-1 (eBook)
https://doi.org/10.1007/978-3-030-24139-1

© The Editor(s) (if applicable) and The Author(s), under exclusive license to Springer Nature Switzerland AG 2019
This work is subject to copyright. All rights are solely and exclusively licensed by the Publisher, whether the whole or part of the material is concerned, specifically the rights of translation, reprinting, reuse of illustrations, recitation, broadcasting, reproduction on microfilms or in any other physical way, and transmission or information storage and retrieval, electronic adaptation, computer software, or by similar or dissimilar methodology now known or hereafter developed.
The use of general descriptive names, registered names, trademarks, service marks, etc. in this publication does not imply, even in the absence of a specific statement, that such names are exempt from the relevant protective laws and regulations and therefore free for general use.
The publisher, the authors and the editors are safe to assume that the advice and information in this book are believed to be true and accurate at the date of publication. Neither the publisher nor the authors or the editors give a warranty, expressed or implied, with respect to the material contained herein or for any errors or omissions that may have been made. The publisher remains neutral with regard to jurisdictional claims in published maps and institutional affiliations.

Cover illustration: Paul Biris/Getty Images

This Palgrave Macmillan imprint is published by the registered company Springer Nature Switzerland AG
The registered company address is: Gewerbestrasse 11, 6330 Cham, Switzerland

For L.A.

Preface

When compared to the Catholic and Protestant Churches of various denominations, Orthodox Churches have retained the loyalty of larger proportions of their respective national populations and have remained more uniformly conservative and more connected to nationalism. Of course, one can look to Poland, Croatia,[1] and Slovakia[2] for examples of post-socialist states where declared religiosity among Catholics remains high (above 80% in the cases of Poland and Croatia). But a wide-ranging survey conducted by the Pew Research Center in 2015–2016 in seven post-socialist countries found that belief that there is a God was highest in Romania, Bosnia–Herzegovina, and Serbia, followed by Croatia and Poland (tied for fourth place). Where tolerance of homosexuality was concerned, the percentage of people who felt that homosexuality was morally wrong was highest in Romania (82%), Bosnia–Herzegovina (81%), Serbia (69%), and Bulgaria (58%), with somewhat lower figures in Croatia (49%) and Poland (48%).[3] Even more striking perhaps is the fact that while declared religiosity declined somewhat in Poland in the years 1991–2015, from 96% in the earlier year to 87% in 2015, in Bulgaria the proportion of adults describing themselves as Orthodox Christians actually rose from 59% in 1991 to 75% in 2015.[4]

The question arises how to account for the tendency in Orthodox countries to maintain higher levels of religiosity than Catholic countries. A comparison of rates of religiosity with rates of urbanization, education, and intolerance of homosexuality is revealing (Table 1).

Table 1 Rates of religiosity, urbanization, education, homophobia (2015–2016)[a]

	Belief in God	% homophobic	Education[b]	% urbanization
Romania	95	82	3.1	54
Bosnia–Herzegovina	94	81	N/A	48.2
Serbia	87	69	3.9	56.1
Bulgaria	77	58	4.1	75
Hungary	59	53	4.6	71.4
Croatia	86	49	4.6	56.9
Poland	86	48	4.8	60.1
Czechia	29	21	5.8	73.8

[a]Rates for belief in God and homophobia derived from the Pew study, 2015–2016. Other figures derived from the CIA World Factbook on 7 April 2019 and reflected the latest data
[b]Proportion of the GDP spent on education

What is immediately apparent is that there is a 100% correlation between belief in God and the conviction that homosexuality is morally wrong as well as an inverse correlation with the percentage of GDP spent on education. In other words, the better educated people are, the less likely they are to believe in God and the more likely they are to be accepting of homosexuality. By contrast, the level of urbanization is a less certain guide, even if the country with the highest rate of urbanization, the Czech Republic, is also the least religious and the most tolerant of homosexuality.

There have been a number of volumes devoted to the Orthodox Church published in recent years, among them two edited by Lucian Leustean, who has contributed the afterword to this volume.[5] It is our collective hope, nonetheless, that, by focusing on the themes of conservatism, nationalism, and intolerance, we may shed some additional light on the world of Orthodoxy.

Saksvik, Norway   Sabrina P. Ramet
April 2019

Notes

1. "Religious Belief and National Belonging in Central and Eastern Europe," *Pew Research Center*, 10 May 2017, at http://www.pewforum.org/2017/05/10/religious-belief-and-national-belonging-in-central-and-eastern-europe/ [last accessed on 7 April 2019].
2. Kelsey Jo Starr, "Once the Same Nation, the Czech Republic and Slovakia Look Very Different Religiously," *Pew Research Center*, 2 January 2019, at https://www.pewresearch.org/fact-tank/2019/01/02/once-the-same-nation-the-czech-republic-and-slovakia-look-very-different-religiously/ [accessed on 7 April 2019].
3. "Religious Belief and National Belonging."
4. Ibid.
5. Lucian Leustean (ed.), *Eastern Christianity and the Cold War, 1945–91* (London: Routledge, 2010); and Lucian Leustean (ed.), *Eastern Christianity and Politics in the Twenty-First Century* (London: Routledge, 2014).

Contents

1 The Orthodox Churches of Southeastern Europe:
  An Introduction 1
  Sabrina P. Ramet

2 Faith, Nation, and Structure: The Diachronic Durability
  of Orthodox Churches in the Balkans 15
  David B. Kanin

3 Conservative Orthodoxy in Romania 41
  Lucian Turcescu and Lavinia Stan

4 The Bulgarian Orthodox Church: Authoring
  New Visions About the Orthodox Church's Role
  in Contemporary Bulgarian Society 53
  Daniela Kalkandjieva

5 The Church, the Nation, and the State: The Serbian
  Orthodox Church After Communism 85
  Jelena Subotić

6 Orthodoxy and Antisemitism: The Relationship
  Between the Serbian Orthodox Church and the Jews 111
  Francine Friedman

7	The Orthodox Church of Greece Altuğ Günal and Zeynep Selin Balcı	131
8	The Macedonian Orthodox Church in the New Millennium Zachary T. Irwin	167
9	Navigating the Challenge of Liberalism: The Resurrection of the Orthodox Church in Post-Communist Albania Isa Blumi	197
10	The Orthodox Church of the Czech Lands and Slovakia: Survival of a Minority Faith in a Secular Society Frank Cibulka	223

Afterword: Why Are Orthodox Churches Prone to Political Mobilization Today?	249
Further Reading	257
Index	263

Notes on Contributors

Zeynep Selin Balcı is a Ph.D. candidate in International Relations at Ege University where she works as research assistant. She holds an M.A. in International Relations from Ege University and a B.A. in International Relations and European Union from the Izmir University of Economics, with full scholarship. Her research interests center on humanitarian intervention and the duty to protect civilians. She is also interested in the politics of South Caucasia and the nation-building processes of mostly post-Soviet countries. Apart from academic studies, she enjoys trekking, cycling, and non professional novel writing.

Isa Blumi (Ph.D., NYU-Joint Program in History and Middle Eastern and Islamic Studies, 2005) is a Docent/Associate Professor of Middle Eastern and Turkish Studies at Stockholm University. He is the author of six books, among them, *Destroying Yemen: What Chaos in Arabia Tells Us About the World* (University of California Press, 2018); *Ottoman Refugees, 1878–1939: Migration in a Post-Imperial World* (Bloomsbury Press, 2013); *Foundations of Modernity: Human Agency and the Imperial State* (Routledge, 2012) and *Reinstating the Ottomans: Alternative Balkan Modernities* (Palgrave Macmillan, 2011). He contributed a chapter to *Religion and Politics in Central and Southeastern Europe: Challenges Since 1989*, edited by Sabrina P. Ramet (Palgrave Macmillan, 2013).

Frank Cibulka (Ph.D., Pennsylvania State University, 1983) is a specialist in East European Studies. From 1983 to 2001, he taught in the Department of Political Science at the National University of Singapore, reaching the rank of Senior Lecturer. During 2002 to 2004, he was elected as academic visitor at Oxford University as a Senior Associate Member of St. Antony's College. During 2004 to 2016, he taught as an Associate Professor of Humanities and Social Sciences at Zayed University in Abu Dhabi, in the United Arab Emirates. Since January 2017, he is employed there as an Adjunct Associate Professor in the University College at Zayed University. His best-known works so far are *Gorbachev and Third World Conflicts*, co-edited with Jiri Valenta (Transaction Press, 1990) and *China and Southeast Asia in the Xi Jinping Era*, co-edited with Alvin Cheng-Hin Lim and Trin Aiyara (Lexington Books, 2018).

Francine Friedman (Ph.D., Claremont Graduate School, 1977) is Professor of Political Science and has been at Ball State University since 1990. Professor Friedman teaches international relations, Russian and East European politics, terrorism, international decision making and negotiation, and ethnic conflict. Her primary research interests focus on the former Yugoslavia, especially Bosnia and Herzegovina. Professor Friedman is also the Director for the Ball State University Jewish Studies program. She is the author of *The Bosnian Muslims: Denial of a Nation* (Westview Press, 1996) and of *Bosnia and Herzegovina: A Polity on the Brink* (Routledge, 2004). Her current research focuses on the Jewish community of Bosnia and Herzegovina.

Altuğ Günal (Ph.D., Dokus Eylul University, 2011) born in Tekirdağ is a lecturer at the "International Relations Department" of Ege University in İzmir/Turkey and the head of "Balkans and Cyprus Desk" at Ege Strategic Research Center. He has conducted doctoral or postdoctoral research at Exeter University/United Kingdom, Aalborg University/Denmark, NTNU/Norway, and the University of Zagreb/Croatia. He is a specialist in Balkan issues, the Cyprus issue, humanitarian interventions, federations, and the European Union. He contributed a chapter on Serbia to *Contemporary Balkan Politics* (Gazi Press, 2012) and has published several articles in academic journals including: *Aegean Academic View*, *Journal of Cyprus Studies*, and *Strategic Research Center* of the Turkish Military Forces. He also contributed a chapter to *Civic and Uncivic Values in Kosovo: Value Transformation, Education, and Media*, edited by Sabrina P. Ramet, Albert Simkus, and Ola Listhaug (Central European University Press, 2015).

Zachary T. Irwin (Ph.D., Pennsylvania State University, 1978) born in Port Jervis, New York, is an Associate Professor Emeritus of Political Science at the Behrend College of Pennsylvania State University in Erie. He has contributed chapters to several books edited or co-edited by Sabrina Ramet—among them, *Religion and Nationalism in Soviet and East European Politics*, rev. ed. (Duke University Press, 1989), *Beyond Yugoslavia: Politics, Economics, and Culture in a Shattered Community*, co-edited with Ljubiša S. Adamovich (Westview Press, 1995), *Democratic Transition in Slovenia: Value Transformation, Education, and Media*, co-edited with Danica Fink-Hafner (Texas A&M University Press, 2006), *Bosnia-Herzegovina Since Dayton: Civic and Uncivic Values*, co-edited with Ola Listhaug (Longo Editore, 2013), and *Building Democracy in the Yugoslav Successor States: Accomplishments, Setbacks, and Challenges Since 1990*, co-edited with Christine M. Hassenstab and Ola Listhaug (Cambridge University Press, 2017). His articles have appeared in *East European Quarterly, Problems of Communism, South Asia*, and other journals.

Daniela Kalkandjieva (Ph.D., Central European University, 2004) is a postdoctoral researcher at Sofia University St. Kliment Ohridski. Her main publications include her monographs *The Bulgarian Orthodox Church and the State, 1944–1953* (Sofia: Albatros, 1997) and *The Russian Orthodox Church, 1917–1948: From Decline to Resurrection* (Routledge, 2015) as well as multiple studies on the Bulgarian Orthodox Church, e.g., "The Bulgarian Orthodox Church at Crossroads: Between Nationalism and Pluralism" in Andrii Krawchuk and Thomas Bremer (eds.), *Orthodox Christian Encounters of Identity and Otherness: Values, Self-Reflection, Dialogue* (Palgrave Macmillan, 2014); and "The Bulgarian Orthodox Church" [Българската православна църква] in Lucian N. Leustean (ed.), *Eastern Christianity and Politics in the Twenty-First Century* (Routledge, 2014).

David B. Kanin (Ph.D., Fletcher School of Law and Diplomacy, Tufts University, 1976) is Professorial Lecturer in European Studies at the School of Advanced International Studies of The Johns Hopkins University, Analytic Director with Centra Technology and Adjunct Professor of National Security at the Daniel Morgan Graduate School of National Security. In 2010, he retired as a senior analyst after a 31-year career with the Central Intelligence Agency. He spent much of his last decade at the Agency as founding member of the Red Cell, an alternative analysis and brainstorming group. Dr. Kanin's responsibilities included challenging Agency judgments on topics worldwide and presenting alternative worldviews to senior policymakers. From 2007 to 2009, he served as Director of Long-Range Identity Studies on the National Intelligence Council. He served as senior political analyst on the Director of Intelligence's Interagency Balkan Task Force during the wars that followed the collapse of former Yugoslavia in the 1990s. From 1993 to 1996, he was Deputy National Intelligence Officer for Europe, in which capacity he managed the production of National Intelligence Estimates and other Community products on Balkan and wider European issues. Before then he worked as an analyst on European security issues, Yugoslavia, North Korea, and counterintelligence. He was a member of the US delegation to the Madrid Review conference of the Conference on Security and Cooperation in Europe in 1981 and the Rambouillet peace talks on Kosovo in 1999. He was born in Milwaukee, Wisconsin.

Sabrina P. Ramet (Ph.D., UCLA, 1981) is a Professor Emerita of Political Science at the Norwegian University of Science and Technology (NTNU) in Trondheim, Norway. She is the author of 14 books—most recently of *Alternatives to Democracy in Twentieth-Century Europe: Collectivist Visions of Modernity* (Central European University Press, 2019). She is also editor or co-editor of 36 previous books—35 published to date and one in production—among them, *Religion and Politics in Central and Southeastern Europe: Challenges Since 1989* (Palgrave Macmillan, 2014).

Lavinia Stan (Ph.D., University of Toronto, 2001) is Jules Leger Research Chair in the Department of Political Science at St. Francis Xavier University, Canada. Her publications, prepared jointly with Lucian Turcescu, include *Justice, Memory and Redress: New Insights from Romania* (Cambridge Scholars, 2017), *Church, State and Democracy in Expanding Europe* (Oxford University Press, 2011), and *Religion and Politics in Post-Communist Romania* (Oxford University Press, 2007). Stan's research focuses on religion and politics in Central and Eastern Europe, as well as transitional justice in post-communist countries.

Jelena Subotić (Ph.D., University of Wisconsin-Madison, 2007) is a Professor of Political Science at Georgia State University. She is the author of two books—*Hijacked Justice: Dealing with the Past in the*

Balkans (Cornell University Press, 2009) and *Yellow Star, Red Star: Holocaust Remembrance After Communism* (Cornell University Press, 2019) and more than twenty scholarly articles on human rights, transitional justice, and identity politics in the Western Balkans. She also contributed a chapter to *Building Democracy in the Yugoslav Successor States: Accomplishments, Setbacks, and Challenges*, edited by Sabrina P. Ramet, Christine M. Hassenstab, and Ola Listhaug (Cambridge University Press, 2017).

Lucian Turcescu (D.Th., St. Michael's College of the University of Toronto, 1999) is a Professor and the Chair of the Department of Theological Studies at Concordia University (Canada). He has published six scholarly books as author, co-author, or editor, and over three dozen articles. One of his books was published in a Romanian translation. His recent books include *Religion and Politics in Post-Communist Romania* (Oxford University Press, 2007), *Church, State and Democracy in Expanding Europe* (Oxford University Press, 2011), and *Justice, Memory and Redress: New Insights from Romania* (Cambridge Scholars, 2017)—all three co-authored with Lavinia Stan—as well as *The Reception and Interpretation of the Bible in Late Antiquity: Proceedings of the Montreal Colloquium in Honour of Charles Kannengiesser*, co-edited with L. DiTommaso (E. J. Brill, 2008).

CHAPTER 1

The Orthodox Churches of Southeastern Europe: An Introduction

Sabrina P. Ramet

Abstract Whether in Southeastern Europe or elsewhere, the Orthodox Church has been characterized by profound conservatism and an enduring conviction of its unique monopoly on religious truth. From these two features spring also an intolerance of other religious bodies as well as of sexual minorities, who, according to Orthodox doctrine, defy God's eternal law. But the Orthodox Church does not restrict itself to broadly understood theological and moral matters, but has also, across the centuries, presented itself as the champion of the various nations of Southeastern Europe. These themes—conservatism, intolerance (extending to both religious intolerance and homophobia), and nationalism provide the thematic underpinnings of this volume.

Every religious faith is characterized by both continuity and evolution. Factors promoting continuity in the Orthodox communion have included Scriptures, documents adopted to define the faith (such as the

S. P. Ramet (✉)
Department of Sociology and Political Science,
Norwegian University of Science and Technology, Trondheim, Norway
e-mail: sabrina.ramet@ntnu.no

Orthodox Church's Social Concept[1]), the formal training of clergy at seminaries and schools of theology, and the socialization of the young. To this set of factors promoting continuity, one may add "Clifford Geertz's concept of 'spiritual afterimages' which refers to 'reflections, reverberations, [and] projections' of religious experience in daily life. Formed in an earlier point in the nation's history as moral imperatives and sentiments that continue to guide national development" these *afterimages* "leave a distinct mark on the country's political, social, and economic practices."[2] Factors promoting evolution have included reforms (such as Patriarch Nikon's reform of Russian Orthodoxy in the seventeenth century), councils at which articles of the faith have been defined (such as the Council of Chalcedon held in 451, which decreed that Jesus of Nazareth had two natures—divine and human—rather than one nature which was simultaneously divine and human[3]), and internal dissent (among which the abortive Living Church movement within the Russian Orthodox Church in the 1920s may be recalled).

However, Orthodox believers interpret the deliberations of the councils above all as clarifications or judgments and prefer to stress the unchanging core of the Orthodox faith, while acknowledging that the world in which the Church lives continues to change. The Orthodox are convinced that they hold a monopoly on doctrinal Truth and, for the Orthodox, doctrine is crucial. The intense quarrel with the Western (Catholic) Church about the *filioque*—whether the Holy Spirit proceeded from the Father and the Son, as Catholics maintain, or just from the Father, as Orthodox maintain—was one of two decisive arguments (the other being the pope's claim to primacy in the Christian world) which finalized the split between the Catholic and Orthodox Churches in the eleventh century[4] and it is still a point of dispute between these two ancient Churches. It was, furthermore, and still is a dispute about doctrinal Truth, and the Orthodox Church, as a body which stresses doctrine and prizes Truth, wants nothing less than to bring all Christians into communion with itself, which in practice means that all Christians should accept Orthodox doctrine.[5]

The Orthodox Church prides itself on being a *conservative* Church, doing its best to safeguard what it considers traditional values. But this has not prevented the appearance of alternative voices, even currents, within the Church, such as pro-European moderates within the Serbian Orthodox Church who appeal to "Orthodox notions of a God-given, unique personality" and theological arguments to promote the idea of a "voter-citizen" in a democratic setting.[6] More particularly, moderates anywhere in the Orthodox world do not exclude the possibility that non-Orthodox could be members of the one true Church—understood as transcending any earthly embodiments—and argue that "there are many different ways of being related to this one Church, and many different ways of being separated from it."[7] But conservatives, who constitute the majority of Orthodox bishops and ordinary clergy, argue on the contrary that only the Orthodox are members of the one true Church. Thus, moderates have remained in a minority; indeed, anti-Westernism in the Serbian Church, for example, increased between the two world wars, with Serbian clergy engaging in dysphoric rumination about their Church's alleged "centuries-long suffering and martyrdom."[8] Against the moderates, the anti-Westernizers have promoted values of humility, obedience, and national pride, which is easily translated into nationalism. Indeed, in viewing the Orthodox Churches of Southeastern Europe, one can identify three syndromes which are common throughout the region: nationalism, conservatism, and intolerance of other religious bodies but also of sexual minorities, both of which are seen as threatening, if not undermining, traditional values.

Nationalism. On the one hand, it may be conceded that joy in the achievements of one's people and care for their welfare is a positive thing (as the Roman philosopher Cicero, among others, noted). So too are treasuring of one's culture and the engagement to remember the history of the nation (as recommended in his *Considerations on the Government of Poland* by Jean-Jacques Rousseau). On the other hand, nationalism, when understood as entailing hostility or mistrust or resentment toward other nations or simple prejudice, as well as the claim that the desires and needs of one's own nation and its members take precedence over the rights and needs of other nations and their members, is dangerous. Anti-Semitism may still be found in the Orthodox Churches of Southeastern Europe. For example, in Romania, there were reports, in 2014, "of a range of anti-Semitic incidents, including desecrations of synagogues, anti-Semitic sermons by Orthodox priests, Holocaust denials, and events commemorating former pro-Nazi leaders of the Legionnaire Movement."[9] But there are also other "out-groups" specific to each respective Orthodox Church, whether Macedonians and Turks in the case of the Greek Orthodox Church, Croats and Albanians in the case of the Serbian Orthodox Church, or the hostility found among at least some Macedonian Orthodox vis-à-vis the Albanian Orthodox Church.[10]

Where the Bulgarian Orthodox Church is concerned, Spas T. Raikin has highlighted the nationalism of that religious body as its defining characteristic.[11]

Vladimir Solov'ev (1853–1900), one of the greatest Orthodox theologians of the nineteenth century, distinguished between nationality or nationhood and nationalism. In an 1884 essay, Solov'ev characterized nationhood as "a living force, both natural and historical, which itself must serve the highest idea, and by that service give meaning to and justify its own existence."[12] Referring to the Gospels, Solov'ev further argued that nurturing and celebrating one's own national culture and people can be positive, so that nationhood "ceases to be a boundary, and becomes the basis of a positive union" with all the rest of humankind.[13]

Conservatism. Whether one thinks of Orthodox Churches in Southeastern Europe or Orthodox Churches in Russia or elsewhere, the defense of "traditional values" looms large. Traditional values are usually understood, nowadays, as including heterosexual marriage, sex for procreation not for pleasure, abstinence from sex before or outside marriage, hostility to feminism, a ban on abortion, and the doctrine of complementarity in the roles of men and women.[14] But to this list of contested values, one may also add honesty, truthfulness, honor, and personal morality, which have been championed, for example, by the Russian Orthodox Church.[15] Summarizing the perspective of Serbian theologian Justin Popović (1894–1979), Mirko Đorđević wrote that

> For his theanthropic philosophy of life, death, and the sacred, human being[s], society, the nation, and the state must accommodate themselves to the Church as the eternal ideal, but under no circumstances need the Church seek accommodation with them, and even less should it serve them.[16]

Just to repeat: for Popović, the Church was not supposed to serve human beings or society. It is, rather, the Kingdom of God on earth.

Like the Catholic Church and other Christian faiths, the Orthodox Churches reject the notion that two people of the same sex have any business sharing a life together, but typically balance this by underlining that gays and lesbians should not be hated or ridiculed. One example was a set of "Policy Statements on Contemporary Moral Issues," issued by the Bulgarian Eastern Orthodox Diocese of the USA, Canada, and Australia in 2004. In this document, the Bulgarian Diocese declared that

"The practice of homosexuality is unacceptable according to the teachings of the Orthodox Church. Nevertheless, those who express hatred, ridicule or animosity towards people with a homosexual orientation act contrary to the central Christian ethos of love and compassion for all people."[17] In Romania, the local Orthodox Church objected vociferously to the provision in the European Convention of Human Rights (ratified by post-communist Romania), which recognizes the right of both heterosexuals and homosexuals to choose their partners. Patriarch Teoctist even "addressed the nation on the state television,…characterizing homosexuality as 'a sin that has nothing to do with human rights.'"[18] Or again, in Macedonia, a representative of the Macedonian Orthodox Church presented a speech at the fifth session of the National Council for Euro-Integration in May 2009, denouncing the notion that sexual orientation be included in the prohibition against discrimination.[19] In consonance with this attitude, Orthodox hierarchs and ordinary clergy have repeatedly expressed their opposition to gay pride parades, whether in Belgrade[20] or Bucharest[21] or Sofia[22] or Thessaloniki[23] or elsewhere. While Orthodox hierarchs have repeatedly excoriated gays and lesbians, they have devoted comparatively little time to criticizing men for beating their wives. Indeed, in Serbia, wife-beating was even held up at one point as constituting the essence of the Serbian family.[24]

Intolerance. The Orthodox Church is by no means the only religious association to be convinced that its own religious faith is the one, true faith and that all other religious faiths are in error, if not abominations. For the Orthodox, Catholics are schismatics, while Protestants are relativists.[25] The consequence is a fundamental disinterest in ecumenism: using ecumenical fora to spread the word about Orthodoxy would be one thing, agreeing to hear other points of view would be quite another. It was in this spirit that, in the course of 1997–1998, first the Georgian Orthodox Church and then the Bulgarian Orthodox Church withdrew from the World Council of Churches and the Conference of European Churches. Subsequently, the Russian Orthodox Church announced that it was "suspending" its participation in events of the World Council of Churches. The Orthodox Church has been happy to collaborate (up to a point) with Western Christian Churches in criticizing abortion and sexual minorities, for example, even while holding them at arm's length, but the European Union, by contrast, is seen by the Orthodox Church, as well as by the conservative wing of the Catholic Church for that matter, as involving an assault on conservative and traditional values, the promotion of homosexuality and pornography, and the celebration of allegedly "false" rights and freedoms. Serbian bishops expressed their concern in this way in their 2008 Easter message: "A monstrous globalist civilization is being created according to the criteria of a degenerate morality, without the yeast of the eternal meaning of human life. Such a civilization cannot survive as long as it is in opposition to resurrected Christ...."[26]

Intolerance lies at the very core of the Orthodox faith because the Orthodox believers are convinced that, in order to achieve "salvation"—which is to say to be admitted to Heaven after death—they are obliged to do everything they can to assure that others can also be saved.[27] The Orthodox Church alone, so they say, possesses the Truth. Since admission to Heaven depends—at least in general—on accepting the Church's allegedly true doctrines and breaking with what the Orthodox consider heresy and schism, it follows, as Serbian theologian Radovan Bigović has put it, that "The Church does not support any attempts to relativize the Truth...She hates sin and deviation from the Truth."[28]

Orthodox clerics speak of reconciliation, of ending disunion, but this is allowed only on Orthodox terms. As Timothy Ware, also known as Metropolitan Kallistos of Diokleia, has put it,

> Because they believe their Church to be the true Church, Orthodox can have but one ultimate desire: the reconciliation of all Christians to Orthodoxy...
>
> Yet there is one field in which diversity cannot be permitted. Orthodoxy insists upon unity in matters of faith. *Before there can be reunion among Christians, there must first be full agreement in faith...*It is unity in faith that matters...[29]

In those countries where the archives of the respective security services (secret police) have been opened to the public—which is to say, where Orthodox societies are concerned, in Romania and Bulgaria—it has come to light that leading hierarchs of the Orthodox Churches met with agents of the communist security services on a regular basis for purposes of sharing information.[30] Indeed, after a brutal induction into the communist system, the Orthodox Churches of Romania[31] and Bulgaria[32] found themselves in a symbiotic relationship with their respective communist regimes and, accordingly, the sudden transition to pluralism and entry into the European Union has been difficult. Under communism, it was difficult for foreign-based religious groups, such as Mormons, Scientologists, and others, to proselytize; after 1989, interreligious competition increased and Orthodox Churches were thrust on the defensive. They have also found themselves on the defensive as regards their concept of "traditional values," including their disapproval of same-sex unions. And the rash of new legislation including ratifications of European conventions on human rights has threatened these Churches' claims to a monopoly on moral authority. For all of these reasons, the Orthodox Churches of the post-socialist countries in Southeastern Europe have plenty of reasons to be skeptical of the benefits, whether supposed or real, of local brands of democracy.

Summary. The Churches discussed in this volume include both cases in which the local Orthodox Church embraces the majority of the nation's population (Bulgaria, Greece, Macedonia, Romania, and Serbia) and cases in which the Orthodox Church is a minority Church (Albania, and the Czech Lands and Slovakia).

As the figures in Table 1.1 show, the countries with the largest percentage of the population belonging to the Orthodox community are Serbia, Romania, Greece, and Bulgaria.

Chapter 2, written by David Kanin, examines the historical legacy of Orthodoxy in the region and highlights the association of bishops in Bulgaria, Macedonia, Montenegro, and Serbia with their respective communities' national projects. Kanin introduces the concept of *sacred time*, which he defines as "direct perception of individual presence at, participation with, and experience of the seminal miracles, events, and state of mind produced by the contact between the person in question, sacral personages of a faith, and God." Sacred time is, thus, an experience of the supernatural and can be engendered, among other ways, by the viewing of relics. The Churches' nationalism, manifested in the Serbian case in that Church's strong stance against Kosovo's independence, is also a vehicle for sacred time, thus giving extra force to nationalist claims.

The remaining chapters in this book focus on individual national Churches, beginning with a chapter on the Romanian case by Lavinia Stan and Lucian Turcescu. In terms of number of adherents, the Romanian Orthodox Church is clearly the largest Orthodox community in the region, with 18.82 million members in 2014, far ahead of second-place Greece (with 10.72 million members) and third-place Serbia (with 6.37 million members).[33] As the authors note, the Romanian Orthodox Church has paid less attention to abortion, which has fired

Table 1.1 Percentage of each nation belonging to the Orthodox Church (in %)

	% Orthodox	Year
Serbia	88	2015/16
Greece	81–90	2015
Romania	86	2015/16
Bulgaria	75	2015/16
Montenegro	72.1	2011
Macedonia	64.8	2002
Albania	6.8	2011
Czech Republic	1.0	2015/16
Slovakia	0.9	2014
Poland	0.7	2017

Sources Figures for Albania, Greece, Kosovo, and Macedonia, from the CIA, *World Factbook*, at https://www.cia.gov/library/publications/the-world-factbook/ [last accessed on 22 December 2018]; figures for Bulgaria, the Czech Republic, Romania, and Serbia from Pew Research Center, *Religious Belief and National Belonging in Central and Eastern Europe* (10 May 2017), at http://www.pewforum.org/2017/05/10/religious-belief-and-national-belonging-in-central-and-eastern-europe/ [accessed on 29 June 2018]; figure for Slovakia from *NationMaster*, at https://www.nationmaster.com/country-info/profiles/Slovakia/Religion [accessed on 22 December 2018]; and figure for Poland from Study shows 95% of Poles are religious, *Radio Poland* (13 February 2017), at http://thenews.pl/1/11/Artykul/293281,Study-shows-95-of-Poles-are-religious [accessed on 22 December 2018]

the Catholic Church across Europe and beyond, than it has to defending conservative values at the expense of same-sex couples. The Romanian Church continues to display a nationalist countenance while betraying blanket intolerance of other religious communities.

This is followed by an examination of the Bulgarian Orthodox Church, which embraced just over 6 million adherents in 2015, according to *The Sofia Globe*.[34] As Daniela Kalkandjieva recounts, the Bulgarian Church proved to be hostile to other faiths and has nurtured an ambition to regain the ecclesiastical hegemony it enjoyed in pre-communist times. The Church in Bulgaria has both opposed efforts to extend some form of legal recognition to same-sex couples and rejected the Istanbul Convention (drafted in 2011 and signed by 46 countries by January 2018) on preventing and combating domestic violence against women. By 2012, the Bulgarian Orthodox Church succeeded in retrieving its property rights over extensive lands, forests, and non-religious urban buildings which had been seized by the communists more than half a century earlier. However, as Kalkandjieva relates, the Church was internally divided from 1992 until 2012 between two rival synods, each claiming legitimate leadership. But the Church's prestige was more particularly threatened by the revelation in 2012 that 11 of the then-15 members of the Holy Synod had collaborated as informers for the communist-era secret police.

The Serbian Orthodox Church—the subject of Chapter 5—is, *in proportional terms*, probably the largest Orthodox community in the region, with 88% of Serbs reporting that they are Orthodox. (In Greece, somewhere between 81 and 90% of Greeks are thought to be Orthodox.) Written by Jelena Subotić, this chapter carefully follows the themes of this volume, while paying especially close attention to the Church's responses to the presence of sexual minorities in the country and to Kosovo's status as an independent state. In a striking expression of its nationalism, the Serbian Church announced in spring 2018 that it was changing its official name to the Serbian Orthodox Church—*Patriarchate of Peć*, signaling its continued recollection of Ottoman times when the Church had its headquarters in the city of Peć in Kosovo now known by its Albanian name of Peja.[35] The Ottoman legacy is also part of the story of homophobia in Serbia since, as human rights activist Ivan Janković has explained, Serbs opposed to Ottoman rule in their country marshaled accusations of alleged Turkish sodomizing of young Serbian boys in order to energize outrage and anger against the Turks.[36]

The Serbian case is the subject also of Francine Friedman's chapter, but here the focus is specifically on the relationship between Serbian Orthodoxy and anti-Semitism. The chapter begins with a retrospective review of the ideas and career of the still controversial pro-fascist Bishop Nikolaj Velimirović (1881–1956), who was canonized in 2003. The chapter also discusses the current orientation of the Church as regards the small Jewish communities in Serbia and the Republika Srpska.

Chapter 7, by Altuğ Günal and Zeynep Selin Balcı, takes up a subject of the Greek Orthodox Church, noting that it continues to fight secularizing tendencies in society, to portray itself as the protector of Greek national identity, and to oppose same-sex marriage and LGBT rights. The Greek Church sided with Greeks who were opposed to admitting Macedonia, even if renamed North Macedonia, into the European Union and, like other Orthodox Churches, sees itself as keeping vigilance over the eternal Truths handed down centuries if not millennia ago. The Church has also stood firm against same-sex rights, with Metropolitan Ambrose of Kalvrta, for example, posting a controversial blog in 2015 in which he termed homosexuality a "sin" and called on the faithful to oppose same-sex relations. Posted about the time that the Greek parliament was voting, by a margin to 193 to 56, to register same-sex civil partnerships, the blog became the subject of a lawsuit resolved only in March 2018, with the acquittal of the Metropolitan of any intention to incite anti-gay violence.[37] In spite of the bishop's objection, same-sex partnerships, thus, have legal status in Greece since 24 December 2015.

The only existentially controversial case discussed in this volume involves the Macedonian Orthodox Church, which is still struggling to win canonical recognition. As Zachary Irwin relates, the Macedonian Church has had to face both an external challenge from the Serbian Church, which views the Macedonian Church as a schismatic body, and internal problems, such as the case of Bishop Jovan Vraniškovski, who defected to the Serbian Church. As with the other Orthodox Churches already discussed, the Macedonian Church displays the typical Orthodox syndrome of conservatism, nationalism, and intolerance.

This brings us to the two minority Churches: the Albanian Orthodox Church and the Orthodox Church of the Czech Lands and Slovakia. Both of these Churches are small, but they are included in this volume in order to show how an Orthodox Church behaves when it is not hegemonic. For the Albanian Orthodox community, as Blumi relates, there have been three chief challenges since 1990: first, since the collapse of communism, the country has been exposed in various ways to liberal values, such as acceptance of same-sex values—an acceptance which the Church is not ready to embrace; second, there has been a bitter conflict over properties confiscated from the Church by the communists, which have been turned to other uses and which ecclesiastical leaders want to retrieve; and third, there has been the long process of replacing Greek bishops with Albanian bishops in what is an *Albanian* Church. On this last point, Blumi notes that, since 1992, 165 Orthodox clergy have been ordained, all of them Albanians. The following chapter—contributed by Frank Cibulka—focuses on the most unique case in this volume: first, by contrast with other Churches discussed herein, the Orthodox Church of the Czech Lands and Slovakia is not a hegemonic, majority Church but, on the contrary, a minority Church in both the Czech Republic and Slovakia; and second, this Church is operating, as Cibulka notes, "in one of the most secularized and atheistic countries in the world." As if this combination of factors were not enough of a challenge, the Church has also recently experienced an internal power struggle, leading the Ministry of Culture to suspend restitution payments to the Church in late 2014.

Finally, in an afterword for this volume, Lucian Leustean offers his reflections on the patterns of behavior of these Churches, on the values they espouse, and on the lessons to be learned. In a striking passage, Leustean notes that "Orthodox Churches have become politically stronger when states have failed to provide social support for a population in need." In such circumstances, Orthodox Churches have typically filled the void.

Acknowledgements I am grateful to Professors Jerry Pankhurst and Lucian Turcescu for comments on earlier drafts of this chapter as well as to Dr. Daniela Kalkandjieva for her useful input.

Notes

1. See Olga Hoppe-Kondrikova, Josephien Van Kessel, and Evert Van Der Zweerde, "Christian Social Doctrine East and West: The Russian Orthodox Social Concept and the Roman Catholic Compendium Compared," in *Religion, State and Society*, Vol. 41, No. 2 (2013), pp. 199–224, https://doi.org/10.1080/09637494.2013.800777.
2. Jerry Pankhurst, "Religious Culture: Faith in Soviet and Post-Soviet Russia," *Center for Democratic Culture* (2012), at http://digitalscholarship.unlv.edu/russian_culture/7/ [last accessed on 21 April 2019], no page numbers.
3. Not all Christians were prepared to accept the decision of the Council of Chalcedon, and several Church bodies, including the Armenian Apostolic Church and the Coptic Orthodox Church of Alexandria, held at one time to the doctrine that Jesus of Nazareth had one nature, both divine and human; this doctrine was called Monophysitism. At this point in time, this dispute has lost its salience and what used to be called "Monophysite" Churches are now referred to as non-Chalcedonian Churches.
4. The traditional date for the final split is, by convention, given as 1054. Regarding the *filioque* controversy, see Timothy Ware, *The Orthodox Church: An Introduction to Eastern Christianity*, new ed. (Milton Keynes: Penguin Books, 2015), pp. 48–49, 52–54, 56, 307.
5. Ibid., p. 303; also Mirko Đorđević, "The Testamentary Thought of Justin Popović," in *Forum Bosnae*, No. 49 (2018), at https://www.ceeol.com/search/viewpdf?id=240609 [accessed on 22 December 2018], p. 187.

6. Klaus Buchenau, "Orthodox Values and Modern Necessities: Serbian Orthodox Clergy and Laypeople on Democracy, Human Rights, Transition, and Globalization," in Ola Listhaug, Sabrina P. Ramet, and Dragana Dulić (eds.), *Civic and Uncivic Values: Serbia in the Post-Milošević Era* (Budapest and New York: Central European University Press, 2011), p. 125.
7. Ware, *The Orthodox Church*, p. 301.
8. Buchenau, "Orthodox Values," p. 113.
9. U.S. State Department, *Romania 2014: International Religious Freedom Report*, at http://www.state.gov/documents/organization/238636.pdf [accessed on 19 September 2016], p. 1.
10. See Naser Pajaziti, "Issue of Albanian Orthodox in FYROM Has Caused Ethnic and Religious Debates," *Independent Balkan News Agency*, 5 December 2014, at http://www.balkaneu.com/issue-albanian-orthodox-fyrom-caused-ethnic-religious-debates/ [accessed on 19 September 2016].
11. Spas T. Raikin, "The Bulgarian Orthodox Church," in Pedro Ramet (ed.), *Eastern Christianity and Politics in the Twentieth Century* (Durham, NC: Duke University Press, 1988), pp. 160, 179.
12. Solov'ev, "About Nationhood and Russia's National Affairs" (1884), as quoted in Judith Deutsch Kornblatt, "Vladimir Solov'ev on Spiritual Nationhood, Russia and the Jews," in *The Russian Review*, Vol. 56, No. 2 (April 1997), p. 175.
13. Solov'ev, *The Justification of the Good* (1894–1898), as quoted in Kornblatt, "Vladimir Solov'ev," p. 172 (emphasis removed).
14. For a straightforward explanation and critique of the doctrine of complementarity, see Maureen Fiedler, "Complementarity of the Sexes: A Trap," *National Catholic Reporter*, 14 November 2014, at https://www.ncronline.org/blogs/ncr-today/complementarity-sexes-trap [accessed on 19 September 2016].
15. William C. Fletcher, "The Russian Orthodox Church and a Work Ethic," in Sabrina Petra Ramet and Donald W. Treadgold (eds.), *Render Unto Caesar: The Religious Sphere in World Politics* (Washington, DC: American University Press, 1995), pp. 293–294. See also Kristina Stoeckl, "The Russian Orthodox Church as Moral Norm Entrepreneur," in *Religion, State and Society*, Vol. 44, No. 2 (2016), pp. 136–144, https://doi.org/10.1080/09637494.2016.1194010.
16. Đorđević, "The Testamentary Thought," p. 185.
17. Bulgarian Eastern Orthodox Diocese of the USA, Canada, and Australia, Bulgarian Patriarchate, "Policy Statements on Contemporary Moral Issues" (2004), at http://www.bulgariandiocese.org/policies.html [accessed on 19 September 2016].

18. Sabrina P. Ramet, *Nihil Obstat: Religion, Politics, and Social Change in East-Central Europe and Russia* (Durham, NC: Duke University Press, 1998), p. 198. See also Lucian Turcescu and Lavinia Stan, "Religion, Politics and Sexuality in Romania," in *Europe-Asia Studies*, Vol. 57, No. 2 (March 2005), pp. 291–310, https://doi.org/10.1080/09668130500051924.
19. Cf. Slavcho Dimitrov, "The Triumphant Distribution of the Heteronormative Sensible: The Case of Sexual Minorities in Transitional Macedonia, 1991–2012," in Christine M. Hassenstab and Sabrina P. Ramet (eds.), *Gender (In)Equality and Gender Politics in Southeastern Europe: A Question of Justice* (Basingstoke: Palgrave Macmillan, 2015), p. 236.
20. Cf. Rada Drezgić, "Orthodox Christianity and Gender Equality in Serbia: On Reproductive and Sexual Rights," in Hassenstab and Ramet (eds.), *Gender (In)Equality and Gender Politics*, pp. 306–307. Concerning the sexual conservatism of the Serbian Orthodox Church, see also Radmila Radić and Milan Vukomanović, "Religion and Democracy in Serbia Since 1989," in Sabrina P. Ramet (ed.), *Religion and Politics in Post-Socialist Central and Southeastern Europe: Challenges Since 1989* (Basingstoke: Palgrave Macmillan, 2014), p. 193.
21. "Clashes Mark Romanian Gay Pride," *BBC News*, 4 June 2006, at http://news.bbc.co.uk/2/hi/europe/5045352.stm [accessed on 19 September 2016]. See also Lavinia Stan and Lucian Turcescu, *Religion and Politics in Post-Communist Romania* (Oxford: Oxford University Press, 2007).
22. "Bulgarian Orthodox Church Declares Opposition to Sofia Pride," *novinite.com*, 16 June 2016, at http://www.novinite.com/articles/174944/Bulgarian+Orthodox+Church+Declares+Opposition+to+Sofia+Pride [last accessed on 21 April 2019].
23. Mary Harris, "Greek Church Prays for LGBT Abnormality, Ahead of Thessaloniki Pride," *Greek Reporter*, 24 June 2016, at http://greece.greekreporter.com/2016/06/24/greek-church-prays-for-lgbt-abnormality-ahead-of-thessaloniki-pride/ [accessed on 19 September 2016].
24. In Serbia in a striking reflection of the patriarchal culture of wife-beating, when Sonja Licht, a highly regarded feminist, demanded that the legislature adopt legislation to combat wife-beating, one legislator snapped, "Don't speak to me about a law against violence in the family. It would destroy the essence of the Serbian family." As quoted in Marlene Nadle, "For Men Only? No!" in *World Monitor* (May 1992), p. 46.
25. Sabrina P. Ramet, "The Way We Were—And Should Be Again? European Orthodox Churches and the 'Idyllic Past'," in Timothy A. Byrnes and Peter J. Katzenstein (eds.), *Religion in an Expanding Europe* (Cambridge: Cambridge University Press, 2006), p. 156.
26. As quoted in Buchenau, "Orthodox Values and Modern Necessities," p. 128.

27. Radovan Bigovic, *The Orthodox Church in 21st Century*, trans. from Serbian by Petar Serovic (Belgrade: Konrad Adenauer Stiftung, 2011), p. 108.
28. Ibid., p. 107.
29. Ware, *The Orthodox Church*, pp. 302–303 (Ware's emphasis).
30. Documented in Sabrina P. Ramet, "Religious Organizations in Post-Communist Central and Southeastern Europe: An Introduction," in Ramet (ed.), *Religion and Politics in Post-Socialist Central and Southeastern Europe*, pp. 9–10.
31. See Lucian Turcescu and Lavinia Stan, "The Romanian Orthodox Church," in Lucian N. Leustean (ed.), *Eastern Christianity and Politics in the Twenty-First Century* (London: Routledge, 2017), pp. 95–98.
32. Daniela Kalkandjieva, "The Bulgarian Orthodox Church," in Leustean (ed.), *Eastern Christianity and Politics*, pp. 125–129.
33. "Religion > Christian > Orthodox > Orthodox Population: Countries Compared," *NationMaster*, at https://www.nationmaster.com/country-info/stats/Religion/Christian/Orthodox/Orthodox-population [accessed on 22 December 2018].
34. *The Sofia Globe* (n.d.), at https://sofiaglobe.com/2017/11/12/81-of-bulgarias-population-are-orthodox-christians-but-22-of-them-are-atheists-or-agnostics-2/ [accessed on 21 April 2019].
35. Srdjan Garcevic, "Serbia's Church Should Stop Alienating Liberals," *Balkan Insight*, 16 April 2018, at https://balkaninsight.com/2018/04/16/serbia-s-church-should-stop-alienating-liberals-03-28-2018/ [accessed on 21 April 2019].
36. Ivan Janković, as summarized in Milan Radonjic, "How Opposition to the Ottomans Nurtured Serbia's Homophobia," *Balkan Insight*, 22 June 2018, at https://balkaninsight.com/2018/06/22/how-opposition-to-the-ottomans-nurtured-serbia-s-homophobia-06-20-2018/?nocache [accessed on 21 April 2019].
37. "Greek Metropolitan Found Innocent of Homophobia—Hate Speech Charges," *Orthodox Christianity*, 19 March 2018, at http://orthochristian.com/111586.html [accessed on 22 December 2018].

CHAPTER 2

Faith, Nation, and Structure: The Diachronic Durability of Orthodox Churches in the Balkans

David B. Kanin

Abstract Those in charge of Orthodox Christian Churches have remained lashed to the national identities they nurtured, and have attempted to revive the sense that nationalism is modern and progressive—but also an essential piece of sacred time. The latter concept involves the direct perception of individual presence at, participation with, and experience of the seminal miracles, events, and state of mind produced by contact between the person in question, sacral personages of a faith, and God. The constructed, iconic past associated with sacred time in a nationalist framework is more than "theology" and anything but an anachronistic experience. Religious and nationalist entrepreneurs synchronize their visions of sacred times to harness the imaginations of the faithful and overcome local resistance to nationalism. The Orthodox Churches of the Balkans have both faith and nationalism in their tool kits and over centuries have used them to survive religious, social, economic, and political challenges—even as they have squabbled with each other.

D. B. Kanin (✉)
Johns Hopkins University,
School of Advanced International Studies,
Washington, DC, USA

© The Author(s) 2019
S. P. Ramet (ed.), *Orthodox Churches and Politics in Southeastern Europe*, Palgrave Studies in Religion, Politics, and Policy,
https://doi.org/10.1007/978-3-030-24139-1_2

The current concern with the efficacy of secular, liberal modernism and its international order will prove more than a momentary phenomenon. The material order offers only material benefits—slogans like "freedom" and "democracy" maintain their appeal only when coupled with a credible promise of prosperity. Mark Juergensmeyer has pointed out that secular nationalism fails to inspire the way a combination of religion and identity can, especially where the secular order has failed to deliver on promises of political freedom, economic prosperity, and social justice.[1]

It remains an open question whether even successful political and economic states can fend off challenges from faith-based and other communal appeals. Rival communal belief systems have the advantage of speaking directly to affective, spiritual needs and providing meaning to peoples' lives. In this context, the return of organized, muscular religion as a central concern to governments—underscored by the revival of the various flavors of Islam as centrally important geostrategic actors—provides a central challenge to the teleology of civic democracy, multicultural integration, and "rule of law." Nationalism, in the nineteenth century viewed by adherents as a component of modernity, now has become a challenger to it.

The Orthodox Churches of the Balkans have both faith and nationalism in their tool kits and over centuries have used them to survive religious, social, economic, and political challenges—even as they have squabbled with each other. This chapter will consider the impact of these churches in their region as diachronic actors able to maintain influence and/or be useful to successive synchronic political powers.

The backdrop for this analysis is the idea of sacred time, direct perception of individual presence at, participation with, and experience of the seminal miracles, events, and state of mind produced by the contact between the person in question, sacral personages of a faith, and God. For some, this heightened spiritual experience can be inspired by foundational oral narratives, sacred texts, or charismatic preachers, but it is just as likely to involve an affective sense of personal experience transcending anything associated with religious authority. Sacred time is not momentary, linear or perishable; it is temporal Platonic form. Transubstantiation of the blood and body of Christ during the Catholic mass or performance in passion plays, perceived connection by those Jews engaged in the study of the written Torah with the tradition of the Oral Torah—the presence on Mt. Sinai of the souls of all future commentators on the law as that law is being given by God to Moses—or a sense of behaving according to the guidance of the Prophet's closest companions or carrying out acts of jihad lead people from secular into sacred time. The viewing of relics associated with any faith can have the same impact on the faithful. Some erudite, sophisticated, or jaded figures of faith will recoil from those who embrace or seek out the rapture of sacred time. Other religious authorities and institutions—no matter how nationalistic or otherwise "of" this world they become—will seek to catch this spiritual lightening in a bottle and use the appeal of sacred time as a bedrock of communal legitimacy. The constructed, iconic past associated with sacred time in a nationalist framework is more than "theology" and anything but an anachronistic experience. Religious and nationalist entrepreneurs synchronize their visions of sacred times to harness the imaginations of the faithful and overcome local resistance to nationalism.[2]

When hundreds of thousands of Serbs communed with the relics of Tsar Lazar at the battlefield of Kosovo Polje in 1889 and 1989, their celebration of the events of 1389 gave them a direct connection to what happened at that spot—the rituals of memory enabled them to believe they were joining the event's protagonists right then, right there. The experience of presence defined the faith and nation that—when in the appropriate frame of mind—constitutes "Serbia." Similarly, Greek Orthodox priests and officers existed in sacred time if it is true they reconsecrated the church of Hagia Sophia in Constantinople in 1919, "resuming" the service at the point tradition says it was interrupted by conquering Ottoman troops in 1453. This possibly apocryphal story highlights the fact that Athens used the dream of some Greeks for a reconstructed Greek and Orthodox Empire buttressed by Greek communities in Asia Minor with ancient pedigrees, access to Homeric and classical literature, the Orthodox faith, and modern Greek nationalism.

Maria Todorova chronicled something along these lines in her narrative on the history of the search for the burial site of the Bulgarian resistance hero Vasil Kunchev—the "Ivan Levsky" celebrated by the Bulgarian Orthodox Church, Bulgarian Communist party, and Bulgarian national entrepreneurs.[3] Todorova's work included iconic (literally) images of the 1980s that bathed Levsky in angelic halos. The discussion here will consider why the Orthodox Churches in the Balkans have been well positioned to bring their flocks into sacred time and have so often done so for the sake of communal cohesion and the interests of the hierarchical authority of both sacred and secular elites.

Various appeals to "tradition" can become conceptual cousins to sacred time. Arno Mayer considered one version as the "persistence of the old regime."[4] His thesis that the aristocracy, not bourgeoisie, drove Europe in the nineteenth century and into World War One ran against the teleology of modernism and reexamined the pull of tradition on the "modernizing" classes. With tongue in cheek, David Cannadine took a look at a related phenomenon he called "Ornamentalism,"[5] which played off Edward Said's more famous book of a similar sounding title[6] to consider how some colonized individuals eagerly embraced imperial decorations and honors. Faith, honor, and other affective pulls provide entrepreneurs of community and their targeted communities with versions of sacred time that provide meaning and orientation.

The struggle for control over sacred time also enables intercommunal conflict and such endogenous contention as struggle between hierarchs and lower clergy on national, regional, and local levels. In the Balkans, the relationship among sacred time, nationalism, and residues of the—related—Byzantine and Ottoman systems inform translation of (and resistance to) various forms of Western-imposed modernity.

The Backdrop of Tradition

It is fair to say Orthodoxy in the Balkans "embodied and expressed the ethos of the Serbian people to such a degree that nationality-religion fused into a distinct 'Serbian faith'."[7] It should be noted that Albanian Orthodoxy was something of an exception; Christians in that region divided roughly between Catholic north and Orthodox south after 1054, with the latter ruled by Greek clergy and Greek-language liturgy.[8] The Patriarch in Constantinople still picks the Albanian primate, a Greek, although Albanians gradually have succeeded to other bishoprics.

This was not modern nationalism, of course, but the idea that Orthodox Slavs in the Balkans were different from Greek-speaking elites in the capital clearly already existed. The Peć Patriarchate was disbanded after the Battle of Smederevo in 1459, but bickering over the use of Greek or Slavonic rites continued, even after the Ottomans chose to inherit the patriarchal establishment as a political and social tool. Bishop Pavel of Smederevo attempted unsuccessfully to organize a "Serbian" Church between 1528 and 1533, and the patriarchal title returned to Peć—with the Sultan's approval—in 1557. Slavic historians would write of the "double yoke" of the Ottomans and the Orthodox hierarchy.[9]

The Ottomans formalized this relationship in the *Taife* arrangement that becomes the much discussed "*Millet*" system—nothing like this had existed in a Byzantine Empire in which Jews faced persecution and Catholic colonies in Constantinople from Venice and Genoa largely were restricted to residences across the Golden Horn. Multiple authors have raised objections to facile use of the "*Millet*" concept,[10] but their various takes on the historical, economic, and social complexity of Ottoman structural toleration of "Peoples of the Book" do not negate the fact that the Empire organized a system of structural religious administration that helped define communal autonomy and identity.

The Orthodox Patriarch often was more rigid than the Sultan in the enforcement of Orthodoxy in organizational as well as religious practice, an issue that would exacerbate the Patriarch's confrontation with both nationalism and imperial reform efforts after 1798. Sacred and secular time among Balkan Christians came under the purview of Greek priests and the "Phanariot" aristocracy, Greeks who administered much of the Balkans for the Sultan but also could provide administrative support for the ecclesiastical interests of a Patriarch who lived in the "lighthouse" district of the capital that gave the Phanariots their name. It is important to remember that the patriarchal hierarchy and its Phanariot allies first fought intensely against nationalism—including Greek nationalism—before a fractured Orthodox ecclesiastical universe became identified with the nationalisms and sacred spaces they enabled, nurtured (even under Communism), and continue to promote today.[11]

The Greek War of Independence had an ambiguous impact on the Ecumenical Patriarch and on religious and secular politics. The creation of a "Greek" Orthodox Church was a direct challenge to the Byzantine roots of the Patriarch's credibility, leading immediately to tensions between the two establishments.[12] This issue became part of a three-cornered struggle to define Greek identity that lasted until the defeat of the Greek invasion of Anatolia after World War One. Phanariots remained Greeks who were loyal to the Ottoman system that privileged them, and would remain engaged in efforts to preserve an imperial system that since the last years of the eighteenth century had proven predictions of its collapse wrong. The Patriarch in Constantinople had little reason to risk the privileges his hierarchy enjoyed. The clergy focused largely on protecting its status against the various nationalisms. Greek nationalists split over the question of how Greece should be constituted—should it be a modernizing Greek national state or the core of a restored Byzantine Empire with its capital eventually restored in Constantinople?

The Patriarch and the Greek Orthodox Church had in common their interest in maintaining the Greek-language liturgy, which put them on the same side of disputes with nationalist or nationalizing priests in the other Balkan Orthodox Churches. The Patriarchate spent the nineteenth century in a rearguard action against efforts by Serbs, Bulgarians, Albanians, and Montenegrins to tie their Churches to emerging national communities. Successful Serbian and Greek separation from Constantinople precluded spiritual and, to an extent, administrative patriarchal obstruction. The effort by Bulgarians to do the same was met with a much more determined resistance. The Sultan created an "exarchate" in Bulgaria rather than an autonomous Church, which satisfied neither side but dissatisfied the Patriarch more.

The Patriarch refused to accept the principle that the faith could be divided by national identity and formally anathematized it as "phyletism" at the Great Council of Constantinople in 1872. Nevertheless, the norm developed that there can be no more than the single ecumenical church on any territory and morphed into a conflict between multiple nationalizing Churches for control over local resources, administration, liturgy/religious services, and education.

Very quickly, Greek and Bulgarian priests helped organize rival establishments in Bulgaria proper and in "Macedonia," the territory and identity of which has been in dispute ever since. As will be discussed below, the Serbian and Macedonian Orthodox Churches have fought over much the same ecclesiastical and practical ground ever since Tito first moved to create an autonomous Macedonian Orthodox Church in 1958. (It declared itself autocephalous in 1967.)

In its "Tarnovo Constitution" of 1879, the Bulgarian government claimed sovereignty over the Bulgarian Orthodox Church. Church hierarchs believed something like the opposite was true.[13] Those local Bulgarians who cooperated with their Greek neighbors became saddled with the epithet "*Grakomani*" (the Patriarchate called them "Bulgarian-speaking Greek activists"). A Bulgarian commander was quoted as saying he did not kill "real" Greeks, just the *Grakomani*.[14] The Bulgarian state helped "its" Church's cause by defining all Orthodox believers living in Bulgaria as "Bulgarian," a practice also observed in Greece and Serbia but not Russia.[15]

This is a period when the Russian Orthodox had its own problems with conflicts among national churches in the Balkans. Ebbing Ottoman power in the region meant Russian clerics could no longer simply appeal to be the protector of all Christians under the Sultan's sway. Now they felt pressure from churches in Serbia, Bulgaria, and Greece—as well as from doctrinal patriarchal authority—to choose sides. The Russian Orthodox Church, under the watchful eyes of the government in St. Petersburg, walked a fine line between, for example, supporting pan-Slavism among Bulgarian Orthodox clerics and maintaining obedience to the denunciation of phyletism at the Great Council of Constantinople.[16]

The struggle among Orthodox Churches, nationalizers, and residual Phanariot authority to control popular experiences with sacred time came to head during the series of uprisings that emerged from the iconic "Ilinden" events in 1903. Nationalizing clergy, by combining religious rites with participation in armed activity, brought combatants/parishioners into the sacred time involved in the ritualized trial by fire of the nation in the struggle against the relevant Other.

Bulgaria stressed its intention to absorb Macedonian identity by changing the language of its constitution to permit adherence by these insurgents to "Bulgarian" identity.[17] Local Greek and Bulgarian priests fought with guerrilla bands. In general, the higher clergy tended toward Greek or Phanariot sympathies, while many priests on the ground tended to identify as Bulgarian. The patriarchal appointment of a Greek Bishop (Constantine) to Varna provoked a serious wave of local violence—citizens initially were successful in forcing the ship carrying the bishop to retreat from the port and return to Istanbul. The Patriarch sent the bishop back, which ensured that fighting spread to Plovdiv and other towns with Greek churches; mobs sacked them and local Bulgarian clergy reconsecrated them with Bulgarian saints' names.[18] Albert Sonnichsen, an American journalist who accompanied a Bulgarian fighting group in Macedonia during the uprisings, also reported that in 1906 Bulgarians (which was how he uniformly identified the Slavic population of Macedonia except in the title of his book) refused to permit patriarchal bishops to return to their appointed places.[19]

However reliable this narrative is, it is clear priests on both sides fought, urged others to fight, organized spy networks, and otherwise participated in a lethal competition to control space and define sacred time. This pattern continued through the Balkan Wars of 1912–1913, the second of which inundated efforts before and during the first at reconciliation among the Orthodox Churches.[20] According to the Carnegie Commission report on those conflicts, the Serbian Orthodox Church teamed up with the Greeks in Macedonia against the exarchate. "'Patriarchism' and 'exarchism' became the rallying cry of the two conflicting nations."[21] The report said that the most difficult among combatants to "subdue" were the priests.[22] Dragostinova notes the pattern of forced conversions on all sides.[23]

The instability and warfare in the decade before World War One carried over into it. The Greek government of Eleftherios Venizelos was suspicious of patriarchal efforts to react to its being shut out of Bulgaria by strengthening its hold over the national Greek Orthodox Church. Memories of Greek atrocities in Macedonia during and after the Second Balkan War motivated reprisals when Bulgaria occupied Macedonia after Sofia's participation in the Central Powers' invasion of Serbia in 1915.[24]

The end of the war brought about a Serbian-dominated Yugoslavia, a divided Greece, and a defeated Bulgaria. The Patriarchate survived the Ottoman collapse, but Phanariot administration did not. The Greek government attempted to absorb Bulgarians living in Greece into the "Greek" Orthodox Church.[25] In the wake of the defeat in Anatolia and the departure from there of much of the Orthodox faithful in the population exchange mandated by Treaty of Lausanne, the Patriarchate became almost a vestigial body. Despite tensions, overall the Greek government and Orthodox hierarchy cooperated. The status of the Bishop of Athens grew during the 1920s at the expense of a Patriarch who still lived in Istanbul. The capital's prelate became the "Archbishop of Athens and all Greece."[26] The Church worked to minimize state supervision and opposed enshrining freedom of religion in the Greek constitution.[27]

Bulgaria's church struggled with its state. Aleksandur Stamboliyski, agrarian politician and strongman until his assassination in 1923, forced the Holy Synod to call a Church council designed to constrict it. The hierarchs managed to manipulate this crisis to their advantage, preventing the government from stacking the Holy Synod with pliant bishops.[28] According to Raikin, Tsar Boris opposed a strong church and saw Peter the Great's subordination of the Russia Orthodox Church as his model. Boris used the Church as a tool in holding off the appeal of Communism until World War Two.[29]

The new Yugoslav state, while ruled by a Serbian King and, initially, by a constitution promulgated in the sacred time of the Serbian national day, was more than just a larger Serbia. Disputes among the country's various communities undermined efforts to create a functioning and universally legitimated state. The Serbian Orthodox and Croatian Catholic Churches had a tense relationship. The Catholic Church also had to deal with tensions between its diocese's hierarchy, based in Zagreb, and Franciscan monks and priests' national sentiments propagated an alternative version of sacred time. Serbian Orthodox prelates, who had burnished their own idea of sacred time by participating in such wartime events as the iconic retreat of virtually the entire royal, political, and clerical elite across the battlefield of Kosovo Polje and Albania in 1915,[30] did not hide their desire for a homogeneous greater Serbian kingdom buttressed by a Serbian patriarchal church.[31]

Serbian Orthodox hierarchs bristled at federal legislative efforts to regulate their activities and were particularly displeased when Belgrade, as part of its effort to motivate Croatian loyalty to the kingdom, tried to conclude a concordat with the Roman Catholic Church in 1937.[32] Both national Churches were skeptical of the government's effort to craft what became the agreement (*Sporazum*) under which Serbia and Croatia partitioned Bosnia under the federal umbrella in 1939.[33] Both Churches mobilized national feeling as Europe slid toward another war after 1937. While Catholic Croatia rationalized its relationship with Fascism, the Serbian Orthodox Church presided at a commemoration of the 550th anniversary of the Battle of Kosovo Polje; sacred time at that time was conjured at the Monastery in Ravanica, rather than at the battlefield itself, unlike similar celebrations of nationalism and faith in 1889 and 1989.[34]

The Romanian Orthodox Church hierarchy enjoyed privileges but not dominance in what was a multi-confessional state, although the head of the Orthodox Church ascended to patriarchal status as a result of a law passed by the Romanian government in 1925. This Orthodox Church was tainted more than other Orthodox Churches by the rise of local variants of fascism. The Church's link to Romanian national and cultural identity in a context where it had to compete for souls against Catholic, Uniate, and Protestant Churches may have motivated especially lower-level clergy to associate with the Iron Guard (League of the Archangel Michael). When Bucharest cracked down on the fascists in 1938, 218 Orthodox priests were among those arrested.[35]

World War Two narratives of the performances of priests and hierarchs from all faiths generally follow the patterns evident in previous rounds of fighting. Debates over atrocities allegedly committed or enabled by clerics underscore larger stories of perpetrators and victims. Serbian Orthodox priests attached themselves to royalist Chetniks; one named

Momčilo Djujić commanded a division of fighters.[36] Nevertheless, Max Bergholz's recent, careful study of violence and identity in and around the Bosnian town of Kulen Vakuf presents a complicated picture of wartime intercommunal relations. Bergholz does not deny the metanarrative. Even enemies accepted the Orthodox religion as the basis for being "Serbian"; the Croatian fascist (and Catholic) Ustashe reportedly excluded Orthodox priests and their families from efforts to convert erstwhile Serbs to Catholicism and—by definition—re-designation as "Croat."[37] The Croats attempted to separate Serbs from Orthodoxy by referring to the clerics as "Greek Easterners," a term Serbian clerics reacted to by "Serbianizing" as much of their message as possible. The Croatian fascist policy of destroying all things "Serbian" led to the destruction of the Serbian Orthodox Church in Bihać.[38]

Nevertheless, Bergholz also recorded instances of clerical resistance to violence against neighbors of the other faith/nationality in and near Kulen Vakuf. His research indicates a Serbian Orthodox priest had defended local Muslims against a Serbian mob as early as 1918.[39] Intercommunal tensions grew after the German destruction of the first Yugoslavia in April 1941, leading to serious local atrocities even before the conflict among Chetniks, Partisans, Italians, and Germans jelled, but at least some Catholic and Orthodox priests cooperated to mitigate the horrors as best they could.[40] Anecdotal evidence that efforts to head off violence sometimes did so suggests that research on the relationship between religion and identity during the series of conflicts marking Balkan history should consider Bergholz's findings that violence can inform identity, but that leadership from committed clerics can enable resistance to violence.

The transition from World War Two to the Cold War certainly stressed the Orthodox Churches, but—with the exception of Albania—did not destroy their existence or the integral links between their exercises in sacred time and partly latent nationalisms. The "People's Democracies" practiced versions of cooptation and repression that competed with but failed to replace the Churches as lodestars of identity. Throughout the Communist era, the Communists tended to favor lower clergy over hierarchs, but would not hesitate to use bishops and even patriarchs, if the times and party strategy appeared to require it. In the view of Janice Broun, Bulgaria was something of a special case; by 1944, the Bulgarian Orthodox Church had lost much of its influence and was not equipped to withstand the onslaught of an atheist regime. The regime was able to manipulate its succession struggles and outright schisms.[41]

One geostrategic change taking place during the Communist years was the considerable increase in ideological/political distance between Greece and the East European Orthodox world as a result of its falling on the Western side of Europe's strategic divide after the end of the Greek Civil War. This also meant the monasteries on Mt. Athos and the Patriarch in Istanbul also became many steps more distant from East European clerics and their captured flocks.

This does not mean religion flourished in Greece and withered in the other Balkan countries. Bulgaria's new Communist masters enshrined the Bulgarian Orthodox Church as a "traditional" institution in their 1949 "Law of Confessions," absorbed the Holy Synod into their own administration, and enabled it to "inform" the substance and spirit of a "People's Democratic Church."[42] Pliant Church officials propagated state propaganda to the Bulgarian diaspora. When Communist boss Todor Zhivkov attempted to exclude the Church from his celebration of the 1300th anniversary of the Bulgarian state, Church officials responded with quotes from the Communists' "iconic" founder Georgi Dimitrov praising the Church as a "solid spiritual bridge."[43]

Romania's Communists retained closer ties with their Orthodox Church; like earlier regimes, the Communists recognized that the Church retained great popularity among the public.[44] At times, high state officials entered sacred time; Scarfe noted that Communist officials baptized their children into the Church and suggested that the Romanian Orthodox Church retained more influence over cultural and spiritual life than its counterparts in other East European countries.[45] Party boss Nicolae Ceauşescu's parents were buried according to Orthodox rites, and the Patriarch had good—perhaps close—relations with Ceauşescu and Elena, his influential wife.[46]

The differences between Tito's Yugoslavia and the other Communist states of Eastern Europe provided a unique context affecting the strategies and activities of Serbian and other Orthodox Churches. Yugoslavia was a federal state, not a country with one clear titular national identity congruent with a national Orthodox Church.

In general, Tito's approach was to attempt to ensure Serbs would not be able to dominate his Yugoslavia, and religion was one tool he used to limit their traditional hegemony. During the Communist decades, the Serbian Orthodox Church built a story about itself as God's especially suffering Church, assuring that the sacred time associated with the Battle of Kosovo Polje—June 28—would remain the Serbian national day, as it was in interwar royal Yugoslavia. The trek of the Vojvods in 1689–1690, the catastrophic retreat of virtually the entire national elite across Kosovo and Albania in 1915, the Church's severe losses of priests and parishioners in the world wars (Serbia lost more people per capita than any other participant in World War One), remained—and remains—central to the sacred narrative.

The Serbian Orthodox Church objected to Tito's creation of a Macedonian Orthodox Church, noting claims of jurisdiction over Macedonian believers partly based on a legal and administrative status granted by the Ottoman Sultan and the Ecumenical Patriarch when Serbs receive their status as a *millet* after 1830. A desire to hold on to church properties also was not irrelevant.[47] Macedonian clergy, meanwhile, called for the reopening of the Patriarchate at Ohrid and looked for some sort of contact with the Vatican.[48] Serbian Orthodox officials called for an ecumenical council to settle the issue, but—given the attitude of the Bulgarian Church—it was far from clear that this would lead to a result satisfactory to the Serbian side.

Serbian Orthodox hierarchs worried about their social as well as political flank. A survey conducted in 1966 suggested Catholic and Muslim Yugoslav citizens were more religious than their Orthodox counterparts.[49] Subsequent polls in the 1970s and 1980s had similar results. The Serbian Orthodox Church only had 1 priest for every 5714 believers in the 1980s—a worse rate of clerical representation than other faiths.[50] The Church responded by increasing the number of public ritual celebrations involving historic sites and publicized hierarchs' visits to the Hilandar Monastery on Mount Athos and to Churches in Jerusalem, Antioch, Alexandria, and Moscow. It was not clear whether this appeal to sacred time increased Serbian Orthodox religiosity, but in 1974 the League of Communists of Serbia criticized the Church as being the carrier of the "new nationalism."[51]

Meanwhile, the Serbian Orthodox Church worked to highlight the collective memory of Croatian atrocities against Serbs during World War Two while Yugoslavia's Catholic hierarchy attempted to play down Croatian and clerical responsibility for war crimes. The two such memories with perhaps the highest level of attention and symbolism have been the question of the behavior of Alojzije Stepinac, wartime Archbishop of Zagreb (he held that office from 1937 until his death in 1960), who was tried and convicted by the Communists, and the issue of how many Serbs and others were killed (and by whom) at the death camp at Jasenovac. During the Communist years, the Serbian Orthodox scrutinized the regime's treatment of these issues and demanded financial reparations from the Yugoslav Republic of Croatia. After Tito died, these feuds came into high relief as the durability of the Communist system came into question. On 2 September 1984, 20,000 Serbs attended a Serbian Orthodox ceremony at Jasenovac, held as an explicit answer to perceived efforts by Croats and the Catholic Church to "obliterate" the fact of the slaughter. The Serbs reportedly were able to attract some support for their version of events from Yugoslavia's Jewish Community.[52] The Catholics responded not only with their own narratives of these controversies, but also with an effort to brand the 1690 trek of the Vojvods as an Orthodox invasion of Croatia.

Looking Back to Look Ahead

The demise of the Soviet system in Eastern Europe disoriented political and social life in the Balkans somewhat differently from in the rest of Eastern Europe. The borders of the Poland and Hungary had been decided by the World Wars (although Transylvania remains an irritant between Hungary and Romania), and Czechs and Slovaks agreed on a peaceful process of separation. As in the rest of "Europe," the Cold War diminished Europe's space and importance. In contrast—no matter the rhetoric of Western governments and EU paladins—borders in the Balkans have remained unsettled, Orthodox Church affiliations have remained contested, and dueling religious/national narratives about sacred time have ensured these rivalries continue to fester.

As Communism evaporated, Churches pressed their status as definers of the nation to engage in politics and take positions on intensifying communal rivalries. This was part of an effort to overcome the stain on clerical reputations of collaboration with the Communists (association with pre-war nationalists and fascists was much less of a problem regarding clerics' communal reputations). It also was an attempt to revive the role Orthodox Churches had played in imperial and national contexts before the Balkans had been inundated by the German-Soviet and then the US-Soviet struggles for domination. In addition, the end of the Cold War brought Greece and Bulgaria (and their Orthodox hierarchies) back into the "Balkans," in that the future of the Macedonian piece of a collapsing Yugoslavia led both countries to pick up where they had left off regarding their differing slants on whether "Macedonia" or "Macedonians" exist.

The Orthodox Churches dusted off creation myths and moved to restore their places at the center of communal sacred time and secular space. Clerics in former Communist countries worked to regain properties and restore public faith in priests who had collaborated with the regimes. Meanwhile, the Greek Orthodox Church resisted efforts to distribute Church properties to needy villagers and faced discontent from the "Old Calendarists" who had never accepted adoption of the Western calendar in 1924.[53] The Churches received some help from former monarchs, who looked to connect with traditional elements of national identity even as they presumed to play the modernizing role in their countries that King Juan Carlos played in Spain after Franco's death. The author saw Simeon Saxe-Coburg-Gotha stand close to a televised Easter service of the Bulgarian Orthodox Church shortly before the former Tsar became Bulgaria's Prime Minister.

The Serbian Orthodox Church had had no use for Tito's Yugoslavia and had increasingly played an active role in its demise. Riots in Kosovo in 1968 had sparked public complaint about the regime's lack of protection of churches and monasteries in Kosovo—including a letter from Orthodox bishops to Tito—and intensified the use of processions and other ceremonies to highlight Serbian spiritual attachment to the province.[54] The Church also joined secular Serbian complaints about alleged forced expulsion of Serbs and Montenegrins from Kosovo by ethnic Albanians (and the provincial party leadership). The decentralization during Tito's later years and the decade-long interregnum after his death in 1980 enabled public disputes between the Serbian Orthodox Church and Croatian Catholic Church over contrasting narratives of the atrocities committed during World War Two, and Croatian efforts to use the Catholic shrine of the Virgin at Medjugorje as a rallying point for sacred time and nationalism. A papal reception for nationally minded Macedonian Orthodox clerics in 1985 did not help matters; the Vatican press intruded in inter-Orthodox disputes by supporting pretensions to separation from the Serbian Church expressed by some Montenegrin Orthodox clerics.[55]

The Serbian Orthodox Church continued to use the Hilandar Monastery at Mt. Athos to cement Serbian religious and national identity in a context of sacred time. Church officials referred to it as a "living spiritual holy of holies" and said it and other monasteries were "milestones" of Serbian spiritual space.[56] This "religious statecraft" reportedly did not impress international and NGO observers,[57] reflecting secular modernists' tendency to underestimate the affective appeal of religious identity in conditions where political authorities and outside notables have little legitimacy.

In the context of strife in Kosovo and separatist movements among Macedonian and Montenegrin Orthodox hierarchs and believers, German II—the aging Serbian Orthodox Patriarch—became increasingly nationalistic in his pronouncements and behavior. In 1987, he and the Serbian Orthodox Church called for the partition of Yugoslavia. He also opposed dialogue with Uniates (Catholics who celebrate the Orthodox rite) at a conclave convened by the Ecumenical Patriarch in Constantinople.[58] German and the Church cooperated with Serbian strongman Slobodan Milošević in a nationalistic on-site celebration of the 600th anniversary of the 1389 Battle of Kosovo Polje, attended by an estimated 1 million people (although Milošević reportedly avoided religious services in favor of a celebration of secular nationalism).[59]

The Church had some leverage over the state regarding the use of Kosovo as a central symbol of the nation. Political authorities routinely used—and still use—Serbian religious connections with the province to maintain their territorial claims. Belgrade has consistently continued to refer to "Kosovo-Metohija"—"Metohija" highlighting the monastic estates associated with Serbia's claim to the place. Once it became clear to many inside Yugoslavia that the federation was falling apart, the Serbian Orthodox Church geared up to promote efforts to ensure that post-Yugoslav Serbs in Croatia, Bosnia, Kosovo, Montenegro, and perhaps Macedonia would live in a unified political and religious Serbia—there clearly existed a religious tinge in the nationalists' slogan, "wherever there are Serbs, there is Serbia."

This exposed a contradiction in the Church's approach to politics and security that widened after 1990. On the one hand, it welcomed the collapse of Yugoslavia and its Communist, multicultural, non-Serbian nationalist orientation. On the other hand, in losing the larger context of Yugoslavia's borders, the Serbian Orthodox Church found itself struggling to preserve the political basis for its greater-Serbian ambitions. The Church could pose as the legitimation and spiritual underpinning of Serbdom, but that did little good when attempting to support the preservation of a single entity encompassing Serbian communities wherever they happened to be inside the former federal boundaries. After 1990, many Serbs found themselves living inside newly minted successor states dominated by non-Serbs or, in the case of Bosnia-Herzegovina, without a hegemonic ethnic, religious, or civic community. In addition, the independence of Macedonia and sometimes tense relationship between the

Serbian Orthodox Patriarch and various bishops revived questions related to the pecking order of the Patriarch, the dioceses, and Serbian hierarchs in charge of the old Patriarchates of Ohrid and Peć.

In January 1992, speaking through their Holy Assembly, Serbian Orthodox Bishops sent a letter to Western capitals and the Vatican protesting the growing momentum behind the Christian Democratic support (in Germany, the Netherlands, and elsewhere) for recognizing Slovenia and Croatia,[60] which left the impression of international unconcern about what would happen to the rest of the dying federation. The Serbian hierarchs also protested Vatican efforts to establish a Ukraine-like "Uniate" arrangement permitting south Slav Orthodox believers to declare allegiance to the Catholic Church while keeping their Orthodox liturgy and rites. There were some efforts to establish an ecumenical dialogue between Catholic and Orthodox clerics in Croatia and Bosnia. However—along with the fighting in Bosnia and Croatia, of course—the process of separation and war that first created a Serbian (Orthodox) statelet in the Krajina, but then destroyed that state and the network of politically mobilized communities that had existed there for 400 years inundated any hope of an effective interfaith dialogue.[61]

Nevertheless, the Church generally greeted the implosion of Yugoslavia with undisguised enthusiasm. In 1990, Patriarch German II told a Belgian newspaper that Yugoslavia's partition was "inevitable" and stressed the Serbs' need for their own homogeneous state. He expressed the hope that partition would be peaceful, but Orthodox clerics in Croatia and Bosnia called for Serbs to arm themselves to prevent a repeat of the slaughter of World War Two. Serbian Orthodox and Croatian Catholic bishops, echoing their secular counterparts, criticized each other for fomenting tensions[62] but also met to discuss a partition of Bosnia between Serbs and Croats along the lines of the agreement ("*Sporazum*") arranged in 1939 by Prince Paul, Yugoslavia's royal regent.[63] The Church was involved with a revival of interest in the *gusle*, a stringed instrument used to play folk songs, some of sacred and nationalist orientation. As Yugoslavia was falling apart, *gusles* were given as Christmas presents, taken off the walls of taverns and tuned, and appropriated by Radovan Karadžić, Bosnian Serbian leader, psychiatrist, and would-be interpreter of national ballads. The same instrument was used by Croatian and Bosnian Muslim activists, but became most closely associated with Serbian efforts to draw their community into religious and nationalist sacred time.[64]

The Serbian Orthodox Church's enthusiasm for Yugoslavia's collapse likely was accelerated by the realization that the Church quickly replaced the federal state as a lodestar for Serbian identity. The "*Partizan*" football team—representing the Yugoslav National Army and bearing the name of Tito's wartime movement—had made a pilgrimage to the Serbian Orthodox Hilandar Monastery at the foot of Mount Athos (site of multiple shrines of patriarchal and national Orthodox Churches). Slobodan Milošević did the same in 1991.[65] Resident Superiors and visitors would continue to use Hilandar as a venue for political commentary—Hilandar's Father Metodije spoke out against Montenegro's separation from Serbia via referendum in 2006, and Serbian President Vojislav Koštunica used a trip there to stress Kosovo's link to Serbia "through time."[66]

The Church, while supporting *gusle* wielding Radovan Karadžić in Bosnia and Serbian separatists in Croatia, did not express the same enthusiasm for Milošević. German was dying in 1990 and was unable to rein in bishops who held varying views about a Communist strongman who appeared to have a hold on the Serbian nationalist constituency. After German's death, Pavle, his successor as Patriarch, stressed his support for the Church's role as the spiritual guide to a democratic Serbia, but expressed muted opposition to Milošević.[67] Nevertheless, Pavle clearly was unwilling to directly undermine Milošević's stature; he wrote a patriarchal letter providing authorization for Milošević to negotiate on behalf of the Bosnian Serbs at Dayton in 1995. This overawed Karadžić's reluctance to relinquish pride of place when defeats on the ground had led to deterioration in the Bosnian Serbian position by the autumn of 1995.[68]

The Orthodox Church became the de facto official religion of the Republika Srpska (RS), the Serbian entity authorized by the Dayton Agreement as a constituent piece of the rickety Bosnian state. Orthodox building projects enjoyed official support in that entity, while Catholic and Muslim projects did not. The author was present in Banja Luka during disputes associated with a long-running effort by the RS authorities to delay as long as possible the rebuilding of the Ferhadija Mosque in that town—a process that was underscored by Orthodox Church-sponsored building projects clearly under way in the same city.

The breakup of Yugoslavia, while providing the Serbian Orthodox Church with an opportunity to resume its role as soul of the nation, also enabled non-Serbian Orthodox clergy and believers elsewhere in the former Yugoslavia to continue Tito's effort to use links with their communities to compete with the Serbian Orthodox Church via their own nation-building processes. Macedonian and Montenegrin Orthodox hierarchs acted very much as did the Bulgarian Exarchate against the Patriarch in the 1870s—with Serbian Orthodox bishops and priests playing a role similar to that of the hierarchs in Constantinople during that period. The Serbian Orthodox Church attempted to retain its authority in both cases—Macedonian prelates rejected their Serbian brethren's effort to reverse their 1958 decision to "relinquish" authority over the Macedonian Orthodox Church.[69] This time the Greek Orthodox Church attempted to play a mediating role; no element of the Orthodox universe had made a serious effort to do so in earlier periods. Its efforts to bridge the gaps between Serbian, on the one hand, and Macedonian and Montenegrin prelates on the other were unsuccessful.

They were not helped by the strategy used by some Greek clerics to repeat arguments from the nineteenth century against a separate Bulgarian or "Macedonian" Orthodox Church in support of Greece's post-Yugoslav insistence that the country then calling itself "Macedonia" had no right to use that name.[70] The strength of feelings against Greek clergy willing to accept the existence of a non-Greek Macedonia was expressed when Macedonian Archimandrite Nicodemus Barknias was beaten by Greek border guards in May 1994. This was not the first time he had been assaulted; this priest also had been dismissed from his parish because of his views on the Macedonian question.[71]

However beleaguered it was by its problems with the Serbian Orthodox Church, the Macedonian Orthodox Church took the offensive against the religious as well as ethnic identity of Macedonia's 25% or so Albanian population. It erected a 66-meter cross on Mt. Vodno in celebration of 2000 years of Christianity in Macedonia, which no doubt was meant to convey a provocative message regarding Macedonian identity. Archbishop Mihailo referred to Macedonian Muslims as "lost sheep" he hoped would return to the (Christian) fold—an attitude not too different from that of Catholic and Orthodox officials toward Bosnian Muslims during World War Two. Church officials identified Muslims as having an "ethno-linguistic"—but not religious—identity.[72] Ethnic Albanians responded with a mosque graced with 76-meter minarets—this structure was a victim of fighting in 2001. Both communities shoehorned construction projects into the grandiose "Skopje 2014" project promulgated by the nationalist government then in power. A call in November 2017 by the Macedonian Orthodox hierarchy on the

Bulgarian Orthodox Church to become its "parent" signaled that questions of national identity and sacred time remained open.[73]

Milo Djukanović, a one-time Milošević acolyte who, with international support, morphed into Montenegro's semi-autocratic Big Man, exploited tensions between the Serbian and Montenegrin Churches. He needed to prove to the West that Milošević was acting brutally toward Montenegro as part of an effort to stage-manage Montenegro's separation from the Serbian-dominated federation that was all that remained of Yugoslavia by the mid-1990s. Skirmishes at the border and at the airport in Podgorica—which were as likely provoked by Djukanović as by Milošević—were not doing the trick, so the former highlighted fights between Serbian and Montenegrin clergy as purported evidence of Belgrade's heavy-handed repression.[74]

Serbian Orthodox opposition to the NATO bombing campaign over Kosovo in 1999 was over-determined by the Church's identification with a Serbian state under attack, anger at Western assistance to ethnic Albanian efforts to separate from Serbia, and the presence in Kosovo of the central shrines of the Serbian Orthodox Church. The author witnessed efforts in the early 2000s by US diplomats to convince Serbian clerics that they had nothing to fear from a post-Yugoslav Kosovo they promised would become democratic and multicultural. The prelates invariably responded by highlighting ethnic Albanian brutality toward Serbs and the Serbian Orthodox Church and pointing to evidence of damage done to churches and monasteries by Kosovar Albanians and the US-led bombing campaign. Serbian Orthodox clerics participated in successful Serbian efforts to prevent Kosovo from joining UNESCO.[75] When some members of the Serbian government tried to send a "peace train" into Kosovo in January 2017 to underscore Belgrade's continuing hold on vital transportation routes into and out of the lost province, it festooned its cars with icons and other images connecting the Serbian Orthodox Church with the Serbian nation—and both with continued Serbian sovereignty over Kosovo.[76]

The Kosovo bombing campaign sparked a new Russian effort to stake out its claims to the loyalty of fellow Slavs and Orthodox believers in the Balkans. This predated Vladimir Putin's coming to power in 2000. Russia and NATO had cooperated fairly well during the Bosnian War (1992–1995), but Moscow had been dissatisfied with the role the West permitted it to have after the signing of the Dayton Agreement. In 1999, a Russian official told the author of Moscow's dissatisfaction with its treatment by Washington regarding Balkans affairs and explained that Russian troops seized control of the airport in Prishtina without warning because the USA had reneged on promises to disarm, demilitarize, and disband the Kosovo Liberation Army.

Conclusion: National, Not Ecumenical Orthodoxy

Efforts to gain the loyalty of Balkan Orthodox Churches have become an integral part of Russia's geostrategic approach to the region, but the Russian Orthodox Church has had little more success forging a unified Orthodox hierarchy under its guidance than did the Patriarch in Constantinople in the decades between Greek and Serbian independence and World War One. Disputes among Serbian, Macedonian, and Montenegrin Churches have continued unabated and—along with sectarian disputes among other Orthodox Churches—have frustrated occasional efforts by the Russian Orthodox Church to use a shared notion of sacred time in connection with Russian diplomatic and public relations efforts to line up Balkan national Churches in a unified Slavic Orthodox front.

The most significant of these efforts to date was the attempt to arrange the first Orthodox Ecumenical Council in 1200 years, a meeting decided on by Orthodox hierarchs meeting in Istanbul in March 2014.[77] Russian nationalists picked up on this; Viktor Zaplatin, the Russian head of something called the "Balkan Cossack Army," declared, "the Orthodox world is one world."[78] These latter-day Cossacks, with representation from Serbia, Macedonia, Montenegro, Greece, Bulgaria, and the Serbian entity in Bosnia, called for the partition of Bosnia-Herzegovina. This small group appeared to reflect a Russian desire to use the notion of Orthodox ecumenicism to overawe the Ecumenical Patriarch in favor of the pan-Orthodox supremacy of the Russian Orthodox Church.

Whatever Moscow's intention, the ecumenical effort was made stillborn by the myriad disputes inside Christian Orthodoxy, of which Balkan squabbles were only a part. The Bulgarian Orthodox Church pulled out over a number of procedural issues—and in the wake of its continuing difficulty achieving internal unity.[79] The Bulgarians also had a spat with the Macedonian Orthodox over which should possess the bones of medieval Bulgarian (or Macedonian?) Tsar Samuel. Russian and patriarchal spokesman clashed over (among other things) Russian insinuations that the Patriarch had betrayed Orthodoxy when Byzantine Emperor John VII agreed to submit to papal supremacy at the Council of Florence in 1439.[80]

Serbian and Romanian Orthodox Churches attended, but squabbled over jurisdictional issues. There were comments about the "sly Greeks" from some Slavic quarters.[81] The Russians finally decided not even to come, but took the opportunity to clash with the Ukrainian Church over the conflict in eastern Ukraine. Long-standing rivalry soured the discourse between the patriarchs of Jerusalem and Antioch. Some Churches bolted over their disagreement with the idea of referring to Catholics and Protestants as anything but "heretics." National Churches refused to give equal status to clerics representing mere ethnic groups—the national principle also was protected on its other flank by removing the meeting from Istanbul to Crete, ostensibly because of ongoing tensions between Russia and Turkey.[82] Moscow tried to smooth things over with selected Balkan Churches; the Russian and Serbian Patriarchs met as the Ecumenical Council was losing attendees, and the Russian Orthodox Church returned relics of St. Luka to its Bulgarian Orthodox counterpart.[83] The Russian Orthodox Church welcomed the results of the meeting, but refused to term it "pan-Orthodox." There were reports Russian schools intend to add courses in "Orthodox Culture."[84]

Inter-(or is it Intra-?) Church politics continued to roil after the less than successful meeting ended. The Macedonian Orthodox Church hierarchy asked its Bulgarian counterpart to become its "Big Brother," which reopened the issue of Macedonian identity and the clerical turf wars of the nineteenth century. The Bulgarian Patriarch urged his Holy Synod to "take the hand extended to us by our Macedonian brothers," but—after strong letters from the Ecumenical Patriarch and the Serbian Orthodox Church—the Bulgarian Synod voted 8-5 against accepting this offer.[85] This consideration of a Bulgarian/Macedonian religious alliance, while abortive, threatened to reinforce the traditional Bulgarian claim that the closeness of their languages means Macedonians are actually Bulgarians.

The decision by the Ecumenical Patriarch to recognize the autocephaly of the Ukrainian Orthodox Church had a considerable impact on the Balkans, given demands by the Macedonian and Montenegrin Orthodox Churches for similar status. The Patriarch was careful to underscore the distinction between a Ukrainian Church acting in accordance with Constantinople's version of sacred time and Church history, and the formal subordination of the Archbishop of Ohrid to the Archbishop of Peć.[86] Nevertheless, the Patriarch's support for a separate Church in Kyiv undercut Constantinople's traditional argument against phyletism, cost the Patriarch any residual authority over the half of Orthodox believers who are faithful to the Russian Orthodox Church, and reinforced the cases for autocephaly in Macedonia and Montenegro.

Meanwhile, the Russian Orthodox Church's attempts to maneuver among the conflicting interests of the Serbian, Bulgarian, Macedonian, and Montenegrin Churches have presented Moscow with problems somewhat akin to those it faced in the 1870s. Russian efforts to organize a common Orthodox view of sacred time ran up against the struggles to build nations and national Orthodox Churches during that earlier period that remain centrally relevant to current disputes.

Those in charge of Orthodox Christian Churches in the Balkans have remained lashed to the national identities they nurtured and have attempted to revive the sense that nationalism is modern and progressive—but also an essential piece of sacred time. Politicians continue to seek clerical support as keepers of the national flame,[87] and the Byzantine-like icons remain a flourishing art form.[88] Nevertheless, there are limits to Orthodoxy's influence—the Serbian Orthodox Church failed to prevent newly elected President Aleksandar Vučić from appointing Ana Brnabić, the country's first openly lesbian Prime Minister.[89]

The Churches have succeeded in turning communal memories of the formation of national feeling into a sort of primordial celebration of what has become the sacred time of the nineteenth and earlier centuries. In this sense, their stance is somewhat similar to that of religious Zionists on Israel, with the important exception that, while Christian Orthodoxy was linked to nationalism from the latter's modern inception, many Orthodox rabbis initially were skeptical of the Zionist movement and continued until relatively recently to feel alienated from what started out as a largely secular Israeli state. At the same time, while Jewish Orthodoxy has skillfully used the commotion that is Israeli politics to capture that state, Christian Orthodox Churches remain very much junior partners in contemporary national politics—much as they were during the Byzantine and Ottoman centuries. When comments from hierarchs anger politicians, the formers' spiritual status will not prevent the latter from slapping them down.[90]

Nevertheless, the spiritual and emotional pull of sacred time will continue to serve both clerical and political authorities in the Balkans and elsewhere, especially if the largely material appeal of liberal institutionalism continues to decline. As nations are imagined, whatever is sacred about their constructed pasts will remain in the foreground of politics and security, and will continue to confound Western nation-building and conflict management dogma.

Notes

1. Mark Juergensmeyer, *Global Rebellion: Religious Challenges to the Secular State, from Christian Militias to Al Qa'ida* (Berkeley and Los Angeles: University of California Press, 2008), p. 3.
2. This resistance is analyzed in Pieter M. Judson, *Guardians of the Nation: Activists on the Language Frontiers of Imperial Austria* (Cambridge, MA: Harvard University Press, 2006); Jeremy King, *Budweisers into Czechs and Germans: A Local History of Bohemian Politics, 1848–1948* (Princeton, NJ: Princeton University Press, 2002).
3. Maria Todorova, *Bones of Contention: The Living Archive of Vasil Levski and the Making of Bulgaria's National Hero* (Budapest: Central European University Press, 2009).
4. Arno J. Mayer, *The Persistence of the Old Regime: Europe to the Great War* (New York: Pantheon, 1981).
5. David Cannadine, *Ornamentalism: How the British Saw Their Empire* (Oxford and New York: Oxford University Press, 2001).
6. Edward Said, *Orientalism* (New York: Vintage Books, 1978).
7. Vekoslav Perica, *Balkan Idols: Religion and Nationalism in Yugoslav States* (Oxford: Oxford University Press, 2002), p. 6.
8. Pedro Ramet, "The Albanian Orthodox Church," in Pedro Ramet (ed.), *Eastern Christianity and Politics in the Twentieth Century* (Durham, NC: Duke University Press, 1988), pp. 149–159.
9. Peter F. Sugar, "External and Domestic Roots of East European Nationalism," in Peter F. Sugar and Ivo J. Lederer (eds.), *Nationalism in Eastern Europe* (Seattle and London: University of Washington Press, 1969), p. 31.
10. For example, Idek K. Yosmaoglu, "From Exoticism to Historicism: The Legacy of Empire and the Pains of Nation-Making in the Balkans," in Theodora Dragostinova and Yana Hashimova (eds.), *Beyond Mosque, Church, and State: Alternative Narratives of the Nation in the Balkans* (Budapest: Central European University Press, 2016), pp. 57–79.
11. Ibid., p. 59.
12. Dragostinova, *Between Two Motherlands*, p. 20.
13. Spas T. Raikin, "The Bulgarian Orthodox Church," in Ramet (ed.), *Eastern Christianity and Politics*, p. 162.
14. Dragostinova, *Between Two Motherlands*, p. 33.
15. Dragostinova, "In Search of the Bulgarians: Mapping the Nation Through National Classification," in Dragostinova and Hashimova (eds.), *Beyond Mosque*, pp. 114–115.
16. Lora Gerd, "Russia, Mt. Athos, and the Eastern Question, 1878–1914," in Lucien J. Frary and Mara Kozelsky (eds.), *Russian-Ottoman*

Borderlands: The Eastern Question Reconsidered (Madison: University of Wisconsin Press, 2014), pp. 193–220.
17. Shea, *Macedonia and Greece*, p. 168.
18. Dragostinova, *Between Two Motherlands*, p. 34.
19. Albert Sonnichsen, *Confessions of a Macedonian Bandit: A Californian in the Balkan Wars* (Santa Barbara: The Narrative Press, 2004—Reprint of the 1909 Premier Press edition), p. 64.
20. Dragostinova, *Between Two Motherlands*, p. 79.
21. Carnegie Endowment for International Peace, *Report of the International Commission to Inquire into the Causes and Conduct of the Balkan Wars* (Washington, DC: Carnegie Endowment, 1914), p. 25.
22. Ibid., p. 52.
23. Dragostinova, "In Search of the Bulgarians: Mapping the Nation Through National Classification," in Dragostinova and Hashimova (eds.), *Beyond Mosque*, pp. 121–122.
24. Dragostinova, *Between Two Motherlands*, pp. 88–89.
25. Ibid., p. 222.
26. Theofanis G. Stavrou, "The Orthodox Church of Greece," in Ramet (ed.), *Eastern Christianity and Politics*, p. 193.
27. Ibid., p. 193.
28. Raikin, "The Bulgarian Orthodox Church," p. 163.
29. Ibid., pp. 169–170.
30. During the wars of the 1990s, the author witnessed the treatment of this national trek as sacred time, with a film about these events running as an almost continuous loop on Belgrade television.
31. Perica, *Balkan Idols*, p. 214.
32. Ramet, "Autocephaly and National Identity in Church-State Relations in Eastern Christianity: An Introduction," in Ramet (ed.), *Eastern Christianity and Politics*, p. 14.
33. Perica, *Balkan Idols*, p. 47.
34. Ibid., p. 20.
35. Alan Scarfe, "The Romanian Orthodox Church," in Ramet (ed.), *Eastern Christianity and Politics*, p. 214.
36. Perica, *Balkan Idols*, p. 23.
37. Max Bergholz, *Violence as a Generative Force: Identity, Nationalism, and Memory in a Balkan Community* (Ithaca, NY: Cornell University Press, 2016), p. 81.
38. Ibid., p. 97.
39. Ibid., p. 70.
40. Ibid., p. 52.
41. Janice Broun, "The Schism in the Bulgarian Orthodox Church," *Religion, State, and Society*, Vol. 21, No. 2 (1993), pp. 207–220.

42. Raikin, "The Bulgarian Orthodox Church," pp. 163, 170.
43. Ibid., pp. 175–176.
44. Maura Woodman, "The Romanian Orthodox Church and Post-Communist Democratization," Prezi.com, 3 May 2017.
45. Scarfe, "The Romanian Orthodox Church," p. 220.
46. Ramet, "Autocephaly and National Identity," p. 17.
47. Vasiliki P. Neofotistos, *The Risk of War: Everyday Sociality in the Republic of Macedonia* (Philadelphia: University of Pennsylvania Press, 2012), p. 16.
48. John Shea, *Macedonia and Greece: The Struggle to Define a New Balkan Nation* (Jefferson, NC: McFarland, 1997), p. 174.
49. Perica, *Balkan Idols*, p. 50.
50. Ibid., p. 132.
51. Ibid., p. 52.
52. Ibid., pp. 149–151.
53. Stavrou, "The Orthodox Church of Greece," p. 204.
54. Perica, *Balkan Idols*, p. 45.
55. Ibid., p. 146.
56. Ivan Čolović, *The Balkans: Essays in Political Anthropology* (Baden-Baden: NOMOS, 2011), pp. 26–27.
57. Ibid., p. 184.
58. Perica, *Balkan Idols*, pp. 158–161.
59. Ibid., p. 128.
60. Ibid., pp. 162–163.
61. Neven Duvnjak and Renata Relja, "Orthodox in Croatia After 1990," in *Occasional Papers on Religion in Eastern Europe*, No. 4 (2002).
62. Ibid.
63. Perica, *Balkan Idols*, pp. XXVI, 154.
64. Colovic, *The Balkans*, pp. 123–156.
65. Ibid., p. 159.
66. Ibid., pp. 168–169.
67. *Washington Post* and Associated Press, 15 November 2009.
68. Christopher Bennett, *Bosnia's Paralyzed Peace* (Oxford and New York: Oxford University Press, 2016), p. 77.
69. Shea, *Macedonia and Greece*, p. 101.
70. Ibid., pp. 4–5.
71. Ibid., pp. 141–145.
72. Victor Friedman, "E mos shikjoni kish e xhamija (And Look Not to Church and Mosque): How Albania and Macedonia Illuminate Bosnia and Bulgaria," in Theodora Dragostinova and Yana Hashamova (eds.), *Beyond Mosque, Church, and State: Alternative Narratives of the Nation in the Balkans* (Budapest and New York: Central European University Press, 2016), p. 190.

73. Mariya Cheresheva and Sinisa Jakov Marusic, "Macedonia's Lonely Church Seeks Bulgarian 'Parent'," *Balkan Insight*, 20 November 2017.
74. Perica, *Balkan Idols*, pp. 176–177.
75. *B-92* (Belgrade), 23 May 2017.
76. "Tensions Flare as Serb Nationalist Train Halts at Border," *The Telegraph* (London), 14 January 2017.
77. "Orthodox Churches Will Hold First Ecumenical Council in 1200 Years in Istanbul," *Reuters*, 9 March 2014.
78. As quoted in Jasna Vukovic and Robert Coalson, "Russia's Friends Form New 'Cossack Army' in Balkans," Eurasianet.org, 18 October 2016.
79. See Broun, "The Schism in the Bulgarian Orthodox Church." Bulgarian politicians took sides among competing would-be patriarchs and other hierarchs that involved clerical kidnappings, court challenges, and other adventures.
80. This desperate move was deemed necessary in the context of what the Byzantines recognized was an Ottoman conquest inevitable without Western help. The Church in Constantinople repudiated the deal when it learned of it.
81. Serge P. Brun, "Pneumatophobia: The Orthodox Church in the Wake of the Great and Holy Council," wheeljournal.com, 18 June 2016.
82. Andrew Higgins, "Orthodox Churches' Council, Centuries in Making, Falters as Russia Exits," *New York Times*, 14 June 2016.
83. Ibid.
84. *BBC News*, 30 November 2016.
85. Martin Dimitrov, "Bulgarian Clerics Retreat from Support for Macedonian Church," *Balkan Insight*, 15 May 2018.
86. "Ecumenical Patriarch Rebuffs Macedonian Church's Plea for Recognition," *Balkan Insight*, 18 October 2018.
87. See, for example, "Daily Claims Dacic Is Lobbying Church in Bod to Become PM," *Blic* (Belgrade), 7 June 2017.
88. "Old Art of Icon Making Thrives in Modern Serbia," *Balkan Insight*, 2 June 2017.
89. "Church Does Not Want Gay Prime Minister," *Blic*, 12 May 2017.
90. "Amfilohije Criticized for Incendiary Comments About Montenegro, Kosovo, Interfering in State Affairs," *Politika* (Belgrade), 17 January 2017.

CHAPTER 3

Conservative Orthodoxy in Romania

Lucian Turcescu and Lavinia Stan

Abstract This chapter considers the topics of nationalism, conservatism, homophobia, and religious intolerance in the Romanian Orthodox Church (RomOC, hereafter) after the collapse of communism in 1989. This analysis begins with a brief historical overview of the Church during the pre-communist and communist periods, and then turns its attention to presenting and assessing the above topics in post-communist times.

THE LEGACY OF THE PAST

In Romania, the communist regime (1945–1989) was more repressive than in many other Eastern European countries with, perhaps, the exception of Albania and the Soviet Union. Private property was drastically curtailed, as much as 95% of the economy was state-owned, and political parties other than the Communist Party were banned. The Churches

---

L. Turcescu (✉)
Theological Studies, Concordia University, Montreal, QC, Canada
e-mail: Lucian.Turcescu@concordia.ca

L. Stan
Department of Political Science, St. Francis Xavier University, Antigonish, NS, Canada
e-mail: lstan@stfx.ca

were persecuted during the first two decades of communism in order to force them to collaborate with the authorities in the establishment of the socialist state. Numerous bishops, priests, and lay believers were imprisoned or conscripted for hard labor and, if they came out of prison alive, were coerced into becoming informers for the dreaded secret political police, the Securitate, which acted as the repressive arm of the Communist Party. Many others chose to collaborate with the Securitate out of conviction or opportunism. As the party was aware of the importance of the RomOC for the Romanian population, it tried to use the Church as a most important pawn both with the Romanian citizens and with Western governments, in its foreign policy. The RomOC, in turn, was happy to oblige when the communists, following orders from Moscow, decided to disband the Greek Catholic Church in 1948 and to transfer its places of worship to the Orthodox. The past continues to cast a long shadow over the present, even three decades after the collapse of communism. The names of many collaborators became public only in the 2000s. Some of them were declared non-collaborators, despite overwhelming evidence that they had served the regime and its agents. There is no lustration law in the country, and this is why former collaborators have continued to occupy important positions in the Church hierarchy and theological schools.

NATIONALISM

The scholarly literature dealing with nationalism as an ideology promoting loyalty to the nation-state has distinguished between Western and Eastern nationalism in Europe. Thus, Paul Latawski wrote about the "political," "social," and "territorial" nationalism of the West and the "ethnic" nationalism of the East.[1] Martyn Rady added that, in the West, notions of nationhood were grafted onto older concepts of citizenship, natural rights, and popular sovereignty, all protected by strong states. In the East, by contrast, these concepts were less developed and states lacked the civic and political institutions to protect them when they started to appear in the nineteenth century. As a result, there the nation subsumed the individual, and civic rights took second place to the doctrine of national rights.[2]

Due to its medieval commitment to use Old Church Slavonic as a liturgical language and the Ottoman millet system that allowed the patriarch of Constantinople to have control over Orthodox Churches in the

Balkans, the Orthodox Church in Wallachia and Moldova did not play a role in the country's nation-shaping process. In the middle of the nineteenth century, Romanian Orthodox Metropolitan Andrei Saguna of Transylvania, alongside Greek Catholic leaders, championed the interests of the oppressed and politically underrepresented Romanian majority at a time when his province was part of the Austro-Hungarian Empire. Inspired by Saguna's efforts, the autocephalous RomOC (established in 1885) started borrowing, and by the 1920s monopolized the nationalist discourse centered on the Latin character of the Romanian language and descent, which had helped Transylvanian Romanians to imagine themselves as a nation similar to the Romanians of Wallachia and Moldova. In their turn, Romanian communists abandoned the internationalist discourse of Soviet communism and adopted a heretical version of national communism soon after the death of Joseph Stalin in 1953. In the process, they used the contribution the RomOC had already made to the nation-building process (of course, without giving it credit) in order to acquire additional legitimacy.[3]

Nationalism has been present in the Orthodox religious discourse and practice before, during, and after communism. While aiding the nation-building process, it also promoted an understanding of the Romanian nation as an ethnic, Orthodox nation. Nationalism still played a significant role in Romanian politics during the first decade of post-communism. In the 1990s, the RomOC used nationalism to restore its credibility that had been affected by collaboration with the communist regime. The Church's discourse underscored the link between Orthodoxy and Romanianism, and the importance of preserving the Romanian national identity in the face of growing modernization, globalization, secularization, EU integration, and religious competition. Nationalist messages were delivered through pastoral letters, public declarations by the clergy, theological publications, and the statements released by organizations set up under the Church's aegis. One spectacular manifestation of nationalism occurred on 21 June 1992, when the Holy Synod, RomOC's collective leadership body, undertook the canonization of nineteen Romanian saints and declared the second Sunday after Pentecost the "Sunday of the Romanian Saints." Numerous politicians attended that ceremony, which included the canonization of Prince Stephen the Great (ruler of Moldova in 1457–1504), a national hero known for his intrigues, marital infidelity, and cruelty more than holiness.

The RomOC also unilaterally established the Bessarabian Metropolitanate in 1992 in the independent Republic of Moldova and launched the project of a Cathedral of National Salvation in Bucharest. The Bessarabian Metropolitanate's creation attempted to counter Russian religious influence in the neighboring republic, in the hope that the Republic of Moldova (Bessarabia, as it is known in Romania) would return to Romania, of which it had been a part during the interwar period. The establishment of a religious institution in another country led to a ten-year-long conflict between the new Metropolitanate and successive Moldovan governments, tense relations between Bucharest and Chisinau, and sensitive relations between the Romanian Patriarchate and the Patriarchate of Moscow that continue to this day. Eventually, the Bessarabian Metropolitanate was legally recognized in 2002 by the Moldovan government, but only after the Council of Europe threatened to terminate Moldova's membership in that European body if it did not implement the 13 December 2001 decision of the European Court of Human Rights that ordered the recognition of the Metropolitanate. Even after the official recognition, the clergy of the Bessarabian Metropolitanate faced numerous obstacles and discrimination in their activities.[4]

Another nationalist project is the building of the large Cathedral for National Salvation. The project has received intense attention in Romania, especially because the cathedral is dedicated to "national salvation," not to Jesus or a saint, as is customary in Orthodoxy. Entertained by the RomOC for over a century, when it became evident that the small metropolitan church of Bucharest was unfit to serve as RomOC's cathedral, the project was shelved several times due to lack of financial and political support. It was resurrected by Patriarch Teoctist Arapasu in 1995 on the occasion of the Church's 70th anniversary since its recognition as an independent Patriarchate by other Orthodox Churches. After much bickering and opposition to the project coming from politicians and various atheistic civil society groups, a final location was agreed upon in February 2005 and the land was handed over to the Church. Dealul Arsenalului (Arsenal Hill) lies just behind the Romanian Parliament (formerly, the House of the People), a totalitarian piece of architecture built by Nicolae Ceaușescu in downtown Bucharest. Construction of the cathedral is now in full swing, as the current Patriarch Daniel Ciobotea hoped to officially inaugurate it in 2018, the year marking the centenary of the creation of Greater Romania, and thus to underline again the important connection between Orthodoxy and the Romanian nation.[5] As of the writing of this chapter, the investment costs for the building of the cathedral were estimated at 80 million euros, most of which was contributed by successive Romanian governments from public money.[6]

CONSERVATISM

Like all the other Orthodox Churches around the world, the RomOC takes pride in being a conservative church, teaching its continuity with the early Church of 1800 years ago, promoting some of the misogynistic views of the Church fathers with regard to the roles of men and women in society, and allowing the use of moral and disciplinary rules (known as "Church canons") of 1500 years ago for the regulation of its members' private and public lives. One of the traditional views widely encouraged in Romania is heterosexual marriage. Defending the cause of heterosexual, as opposed to homosexual, marriages has become a much larger project embraced by the Coalition for Family, an umbrella organization bringing together NGOs and a variety of religious groups. The Coalition demanded a referendum to change the country's constitution in order to explicitly state that marriage is only between a man and a woman, not between "spouses," a term which currently leaves open the possibility for homosexual marriages to take place. The Coalition had widespread support in Romania, including from the RomOC and the country's government (a coalition of the Party of Social Democracy, PSD, and Party Alliance of Liberals and Democrats, ALDE). Some of the RomOC hierarchs actively encouraged their priests to participate in a campaign to collect three million signatures, while others insisted that it was an initiative of individual priests, and not an official order of the Church leadership.[7] The referendum was held on 6–7 October 2018 and was declared invalid (and the cause thus defeated) since only 21% of the population participated in it and the minimum participation threshold of 30% was not attained.[8] The opposition parties have accused the government of trying to score political points at a time when it should deal with other important issues, including judicial reforms.

Another issue pertaining to family life and sexuality is that of abortion. In 1966, Ceaușescu introduced a draconian ban on abortion in order to increase the country's workforce. The ban lasted until 1989 and led to numerous women losing their lives by attempting to obtain illegal abortions, tens of thousands of unwanted children being abandoned in orphanages where they suffered from endemic abuse and neglect, and doctors being arrested if they provided abortions. Since 1990, abortion has been legal in Romania as an elective procedure until the 14th week of pregnancy, and available later in the pregnancy for medical reasons. While 1990 recorded close to 1 million abortions in a total population of 22 million, by 2010 that figure declined to under 100,000 abortions and it tended to stay low in subsequent years.[9] After legislation was introduced by the Năstase government in June 2003, women must undergo a psychological checkup before having an abortion. Obstetricians may not perform abortions without notes from psychologists attesting to the mental fitness of the pregnant woman. According to doctors in southeastern Constanța County, the psychological checkup is meant to convince women to carry the pregnancy to term. Women interviewed by local journalists reported that the psychologist could do nothing to change their minds and that the checkup was another method of raising money from a cash-strapped population.[10]

The RomOC is opposed to abortion, but it has a nuanced position determined by its adoption in 2005 of the recommendations of a National Bioethics Committee it set up as an advisory board. Drawing on biblical texts and contemporary scientific knowledge, and taking into account social, psychological, and moral issues, the document offers the following main points with respect to abortion:

a. If a pregnancy endangers the mother's life, the woman's life should be given priority over the child's. This is not because her life is more valuable in itself. Rather, it is due to her relations with and responsibilities for other persons.
b. If genetic investigation reveals an unborn child with abnormalities, we recommend carrying the pregnancy to term thereby observing his right to life. However, this decision belongs to the family after [its members] have been informed by their physician and their father confessor of the crucial moral and physical issues involved. This decision must be made with an eye to the redeeming presence of a disabled [human] being in the life of every person and community.
c. The risk of abortion due to rape or incest must be avoided first of all through education, by teaching citizens not to commit such sins. When pregnancy occurs as a result of rape or incest, the child must be born and given up for adoption, if necessary.

d. Neither a family's economic situation, nor conflict between prospective parents, nor the career of the future mother, nor her physical appearance are moral justifications for abortion.[11]

Thus, the pronouncement is not a blind condemnation of abortion. While not endorsing abortion, the document recognizes instances when abortion may be acceptable. Although titled *Abortion*, the pronouncement also deals with contraception. Contraceptive pills, devices, and surgical procedures to induce temporary or permanent infertility are all condemned because their use is allegedly no less sinful than abortion itself: "The Orthodox Church has always considered the ingestion of medication to cause abortion a grave sin, whose gravity is equal to the sin of abortion." Following the pronouncement, the use of contraception is condemnable also because of the risks it poses to the life and dignity of the woman. No mention is made of risk-free contraceptive methods like the use of condoms, or the Ogino method accepted by the Roman Catholic Church. Since practical considerations like the health of the woman figure prominently in the document's recommendations, it would seem that risk-free contraceptive methods are acceptable and less sinful than other methods. Like the Roman Catholic documents of its kind, *Abortion* does not distinguish theologically between degrees of sinfulness and therefore fails to differentiate between the prevention of conception through the use of contraceptives and the abortion of an already conceived fetus.

Homophobia

In our 2007 book *Religion and Politics in Post-Communist Romania*, we argued that due to the extremely sensitive nature of the issue of abortion, the RomOC did not dare to protest against its legalization in 1990 in order not to alienate the women who had to endure Ceaușescu's anti-abortion policies. Thus, in order to assert its interest in the area of regulating sexuality, right after 1989, the RomOC chose to focus on homosexuality instead, protesting its decriminalization by parliament in 2000 and encouraging Romanians to protest against it. For decades, gays and lesbians kept their sexual orientation secret for fear of prosecution, and many endured long prison terms for the slightest infringement of the communist moral code. After 1989, gay and lesbian groups began lobbying against the ban on homosexual behavior, but their demands met with fierce resistance from the general public, political elites, and religious groups. Several polls conducted after 1990 revealed that a large majority of Romanians (over 60%) did not like homosexuals as neighbors and did not think that the decriminalization of homosexuality was in the country's national interest. Annual US State Department human rights reports reveal that opposition to homosexuality in Romania continues to be high.[12]

In its opposition to the decriminalization under Article 200 of the Criminal Code, the RomOC mobilized numerous resources, from press campaigns to letters sent to MPs and theological writings denouncing homosexuality. Patriarch Teoctist repeatedly came out against "the acceptance of the degradingly abnormal and unnatural lifestyle as normal and legal" and tried to influence the outcome of the parliamentary vote on lifting the ban. True, all of the other religious denominations in Romania came out against decriminalization, but the RomOC was the most vocal of them. The pressure not to decriminalize homosexuality was extraordinary and we documented the many efforts to ban homosexuality in our 2007 book. At one point, Archbishop Nifon of Targoviste announced that the RomOC Synod had decided to ask President Emil Constantinescu not to sign the changes into law, should the Senate also vote for decriminalizing homosexuality, as the Chamber of Deputies had just done. In the end, international pressure from the Council of Europe, which threatened to resume monitoring the Romania's human rights record, played the decisive role in the parliament's decision to decriminalize homosexuality.

It is ironic that a Church that disavows homosexuality was recently rocked by several public scandals involving homosexuality among its clergy. While we want to keep homosexuality separate from pedophilia, it should be noted that some of the clergy mentioned below were not too concerned with the age limit when seeking to engage in sexual relations with younger males. This is perhaps only the tip of the iceberg and many more such scandals will surface, as was the case with the Roman Catholic Church during the recent years. Cristian Pomohaci is a former parish priest, divorced from his wife some ten years ago. In a secret recording that became public in 2017, Pomohaci attempted to attract underage males to have sex with him. The telephone recording contained numerous intimate details about how the two were to have sex. As a result, Pomohaci was defrocked by RomOC, although he continues to have, in the village where he served, numerous supporters who refuse to recognize his defrocking, and who still appreciate him as a hugely popular folkloric music singer.[13] In the other case, Bishop Cornel Onila of Husi was blackmailed by two priests, who wanted to recover the money they had offered to him as bribe in order to get their parishes. To do that, they used several video recordings which also became public. These recordings showed the bishop having sex with male seminary students. Presented with that incontestable evidence, Onila resigned his position as bishop, was defrocked, and remained a simple monk, but continued to deny that it was he in the recordings. Two other bishops are also rumored to have been involved in a homosexual relationship with one another. If that turns out to be true, then a Church that in theory is so opposed to homosexuality, in practice, has to deal with several cases of homosexuality among its clergy and monks, an aspect that does not bode well with its faithful.

In its nationalist drive and fight against the decriminalization of homosexuality, the RomOC was vigorously supported by the extremist Party of Romanian National Unity and the Greater Romania Party, for which Orthodoxy and moral cleanliness represented the quintessence of Romanianism. MPs belonging to those parties proclaimed that Article 200 of the Criminal Code prohibiting homosexual behavior and punishing it with prison term was too lenient toward that "sexual aberration" that was damaging to national pride.

Religious Intolerance

Due to space limitations, we will mention here only one significant incident of religious intolerance manifested by the RomOC. In its 1996 annual report, APADOR-CH presented in detail the campaign launched in Romania against the Jehovah's Witnesses at the instigation of the Orthodox Patriarch Teoctist. On 24 June 1996, Teoctist issued a press release against the intention of the Jehovah's Witnesses to organize an international religious congress in Bucharest on 19–21 July that same year. His protest launched a massive campaign of denigration against the Jehovah's Witnesses, which was conducted by the majority of the mass-media outlets (both printed and audio-visual), including the state-run national television TVR, as well as by politicians and Orthodox associations. The Witnesses were accused of everything from being heretics to being an apocalyptic cult which leads the world to secularization to being a criminal gang and a satanic cult that tries to take over the world in a global conspiracy that represents a big threat to predominantly Orthodox Romania. As a result of the month-long campaign, the congress was moved to other, less prominent venues in the cities of Brașov and Cluj-Napoca. However, the damage was done and Romanians had learned in messages widely disseminated by the printed and audio-visual media that the Jehovah's Witnesses were nothing but a dangerous cult which was strongly opposed by the Orthodox Church leader.[14]

Conclusion

The Romanian Orthodox Church has had a history of conservatism that has touched on the way in which it views nationalism, Romanianness, and the body (including abortion and homosexuality). The present chapter has provided some examples to document the conservatism of Orthodoxy in that country, but further research will be able to show a more detailed and nuanced picture of it.

Notes

1. Paul Latawski, "The Problem of Definition: Nationalism, Nation and Nation-State in East Central Europe," in Paul Latawski (ed.), *Contemporary Nationalism in East Central Europe* (New York: St. Martin's Press, 1995), pp. 1–11.
2. Martyn Rady, "Nationalism and Nationality in Romania," in Paul Latawski (ed.), *Contemporary Nationalism in East Central Europe* (New York: St. Martin's Press, 1995), p. 131.
3. Lavinia Stan and Lucian Turcescu, *Religion and Politics in Post-Communist Romania* (New York: Oxford University Press, 2007), p. 42; Olivier Gillet, *Religion et nationalism. L'idéologie de l'Eglise orthodoxe roumaine sous le régime communiste* (Bruxeless: Editions de L'Universite de Bruxelles, 1997).
4. Stan and Turcescu, *Religion and Politics in Post-Communist Romania*, pp. 52–56. See also Lavinia Stan and Lucian Turcescu, "Church-State Conflict in Moldova: The Bessarabian Metropolitanate," in *Communist and Post-Communist Studies*, Vol. 36, No. 4 (December 2003), pp. 443–465.
5. For details, see Stan and Turcescu, *Religion and Politics in Post-Communist Romania*, pp. 56–63; Lavinia Stan and Lucian Turcescu, "Politics, National Symbols and the Romanian Orthodox Cathedral," in *Europe-Asia Studies*, Vol. 58, No. 7 (2006), pp. 1119–1139.

6. Cristina Radu, "Primăria Capitalei alocă un milion de euro la rectificarea de buget pentru lucrările de la Catedrala Mântuirii Neamului. Consilier: Continuă alocarea aleatorie de la buget. La RATB scădem, dar la Catedrală creștem?" *News.ro*, 11 September 2017, at https://www.news.ro/social/primaria-capitalei-aloca-milion-euro-rectificarea-buget-lucrarile-catedrala-mantuirii-neamului-consilier-continua-alocarea-aleatorie-buget-ratb-scadem-catedrala-crestem-1922403611002017091817201955 [last accessed 1 May 2019].
7. Adriana Stanca, "BOR sprijina oficial initiativa de modificare a Constitutiei: familia, formata din BARBAT si FEMEIE," *Realitatea*, 15 January 2016, at https://www.realitatea.net/bor-sprijina-oficial-initiativa-de-modificare-a-constitutiei-familia-formata-din-barbat-si-femeie_1866714.html [last accessed 1 May 2019].
8. "Rezultatele finale: au votat 21.10% dintre alegatori. Referendumul nu e valid," Digi24 HD (8 October 2018), https://www.digi24.ro/referendum-familie-2018/rezultate-finale-referendum-au-votat-2110-dintre-alegatori-1010305 [accessed 1 May 2019]
9. Institutul National de Statistica, *Demografia in Romania*, October 2013, at http://www.insse.ro/cms/files/publicatii/pliante%20statistice/12_Brosura%20demo.pdf [last accessed 1 May 2019].
10. Stan and Turcescu, *Religion and Politics in Post-Communist Romania*, p. 182.
11. National Committee on Bioethics, *Abortion*, July 2005, at http://patriarhia.ro/content.php?id=78 [accessed 1 May 2019].
12. See the 2016 report from the U.S. State Department, "Romanian 2016 Human Rights Report," at https://www.state.gov/documents/organization/265676.pdf [last accessed 1 May 2019].
13. Viorel Ilisoi, "Secta Pomosoi," *PressOne*, 21 August 2017, at https://pressone.ro/secta-pomohaci/ [last accessed 1 May 2019].
14. "Raportul de activitate APADOR-CH –1996," at http://www.apador.org/aspecte-privind-evolutia-situatiei-drepturilor-omului-in-romania-si-activitatea-apador-ch-raport-1996/ [last accessed 1 May 2019]; Gabriel Andreescu, "Martorii lui Iehova: radiografia unei violări a libertății religioase," *Altera*, No. 3 (1996), pp. 125–172, at http://altera.adatbank.transindex.ro/pdf/4/008Martorii%20lui%20Iehova.pdf [last accessed 1 May 2019].

CHAPTER 4

The Bulgarian Orthodox Church: Authoring New Visions About the Orthodox Church's Role in Contemporary Bulgarian Society

Daniela Kalkandjieva

Abstract This chapter examines the visions which have been advanced by the Bulgarian Orthodox Church to expand and secure its influence in society after fall of communism. While the end of the atheist rule inspired the Church's hierarchy to seek a restoration of the pre-communist dominant status of Orthodoxy as the majority religion, the newly adopted understanding of freedom of conscience and belief as a just and equal treatment of all religious communities impeded the realization of this goal. As a result, the promotion of the Church's positions on the communist past, the form of political governance, nationalism, and traditional values have turned out to be a dynamic process that provokes ambivalent reactions not only in society but also in the community of Orthodox believers.

In 1989, the fall of communism in Bulgaria released the local Orthodox Church from the chains of militant atheism. The change allowed its return

D. Kalkandjieva (✉)
Sofia University St. Kliment Ohridski, Sofia, Bulgaria

© The Author(s) 2019
S. P. Ramet (ed.), *Orthodox Churches and Politics in Southeastern Europe*, Palgrave Studies in Religion, Politics, and Policy, https://doi.org/10.1007/978-3-030-24139-1_4

to the public arena, thus inspiring the Holy Synod to dream about a return to the pre-communist dominant status of Orthodoxy. This ambition, however, has not been fully realized. While in tune with the search of Bulgarian society for continuity with the pre-communist past, the Church has entered into conflict with the effort of people to establish real democracy in their country, which presupposes a just treatment of all local religious denominations. The tensions between these two tendencies are reflected in the legal status of the Orthodox Church in post-communist Bulgaria. Although the new Bulgarian Constitution of 1991 did not recognize Orthodoxy as the dominant faith, it did describe it as the traditional religion in the country (Article 13.3). According to the Constitutional Court, this characterization of Orthodoxy "expresses its cultural and historical role for the Bulgarian state, as well as its present significance for the state life and especially by its impact on the system of official holidays" and does not infringe on the rights of the other religious communities in the country.[1] In 2002, however, the Religious Denominations Act granted *ex lege* recognition to the Orthodox Church (Article 10.2), while requiring the other religious communities to obtain court registration (Article 15).[2]

In 2018, a new amendment of the same bill made another gesture of favor to the Orthodox Church by introducing new rules for state subsidies to the local religious organizations. They distinguish between those religious denominations whose adherents exceeded 1% of the population in the most recent census and those with smaller memberships. In addition, the state subsidy for the denominations from the first group is estimated as a product of the number of their adherents multiplied by 10 levs (about 5 euro), but could not be less than 15 million levs (7.5 million euro). Meanwhile, state support for those from the second group will be administratively assigned (Article 28). As the 2011 Bulgarian census registered a population of 7,364,570 citizens, this means that, until the next census, the first group of religious denominations includes only those that have over 73,646 members. Only two religious communities have such a membership: the Orthodox with 4,374,135 believers or 59.4% of the country population and the Muslims with 577,139 (or 7%).[3] In short, in 2019, the Orthodox Church should receive a subsidy of about 44 million levs (22 million euro).[4]

Furthermore, the political change in 1989 allowed the restitution of those economic assets of the religious communities which had been "nationalized" under communism. As a result, between 1992 and 2012, the

Bulgarian Orthodox Church retrieved its property rights over arable lands, forests, meadows, candle industries, and non-religious urban buildings that significantly improved its economic status. Due to the lack of public registers of these assets, however, society has had no clear idea about their size. Still, there are no doubts that the Orthodox Church has become the biggest landlord in the country after the state. Furthermore, its financial affairs also benefited from a set of laws that decreased the taxation of religious communities. In 2006, the goods and services provided by religious communities in the religious, social, educational, and health sphere were exempted from the VAT.[5] In 2013, churches, monasteries, mosques, and prayer houses were also exempted from local taxes and fees.[6] Despite this financial alleviation, the Orthodox Church refuses to provide information about its income and expenditures. In 2018, the Holy Synod declared that the Church had obtained its possessions mostly through donations and bequests, which as acts of deeply intimate character require that their donors remain anonymous.[7] Such claims, however, contradict the Church's ancient tradition to register the names of its donors and to commemorate them in public during church services. Besides, in addition to personal donations, the Bulgarian Church receives donations in kind and money from national judicial entities as well as from foreign bodies, e.g., from the Greek and the Russian Orthodox Churches.

Although this legal and economic status of the Bulgarian Orthodox Church reveals an increased potential to exert influence on society, it was not accompanied by an increased number of regular churchgoers. According to sociologists, they vary between 3 and 7%. Besides, until 2018, the Holy Synod of the Bulgarian Orthodox Church failed to solicit broad social support for its initiatives. The situation changed in 2018 when the protests of the Orthodox hierarchs against the ratification of the Istanbul *Convention on Preventing and Combating Violence against Women and Domestic Violence* led to its announcement by the Bulgarian Constitutional Court as incompatible with the 1991 Constitution. To understand the reasons behind this process and its dynamics, this chapter analyzes the visions promoted by the Church's leadership and the corresponding reactions of society. They are organized around four major issues dealing with the attitudes of the Orthodox Church and Bulgarian society to the communist past, the form of political government, nationalism, and traditional values.

The Shadow of Communism

The end of the rule of militant atheists in Bulgaria allowed the Holy Synod in Sofia to assume full control over all Orthodoxy-related institutional and religious matters. Between 1992 and 2012, however, its authority was shaken by two crises of distrust. The first of them erupted in 1992 when the secret decision of the Politburo of the Central Committee of the Bulgarian Communist Party from 8 March 1971 for the promotion of Metropolitan Maxim of Lovech as Patriarch of Bulgaria was publicly announced.[8] Not only was his reputation affected by this discovery, but also that of the Bulgarian Orthodox Church. In particular, it provoked a split in the Church's leadership into two rival bodies: Maxim's Synod and the so-called Alternative Synod. The fight between them alienated many Bulgarians from the Church. Besides, the anathema declared by Maxim's Synod on the Alternative one shook the positions of the Bulgarian Orthodox Church in world Orthodoxy.[9] In 1998, the heads of all Orthodox Churches came to Sofia in an attempt to heel the schism. By taking part in the so-called Holy Expanded and Suprajurisdictional Pan-Orthodox Council (31 September–1 October), initiated by Patriarch Maxim, they de facto recognized him as the canonical leader of Orthodox Bulgarians.[10] Under these circumstances, the members of the Alternative Synod agreed to return under Maxim's jurisdiction. The truce, however, lasted only a few days. As soon as the foreign churchmen left Bulgaria, the Alternative Synod revived its activities. In 2002, the Bulgarian state made another attempt to heal the schism—this time by means of law. The new Religious Denominations Act granted an *ex lege* recognition to Maxim's Synod as the proper leadership of the Bulgarian Orthodox Church (Article 10.2), while the Alternative Synod had to obtain court registration (Article 15). Two years later, on the grounds of this bill, the properties of the Alternative Synod were transferred to Patriarch Maxim.[11] The attempts of the former to restore its positions by filing a case at the European Court of Human Rights were in vain.[12] The case was won, but the properties were not returned. Left without means of living, the bishops and priests from the Alternative Synod began to return under Maxim's jurisdiction. In this way, the schism was over by 2012.

Meanwhile, Maxim's victory was darkened by another crisis of distrust. In January 2012, the Committee for Disclosing the Documents and Announcing Affiliation of Bulgarian Citizens to the State Security and the Intelligence Services of the Bulgarian National Army during the communist era announced as agents eleven out of the fifteen then acting members of the Bulgarian Synod.[13] In the next years, the Church's leadership succeeded in stifling this investigation by refusing to submit the personal data necessary for the identification of other Orthodox churchmen and theologians who had formerly collaborated with the communist secret services.[14] Despite this obstruction, however, the efforts of individual researches brought to light new details about this dark side of the recent history of the Bulgarian Orthodox Church.[15] Their studies revealed that not only members of Maxim's Synod collaborated with the former atheist regime, but also those of the Alternative Synod. They also provided evidence that the work of the representatives of the Bulgarian Orthodox Church at the World Council of Churches had been coordinated not only by the national secret services but also by the Soviet ones.[16]

Furthermore, the silence of Orthodox episcopate on the canonization of a score of churchmen who had suffered persecution under communism became another source of discontent in society. Raised by the Union of Orthodox Priests in the first years after the collapse of communism, this issue found the support of the Alternative Synod when it became clear that the new Religious Denominations Act would favor Patriarch Maxim. On 24 October 2002, the former canonized 120 priests and monks murdered by the communist regime.[17] In its turn, Maxim's Synod refused to join this act with the argument that it had been performed by a schismatic body. The end of the schism, however, revived the debate about the canonization of the Church's victims from the communist era. In 2014, the Holy Synod set up a special commission for this purpose. After two years of work, it announced the start of an investigation aimed to lead to the canonization of Metropolitan Boris of Nevrokop, killed by a defrocked priest in 1948.[18] Scheduled for 2018, this act had to coincide with the 130th anniversary of Boris's birth and the 70th anniversary of his death. Both dates passed, but nothing happened. In this way, civil commemoration remains the only opportunity for Orthodox Bulgarians to pay tribute to the Church's victims from the communist times.

While leaving open the question about the religious veneration of these clerics, the Holy Synod of the Bulgarian Orthodox Church glorified Archbishop Serafim (Sobolev)—a Russian émigré hierarch who found asylum in Bulgaria after the Bolshevik Revolution.

In 1921, he was appointed by the Russian Synod Abroad in Sremski Karlovci (Yugoslavia) as the ruling bishop of the Russian émigré communities in Bulgaria. When the Soviet Army occupied Bulgaria in September 1944, he did not flee and soon afterward was accepted under the jurisdiction of the Moscow Patriarchate.[19] In 1946, he became a Soviet citizen. As such, he continued to run the Russian parishes in Bulgaria and died peacefully in Sofia on 26 February 1950.

During his Bulgarian exile, Archbishop Serafim became especially famous among Russian émigrés for his mysticism. On his deathbed, he instructed his disciples to write letters to him, to leave at his grave. Thus, when he was buried in the crypt of the Russian Church St. Nikolay the Wonderworker in Sofia they set up a mailbox there. In 1952, the temple was transformed into the *podvorie* of the Moscow Patriarchate and started functioning as its ecclesiastical embassy at the Bulgarian Orthodox Church. Meanwhile, Sofia citizens also began to seek Serafim's help by leaving letters at his grave. This custom continued after the end of the communist system, and in 2007, the Russian Orthodox Church set up a special commission to discuss the canonization of Archbishop Serafim.[20] As a result, two books appeared that paved the road to this act. The first of them was a short history of the Church, written by Olga Reshetnikova, the wife of Leonid Reshetnikov, a key figure in the Soviet secret services and Director of the Russian Institute for Strategic Studies (2009–2017).[21] The other was a biography of Archbishop Serafim by the Russian Church historian Andrey Kostryukov.[22]

The next step was made in 2014 when a Bulgarian-Russian Ecclesiastical Working Group was set up to discuss Serafim's canonization.[23] The Russian team was headed by Metropolitan Hilarion of Volokolamsk, the Chairman of the Department for External Church Relations of the Moscow Patriarchate, while the Bulgarian one by Metropolitan Yoan of Varna. Another milestone in the realization of this project was the centenary of the consecration of the Russian Church in Sofia celebrated there by a joint Bulgarian-Russian liturgy on 30 November 2014. It was followed by a campaign for the collection of evidence about miracles performed with Serafim's assistance.[24] On 3 February 2016, in the presence of a Bulgarian Church delegation, the Sacred Bishop's Council of the Russian Orthodox Church, held in the Moscow Cathedral of Christ the Saviour, decided for the canonization of Archbishop Serafim.[25] Three weeks later, on 26 February, he was glorified by the Bulgarian Orthodox Church as "Sofia Wonderworker."[26]

This act was not only a demonstration of the sacred bonds between the Bulgarian and the Russian Orthodox Church but created a new spiritual link between the Orthodox Bulgarians and Russia at a moment when the image of the latter was seriously darkened by the annexation of Crimea.

The fall of communism implied changes in the attitude of the Bulgarian Orthodox Church vis-à-vis Western Christianity as well. According to the Sofia Synod, the local Orthodox Church was the only religious body able to save the souls of Bulgarians, who had lost their link with God under communism. Therefore, the Orthodox hierarchs and clerics were especially irritated by the quick spread of new evangelical Churches in post-atheist Bulgaria. As the post-communist state, guided by a liberal understanding of freedom of religion, was not able to secure the monopoly of the local Orthodox Church, Maxim's Synod looked for a religious solution. In 1998, following the example of the Georgian Orthodox Church, it discontinued the membership of the Bulgarian Orthodox Church in the World Council of Churches (WCC). This act was motivated by disappointment with the WCC's inability to stop the proselytism in the former communist countries, where the Orthodox identity of the believers had been seriously injured by the promotion of atheism by the communists during their years in power.[27] According to some observers, this step was provoked by the Synod's distrust in the Church's representatives, appointed with the consent of the former communist regime at international ecumenical organizations.[28] Their hypothesis, however, fails to elucidate why Maxim's Synod did not replace them with more trustworthy persons. It also does not explain the strong anti-ecumenical position of the contemporary Bulgarian Orthodox Church's leadership, which resembles Stalin's ban on the membership of the Orthodox Churches in the countries under Soviet control in the World Council of Churches.[29] On 21 April 2016, the Bulgarian Synod demonstrated once again its anti-ecumenical stance by declaring its disagreement with "Relations of the Orthodox Church with the rest of the Christian World"—one of the key documents of the Holy and Great Council in Crete, scheduled for 16–27 June.[30] Expressing a strong disagreement with its ecumenical spirit, the Bulgarian Synod called for the postponement of the pan-Orthodox forum and later on refused to send a delegation to it.[31]

Meanwhile, the post-Cold War Bulgarian Synod developed a more flexible attitude to the Catholic Church: The former has not fully interrupted the contacts with the Vatican. This approach was demonstrated during the visit of John Paul II (23–26 May 2002), when the Bulgarian Patriarch agreed to give an audience to the Pope, on the condition that he would welcome the latter as a head of state and not as a religious leader.[32] During his stay, John Paul II visited the Patriarchal Cathedral of St. Alexander for the Feast of Saints Cyril and Methodius as well as the famous Rila Monastery.[33] In the next years, however, the dialogue between the two Churches did not become easier. On 5–7 May 2019, Pope Francis also paid a visit to Bulgaria. This time, however, the Holy Synod characterized his trip as entirely a state initiative and warned the Orthodox clerics not to attend the events on the Pope's program.[34] As a result, Francis's contacts with representatives of the Bulgarian Orthodox Church were limited to an audience with Bulgarian Patriarch Neofit. The only Orthodox site that was visited by the Pope was the Patriarchal Cathedral of Saint Alexander Nevski, where he had a private prayer before the throne of Saints Cyril and Methodius.[35]

Playing with Monarchy

Another debate in which the Orthodox Church has been involved after the end of the totalitarian regime concerns the country's mode of government. Although most Bulgarians chose the road toward Western democracy, the monarchy also won popularity among some social groups. It gained many supporters among high-ranking Orthodox churchmen tempted by the idea of restoring the pre-communist union between Orthodoxy and monarchy. In particular, they praised Tsar Boris III (1894–1943) under whose rule the Bulgarian state and Orthodox Church reached the climax of their territorial development. In 1940, the Treaty of Craiova allowed the peaceful return of South Dobrudja to the Bulgarian state and the restoration of the Bulgarian Church's jurisdiction over this area. A year later, as an ally of Nazi Germany, Bulgaria received the control over territories situated in contemporary Serbia, North Macedonia, and Greece, namely the region of Niš, Vardar Macedonia, and Aegean Thrace. These circumstances allowed the Bulgarian Orthodox Church to restore its activities in dioceses which had been under its jurisdiction between 1870 and 1913. At the same time, the praise for Boris III was in tune with particular monarchist sentiments in post-communist Bulgarian society, which were nurtured by his mysterious death on 23 August 1943. The fact that the Tsar had died a few days after his meeting with Hitler inspired many rumors. Some of them claim the Nazis poisoned him because of his refusal to send Bulgarian troops to the Eastern Front, while others suggested that this was done by the Soviets because Boris's popularity would not allow them to include Bulgaria in their postwar zone of influence. All this surrounded the Tsar's name with an aura of martyrdom, which, in post-communist Bulgaria, was able to bring together people from the leftist and the rightist political spectrum.

Furthermore, the popular veneration of Boris III assisted the attempts of the Bulgarian Orthodox Church to regain its most prominent religious site—the Rila Monastery. The quest for its return was launched by Orthodox monks and clerics immediately after the fall of communism. The initiative received the unconditional support of society due to the double significance of this shrine. On the one hand, it is a sacred place that keeps the relics of the most venerated Bulgarian saint, Ivan of Rila. On the other hand, it was a significant landmark of the pre-communist era as the last Bulgarian Tsar, Boris III, was buried there. Loved by people during his lifetime, he did not lose their love after death. Thus, even when the communists came to power, his grave remained a popular pilgrimage site. To halt this practice, in 1946, the communists ordered the exhumation of Boris's remains and their reburial in the Vrana Royal Residence, near Sofia. Three years later, they blew up the new grave. The cult of the dead Tsar, however, persisted. People continued to visit his empty grave at the Rila Monastery, thus linking together the cult to St. Ivan and that of the late monarch. Perceiving this custom as an act of double protest against their regime, the communists undertook another step. In 1961, the Rila Monastery was nationalized and transformed it into a state museum, while the monks were expelled. In 1967, however, under international pressure, the atheist rulers had to allow the functioning of a small monastic community there but imposed a ban on the public performance of religious rites.[36] Therefore, when the question of the return of the Rila Monastery was raised, it received the support of the entire society. In May 1991, it became the first religious site returned to the Bulgarian Orthodox Church. In parallel, a special commission set up at the National Assembly started investigating the case with Boris's remains.[37] It found out that only the Tsar's heart was preserved separately after his autopsy. In 1993, his grave was made anew in Rila Monastery, and his heart was reburied there. In this way, this main religious shrine of the country again bridged the devotion to Orthodoxy with the idea of monarchy.

The mutual affection between the Orthodox Church and the Bulgarian Royal House was demonstrated once more when the son of Boris III, Simeon Saxe-Coburg-Gotha, returned to Bulgaria to serve as Prime Minister (2001–2005). The Religious Denominations Act (2002) adopted during his tenure secured the exclusive place of the Orthodox Church on the religious map of Bulgaria. On 15 December 2014, the Holy Synod demonstrated a new devotion to the idea of the monarchy during a solemn liturgy performed by Metropolitan Nikolay of Plovdiv at his diocesan monastery Saints Kirik and Julita. It was organized to celebrate the Metropolitan's victory in a court case for the restitution of this religious site, previously used as a recreation house of the Union of Bulgarian Architects. On this occasion, in the presence of the Patriarch, the Synod, and Simeon Saxe-Coburg-Gotha, Nikolay promoted his vision of symphony in contemporary Bulgaria:

> ... when the Tsar of Bulgarians is present here, this means that the very idea of statehood is here; that statehood in its transcendent essence stays side by side with the Church in standing up for its rights. ... the Church always has the King in its prayers; and thus the King, i.e., statehood, is always within the Church; and they pray together for Bulgarians and Bulgaria.[38]

Several months later, on 29 April 2015, the Bulgarian Synod decided to pay liturgical homage to Simeon Saxe-Coburg-Gotha. According to the Synod, Simeon's name had to be mentioned during liturgy as the "Tsar of Bulgarians" before the reference to the Orthodox Bulgarian people and their government.[39] The change was justified by the act of royal anointment which Simeon had received together with his baptism in 1937.[40] In order for this decision to enter in force, however, it had to be written down in the minutes of the next summer session of the Holy Synod and approved by its members.

Regardless of this requirement, on 2 May, Patriarch Neofit used the non-approved formula in a solemn open-air liturgy dedicated to the 1150th anniversary of the baptism of Bulgaria.[41] Concelebrated with 27 hierarchs from all Orthodox Churches, this act left the impression of a pan-Orthodox recognition of Simeon as a Tsar.[42] In addition, performed in the presence of the President, the Prime Minister, and many high-ranking state officials of the Republic of Bulgaria as well as in that of the ambassadors of Russia, Greece, Ukraine, and Georgia, this religious homage looked like as a political act.⁴³ Furthermore, its direct transmission by the Bulgarian National Television and Radio multiplied its effect on society. All this provoked a heated debate on the Church's attitude to the secular state. Some observers suggested that the Orthodox hierarchs regarded Simeon as an alternative head of state and even defined their behavior as an attempt to contest the established republican order.⁴⁴ Asked by journalists to comment on the situation, President Rosen Plevneliev responded:

> As the head of the state, I firmly support the constitutional order of the state. I am a republican president. As a humble Christian, I will pray the Holy Synod to reconsider its decision, which has a symbolic meaning and may risk splitting up the Christians in Bulgaria into monarchists and republicans.⁴⁵

The motives for this monarchist drive of the Church's leadership remain an enigma. The fact that this ecclesiastical innovation had disappeared when Plevneliev stepped down from his presidential mandate gives grounds to think that it had been designed as an attack on him. Besides, the Synod's monarchist turn coincided with the attacks of pro-Russian political circles against Plevneliev's systematic support for the international sanctions against Russia after the annexation of Crimea.

THE CHURCH'S MULTIFACETED NATIONALISM

Despite the different assessment of the interplay between Orthodoxy and nationalism, there is a general agreement among scholars that modern Orthodox Churches presenting the religious majorities in their nation-states have played a key role in the promotion of nationalism in their countries at the religious, cultural, and political level. In this regard, the fall of communism in Bulgaria reveals new developments that call for a more careful investigation. It seems that the response of post-communist societies to the religious nationalism of their local Orthodox hierarchy has become much more selective than it was in previous times.

This discrepancy is well demonstrated in the case of St. Nedelya Church in Batak—a town situated in the diocese of Plovdiv. Built in 1813, the temple occupies a special place in Bulgarian national memory as a witness of the tragedy of hundreds of Bulgarians, murdered by Ottoman mercenaries in 1876. For this reason, after the Liberation of Bulgaria, it was unanimously declared a museum-ossuary. Neither the Holy Synod nor the diocesan hierarchs sought its re-consecration and reopening as a parochial church. In 2007, however, the Batak church-museum appeared in the epicenter of passionate public debate, provoked by media publications about a project on the case of Batak as a *lieu de mémoire*.[46] Realized with the financial support of German educational institutions, it involved German and Bulgarian scholars. They planned to close it with a scientific conference at the Institute of Ethnography of the Bulgarian Academy of Science and an exhibition at the National Gallery for Foreign Art in Sofia.

In 2006, one of these scholars, the art historian Martina Baleva, shared her findings in the Bulgarian weekly *Kultura*.[47] The article provoked another Bulgarian historian to publish another article there, accusing Baleva of overestimating the role of foreigners in the building of the image of Batak as a place of national memory and neglecting that of Bulgarians.[48] In turn, she used her right to respond, and the discussion seemed to be over.[49] A year later, however, when Bulgaria joined the European Union, many well-established domestic university professors and politicians fiercely criticized Baleva, accusing her of grant-seeking and national betrayal.[50] The media also joined the debate by playing with the colloquial meaning of the word "myth." In this way, they created an impression that Baleva had tried to present the Batak atrocity as a fake story. Soon she and the other Bulgarian participants in the project were labeled traitors of their nation. In the end, the planned conference and exhibition in Bulgaria were canceled.

In the next years, the debate slowed down its intensity but did not lose its significance for Bulgarian society. In 2011, the Holy Synod decided to canonize the victims of the Batak massacre together with those of another atrocity that had taken place in the village of Novo Selo.[51] In its turn, the municipality of Batak donated the museum-ossuary to Metropolitan Nikolay of Plovdiv. This act triggered a new dispute because the building had the status of a national museum and only the central state authorities were authorized to change its status.[52] The metropolitan, however, did not lose time and transformed the ossuary into a parochial church. The interior was changed, the building was consecrated anew, and regular liturgies began to be performed there. The changes provoked sharp criticism on the part of the museum experts who appealed for the restoration of the authentic appearance of the building and its status as a museum. They pointed out that the washing of human bones with wine and holy myrrh during the canonization of the Batak martyrs had caused them to become moldy.[53] In their turn, the inhabitants of Batak also protested, but on different grounds. They agreed with the canonization of the Batak victims but refuted the introduction of regular liturgies in the temple because it violated the wish of their ancestors. Although their petitions remained without an answer, the people of Batak found a way to demonstrate their respect for the church-ossuary—nobody has chosen it for a baptism, wedding, or funeral.[54] The reactions of museum experts and ordinary people revealed the limits of religion-induced nationalism, which the Holy Synod tried to promote in post-communist Bulgarian society. It turned out to be doubly restricted by the authority of science as well as by people's respect for the will of their forefathers.

At the same time, the tensions between the nationalism of Orthodox hierarchs and that of laymen have obtained international dimensions in the debate on the self-proclaimed Macedonian autocephaly. Both parties perceive the non-canonical Macedonian Orthodox Church as a child of the Bulgarian Orthodox Church. This approach is supported by references to Bulgarian state and Church history. In particular, both churchmen and laypersons stress the role of Ohrid as a major Church see in Medieval Bulgaria, the active part played by the Bulgarians in Macedonia in the nineteenth century struggle for the establishment of an independent Bulgarian Church, and the jurisdiction exercised by the Bulgarian Exarchate over the Orthodox dioceses in present-day North Macedonia between 1870 and 1912. What divides Bulgarian laymen and their hierarchs is their attitude to canon law. In particular, the Bulgarian Holy Synod is obliged to respect the agreement signed with the Ecumenical Patriarchate of Constantinople on 22 February 1945 as a condition for the grant of autocephaly to the then schismatic Bulgarian Orthodox Church. By this agreement, the Bulgarian Church gave up its pretensions over its former dioceses in Aegean Thrace and Vardar Macedonia, thus limiting its jurisdiction within the postwar borders of Bulgaria.

Therefore, while the disintegration of Tito's Yugoslavia and the establishment of the independent state of Macedonia (now called North Macedonia since June 2018) inspired many lay Bulgarians to call for closer relations between their Orthodox Church and the Macedonian one on the grounds of their common Bulgarian origins, the Holy Synod in Sofia has abstained from official engagements with the Orthodox Church in North Macedonia. Besides, the 1945 agreement signed with the Ecumenical Patriarchate of Constantinople has obliged the Bulgarian hierarchy to respect the jurisdiction of the Serbian Patriarchate established over the Macedonian dioceses in the 1920s. Furthermore, the rapprochement of the Bulgarian Orthodox Church with the Macedonian one became additionally complicated in 2002, when the latter split into two bodies: the Macedonian Orthodox Church—Ohrid Archbishopric and the Orthodox Ohrid Archbishopric of Metropolitan Jovan (Vranishkovski). Recognized as a judicial entity by the government in Skopje, the first of these two bodies was proclaimed schismatic by the Serbian Patriarchate. Meanwhile, the archbishopric of Metropolitan Jovan did not receive a similar legal status from the state authorities of North Macedonia but was granted internal autonomy as the canonical branch of the Serbian Patriarchate in North Macedonia, i.e., it can rely on the support of all canonical Orthodox Churches. This situation provoked different responses in the Bulgarian Synod and its lay flock. In particular, the hierarchs are obliged to observe the canonical ban on liturgical communion with schismatics. Had the Sofia Synod entered into such relations with the non-canonical Macedonian Orthodox Church, it would have become schismatic itself and that would have doomed the Bulgarian Church to isolation from the other Orthodox Churches.

In their turn, lay nationalists neglected canonical issues.[55] In their view, the refusal of the Serbian Patriarchate to recognize the self-proclaimed Macedonian autocephalous Church has created an opportunity for the Bulgarian Synod to resolve the Macedonian schism by acting as the "Mother Church" of Orthodox Macedonians. In 2014, the Bulgarian-Macedonian cultural rapprochement allowed concrete steps to be undertaken in this direction. On 11 May, the day on which the Bulgarian Church celebrates the feast of Saints Cyril and Methodius, a delegation of the Macedonian Academy of Science and Arts arrived in Sofia together with Archbishop Stefan of Ohrid, the head of the Macedonian Church. On this occasion, he attended a liturgy served by Patriarch Neofit at St. Alexander Nevski Cathedral in Sofia, but in agreement with canon law, he did not take part in it.[56] In May 2015, Archbishop Stefan paid another visit to Sofia.[57] The intensified contacts stimulated a further elaboration of the idea of the parental rights of the Bulgarian Orthodox Church as derived from the "Bulgarian origin of the official Church in Macedonia."[58] At the same time, the lay advocates of this view defined the autonomous Orthodox Ohrid Archbishopric of the Serbian Patriarchate in North Macedonia as a historically and canonically groundless body.

At the end of the year, the rapprochement between the two Churches was hindered by the engagement of Patriarch Neofit with the cause of the autonomous branch of the Moscow Patriarchate in Ukraine. On 15 December 2015, he sent a letter of protest to Petro Poroshenko, then President of Ukraine. The latter was warned that the attempts of the non-canonically recognized Kyiv Patriarchate to take away the Kyiv Pechorsk Lavra and the Pochayiv Lavra from their legitimate owner—the autonomous Ukrainian Orthodox Church of the Moscow Patriarchate—would destabilize the situation in Ukraine and would prevent "the Orthodox episcopate, clergymen and faithful persons from foreign countries from visiting the aforementioned sacred places, as we do not hold any Eucharistic and Prayerful communion with schismatic structures."[59] Broadcast in English, Russian, and Bulgarian in Orthodox media, this position of the spiritual leader of the Bulgarian Orthodox Church in defense of the autonomous branch of the Moscow Patriarchate in Ukraine against the local "schismatic autocephalies" made impossible the recognition of another schismatic body, namely the non-canonical autocephalous Macedonian Orthodox Church.

Indeed, the relations of the Bulgarian Patriarchate with the Macedonian Orthodox Church of Archbishop Stefan were frozen for more than a year. In November 2017, however, the Macedonian hierarchs expressed their readiness to recognize the Bulgarian Patriarchate as their mother church, if the latter agreed to become the first Orthodox Church recognizing their autocephaly. In their turn, Bulgarian laymen appealed to their Holy Synod to recognize the autocephaly of the Macedonian Orthodox Church. They insisted that this would be "a distinctive achievement of the historical ideal of unity with the Macedonian people in the spiritual realm, a recognition of the common spiritual, cultural and national roots of the two countries."[60] At the same time, they pointed out that an eventual grant of autocephaly by the Serbian Orthodox Church would allow the inclusion of the Macedonian Church in the orbit of influence of the Moscow Patriarchate and respectively of Putin's authoritarian regime. On these grounds, they insisted that the acknowledgment of Macedonian autocephaly by the Bulgarian Church was "the only way to counteract Russian geopolitical interests in the region."[61] What they failed to take into account, however, is the capacity of the Ecumenical Patriarchate of Constantinople to offer a canonical solution to the Macedonian question.

The lay appeal was heard. On 27 November 2017, the Bulgarian hierarchs responded to their Macedonian colleagues with an equally conditional letter. They promised a hand of help if the Macedonian Orthodox Church recognized the Bulgarian Patriarchate as its mother church.[62] From a canonical point of view, however, such an act would be canonically null and void due to the schismatic status of the former. At the same time, the willingness of the Bulgarian Patriarchate to act as the mother church of Orthodox Macedonians fueled criticism from the Holy Synods in Serbia and Greece, who reminded themselves about the existence of canonically recognized Orthodox hierarchy in Macedonia, presented by Archbishop Jovan (Vranishkovski).[63] The Bulgarian lay nationalists were not satisfied either. They accused their hierarchs of refraining from an open demonstration of the motherhood status of the Bulgarian Church. Finally, the Sofia Synod agreed to intercede for the abolishment of the schismatic status of the Macedonian Church within a canonical framework.[64] Accordingly, the two Churches continued the dialogue without entering into liturgical communion. In 2018, the delegation of the Bulgarian Synod that had been visiting the Church of the Holy Sepulchre in Jerusalem every year to fetch the "Holy Fire" for the Easter liturgy started sharing it with the Macedonian Orthodox Church.[65] Such gestures are welcome by the Bulgarian laity. Meanwhile, the recognition of the autocephalous Orthodox Church in Ukraine by the Ecumenical Patriarchate of Constantinople in January 2019 presented another dilemma for the Bulgarian Holy Synod—to recognize or not the Ukrainian one.

Promoting Traditional Values

The promotion of traditional values is a recently emerging area of activities of the Bulgarian Orthodox Church. Until 2012, the Church's efforts in this direction were badly impeded by the schism. Besides, not all visions of the Bulgarian Synod meet the requirements of the post-communist national legislation for the respect of freedom of religion and conscience. As a result, not all attempts of the Holy Synod to impose its visions on the public arena have been successful. This development is well illustrated by the failure of the Orthodox hierarchs to introduce mandatory religious instruction in public schools. In 2007, the achievement of this goal was additionally complicated by Bulgaria's membership in the European Union. Therefore, the Holy Synod had to modify its tactics. Its *Concept for the Study of the Discipline "Religion" in Public Schools* (2008) underlined the right of the Orthodox Church to intervene in the affairs of public school on the grounds of its historical role as "a mother-guardian of the Orthodox Bulgarians," but admitted the rights of Bulgarian citizens to choose whether their children should study Orthodoxy or not. In an attempt to preserve the principle of mandatory study of religion, the Concept proposed the introduction of three sub-disciplines: "Religion-Orthodoxy," "Religion-Islam," and "General Religious Studies" among which students would choose.[66] In the next years, the Holy Synod issued a series of statements and organized round tables, religious processions, and other public events to persuade the state authorities to introduce mandatory confessional and non-confessional study of religion in public schools. The results, however, are far from the expectations. The Ministry of Education and Science introduced elective classes in two religious disciplines: "Christianity" and "Islam" for all 12 grades of the public school, which take place only if a sufficient number of students have opted for them. Today, they are attended by 1% of all students.[67]

Nevertheless, the end of the schism increased the chances of the Holy Synod enhancing the Church's influence on society. In 2012, it adopted a *Strategy for Spiritual Enlightenment, Catechization, and Culture* that addresses the main challenges faced by the Orthodox Church in the contemporary epoch: secularism, globalization, family values, youth morality, etc.[68] Unlike the previous policy of the Orthodox hierarchy, its present efforts are not limited to school students but target the entire society. In addition, the Synod's plans for the implementation of this strategy rely not only on the Church's human resources (episcopate, clergy, and laity) but also on cooperation with the state and municipal authorities working in the sphere of education and culture. Indeed, in the last years, the Orthodox hierarchs abandoned their previous practice of sporadic statements on various social issues and developed a more systematic approach that allows them to take an active part in all public debates on family and traditional values.

As in the case of the education-related statements of the Holy Synod, those on family also provoke different reactions in society. For example, the Orthodox visions on assisted reproduction, surrogate motherhood, and abortion drew fierce criticism among many Bulgarians. It was fueled by the Synod's rejection of the methods of assisted reproduction and surrogate motherhood as incompatible with Christian teachings about family as a union between a woman and a man. In this regard, Orthodox hierarchs have claimed that by involving a third person in the creation of the new life these methods undermine the traditional family.[69] On these grounds, they have prescribed the childless faithful to obey their destiny, to rely on God's wisdom, and not to search for the assistance of contemporary medicine. The only exception permitted is "in vitro fertilization," when the genetic material is taken from spouses of the same family.

Following this logic, the Bulgarian Synod regularly issues statements of protests against the Gay Pride parades organized every June by the Bulgarian LGBT community. According to the Orthodox hierarchs, "homosexuality is a passion against nature which unconditionally causes damages to human personality, family and society and which has pernicious consequences not only for the physical and psychic conditions of people but also for the spiritual one."[70] Although this position is shared by other religious communities, the pride parades receive the support of many citizens who regard them as a human rights manifestation. Similarly, the issue of abortion also divides the liberal and religious sections of society. The former group of citizens emphasizes women's rights, while the second relies on the religious teaching of one or another faith tradition to stress the rights of unborn children. According to the Holy Synod, the child receives his/her body and soul together at the moment of conception. Therefore, it condemns abortion as an act of murder and protests against the use of such terms as "embryo" and "fetus" in legal and medical documents, which use disregards the baby's soul.[71]

In 2015, the migrant crisis created more favorable conditions for the promotion of traditional values. The appeal of the Holy Synod to the national government to stop the entry of migrants into Bulgaria became its first initiative that gained popularity not only among nationalist circles but among the main political parties as well as among many ordinary people.[72] The fear of the non-Christian identity of refugees reinstated the role of the local Orthodox Church as the guardian of Bulgarian national identity. In parallel, the disagreement between the member-states of the European Union on the migrant crisis nurtured euroskeptic moods among Bulgarians. All this facilitated the Synod's efforts to promote its traditional values. In July 2017, invited to a conference dedicated to the 25th anniversary of the present Bulgarian Constitution, Patriarch Neofit stressed before its participants that only legislation that stands upon on the solid fundament of traditional values can be truly effective.[73] He also pointed out that the Orthodox Church and the state must work together for the preservation of moral values that guarantee justice, peace, family, patriotism, and the mutual respect and love between people. In this way, his stance seems to be strongly influenced by the model of a Church-state collaboration set up in Putin's Russia as well as by the Moscow Patriarchate's *Basic Values: The Fundaments of All-National Identity*.[74]

Several months later, the head of the Synod's Public Relations Office, Aleksandra Karamihaleva, reported that the Orthodox Church had become an equal partner of the state in many areas of public life. She also pointed to the changed positions of Western and Eastern European societies regarding Christian values—an idea promoted by Putin in his speech at the Valdai Discussion Club Summit (September 2013).[75] If Western Europe used to protect Christianity when it was suppressed by the communist regimes in Eastern Europe, today, the former is distancing itself from its Christian roots, while the latter has become the last bastion of Christian values, traditions, and morality. Therefore, the contemporary Orthodox Christians bear "the exclusive responsibility to guard, uphold, remind, and spread throughout the secularizing European continent the evangelical truth and Christ's ideal as a measurement and model for human behavior."[76] In this regard, Karamihaleva also referred to the words of the Bulgarian Patriarch that "the Orthodox churchmen, politicians, and public figures from different countries as well as all people of good will around the world should unite their efforts in defense of the original Christian moral values and norms of behavior."[77]

The endorsement of traditional values reached its climax in 2018 when the Bulgarian Synod made a bold statement against the ratification of the Istanbul *Convention on Preventing and Combating Violence against Women and Domestic Violence*. This international act was condemned as incompatible with the teaching of the Orthodox Church about the "two sexes" created by God and Bulgarian public order.[78] The Orthodox hierarchs categorically protested against the introduction of any gender-related concepts and terminology in Bulgarian national legislation. This time, their position was shared by the other religious denominations who issued similar statements. It was also supported by the president and the main political parties. The last word in the dispute on the Istanbul Convention was given to the Constitutional Court which found it incompatible with the Bulgarian Constitution.[79]

In 2019, however, some traditional values were put under question during the public debate on the *Draft Strategy for Child Defense*. According to Orthodox hierarchs, the traditional family is the only proper place for child upbringing, while the planned strategy will allow state officials to intervene in family affairs easily and even to take children away from their parents. In their view, by emphasizing the children's rights and treating the child as an autonomous person, the adoption of this strategy will undermine the hierarchical character of the children-parents relations in the traditional Bulgarian family.[80] What fueled the criticism by society of the Synod's position was its disagreement with the ban on physical child abuse. In addition, many Bulgarians contest the Synod's view that Western liberal methods of education and upbringing are "far from the healthy and conservative values of Christianity" and debauch the morals of youth. As a result, the Holy Synod withdrew its statement on the strategy with the excuse that a Church official had announced it without the necessary consent.

Two months later, it issued a new position.[81] The Synod preserves the thesis about the priority of parental rights in the upbringing of children. It also retains its critical remarks about "good European practices." This time, however, the hierarchs pay more attention to the religion-based arguments in support of their position. They reminded Bulgarians that the Church and family have been established by God to secure the terrestrial and eternal life of man. They also referred to the Bible (1 Corinthians 16:19) to draw a parallel between the Church as the spiritual family of all believers and the family as a "small domestic Church." Finally, the Synod stresses that God has blessed marriage as a union of a man and woman whose love for and care of children are sacred. Thus, no "transitory and fickle political ideologies or ideological projects for redefining the family, reconsidering the parenthood or reshaping child's rights" should infringe God's model after which family has been created. This edited position attracted less criticism in society. It seems that the Church's vision of traditional family is widely shared by Bulgarians, though not always on the grounds of Orthodoxy. What divides the Orthodox Church and society is the issue of the child. Most probably, the reason is the Church's greater regard for the autonomy of human personality and children's rights, developed in Bulgarian society in the course of its democratization and eurointegration.

CONCLUSIONS

Thirty years after the end of the communist rule in Bulgaria, the local Orthodox Church has obtained a special place on the country's religious map. As a representative of the constitutionally recognized traditional religion in Bulgaria, it succeeded in 2002 in gaining an *ex lege* recognition by the Religious Denominations Act and, more recently, a significant state subsidy. In parallel, the post-communist restitution of the economic assets of the religious communities in Bulgaria transformed the local Orthodox Church into a noteworthy economic factor in the country. Finally, the victory of Maxim's Synod over the Alternative Synod allowed the leadership of the Bulgarian Orthodox Church to undertake more systematic measures for expanding its influence not only on its community of believers but also over the entire society. Still, the Holy Synod of the Bulgarian Orthodox Church has faced difficulties to promote its visions in the public arena. The community of Orthodox Bulgarians is not satisfied with the failure of its spiritual leaders to secure a proper religious commemoration of the clerics persecuted under communism. Although the Bulgarian Orthodox Church continues to be seen as a major bearer of national identity in post-communist Bulgaria, tensions have appeared between hierarchs and laymen provoked by their different understandings of nationalism. At the same time, the canonization of Archbishop Serafim seemed to be the most successful policy of the Bulgarian Synod in terms of its flock. This act also pointed to an expanded relationship between the Bulgarian and the Russian Orthodox Church: Based on the common faith, blood, and history during the times of the Soviet domination in Eastern Europe, today makes use of the newly established sacred bonds between the two Churches.

The reaction of Bulgarian society to the behavior of the Orthodox Church's leadership in the public arena is not unilateral either. The majority of citizens condemn the past collaboration of Orthodox hierarchs with the former totalitarian regime and have called for further investigation of this issue. The society also does not accept the monarchist sentiments demonstrated by the Holy Synod. The close relations of the Bulgarian Synod with the Moscow Patriarchate provoke concerns among some Bulgarian citizens, as well. At the same time, society has adopted a selective approach to the traditional values promoted by the Orthodox Church. On the one hand, there is general support for its vision of marriage as a union between a woman and a man, but attempts to impose other limits on the rights and freedoms obtained by Bulgarian citizens after the fall of communism are not welcome.

Notes

1. Constitutional Court of the Republic of Bulgaria, *Judgment No. 2/1998*, 18 February 1998 g., retractable from: www.constcourt.bg [accessed 20 April 2019].
2. "Zakon za veroizpovedaniyata" [Religious Denominations Act], *Darzhaven vestnik* [State Gazette], No. 120, 29 December 2002, at https://lex.bg/laws/ldoc/2135462355 [accessed 20 April 2019].
3. During the national censuses in 1992 and 2001, Bulgarian citizens were obliged to register their belonging to one or another religion in accordance with their own belief or that of their parents and grandparents. In 2011, however, this methodology was abandoned and Bulgarians were free to register or not their religious affiliation. See: "2011 Population Census—Main Results," *National Statistical Institute of the Republic of Bulgaria* (2011), at http://www.nsi.bg/census2011/PDOCS2/Census2011final_en.pdf [accessed 20 April 2019].
4. See Article 28, Para 2 in the Religious Denominations Act, amended in December 2018, *Darzhaven vestnik*, No. 108, 29 December 2018, at https://lex.bg/laws/ldoc/2135462355 [accessed 20 April 2019].
5. "Zakon za danak varhu dobavenata stoynost" [Law on VAT]. See the amended version which is in force since 1 January 2007, *Darzhaven vestnik*, No. 63, 4 August 2006, at https://nap.bg/page?id=472 [accessed 20 April 2019].
6. "Zakon za izmenenie i dopalnenie na Zakona za mestnite danatsi i taksi" [Law on the Amendment of the Law on Municipal Taxes and Fees], *Darzhaven vestnik*, No. 101, 22 November 2013, at http://dv.parliament.bg/DVWeb/showMaterialDV.jsp?idMat=80402 [accessed 20 April 2019].
7. "Stanovishte na Svetiya Sinod na Balgarskata pravoslavna tsarkva otnosno zaknoproekti za izmenenie i dopalnenie na Zakona za veroizpovedaniyata" [Statement of the Holy Synod of the Bulgarian Orthodox Church on the Draft Laws on the Amendment of the Religious Denominations Act], *Bulgarian Patriarchate*, 3 October 2018, at www.bg-patriarchia.bg [accessed 20 April 2019].
8. Stoyan Gruychev, *Cherna Kniga za prestapleniyata i zhertvite na komunizma v Balgariya, 1917–1990 g.* [Black Book on the Crimes and Victims of Communism in Bulgaria, 1917–1990] (Sofia: Zornitsa, 2001), pp. 22–33.

9. Janice Broun has dedicated several articles to the Bulgarian schism: "The Schism in the Bulgarian Orthodox Church," in *Religion, State and Society*, Vol. 21, No. 2 (1993), pp. 207–222; "The Schism in the Bulgarian Orthodox Church, Part 2: Under the Socialist Government, 1993–97," in *Religion, State and Society*, Vol. 28, No. 3 (2000), pp. 263–289; "The Schism in the Bulgarian Orthodox Church, Part 3: Under The Second Union of Democratic Forces Government, 1997–2001," in *Religion, State and Society*, Vol. 30, No. 4 (2002), pp. 365–394; "The Bulgarian Orthodox Church: The Continuing Schism and the Religious, Social and Political Environment," in *Religion, State and Society*, Vol. 32, No. 3 (2004), pp. 209–245.
10. Naum (Dimitrov), Metropolitan of Ruse, "Raskolat v Balgarskata pravoslavna tsarkva in negovoto preodolyavane" [The Schism Within the BOC and Its Overcoming], paper delivered at the conference "The Ukrainian Orthodox Church at the Turn of the Millennium," 28 May 2012, held in the Kiev Ecclesiastical Academy (http://clement.kiev.ua/ru/node/830) and published in Bulgarian on 15 January 2014 at https://dveri.bg/component/com_content/Itemid,100521/catid,280/id,18639/view,article/ [accessed 20 April 2019].
11. Daniela Kalkandjieva, "The New Denominations Act and the Bulgarian Orthodox Church (2002–2005)," in Irimie Marga, Gerald G. Sander, and Dan Sandu (eds.), *Religion zwischen Kirche, Staat und Gesellschaft—Religion Between Church, State and Society* (Hamburg: Verlag Dr. Kovac, 2007), pp. 103–117.
12. Judgment of the European Court of Human Rights (ECHR) on the Case of the Holy Synod of the Bulgarian Orthodox Church (Metropolitan Inokentiy) and others vs. Bulgaria (Application nos. 412/03 and 35677/04), 22 January 2009, at http://hudoc.echr.coe.int/eng?i=001-90788 [accessed 20 April 2019].
13. Decision No. 298/2012 of the Committee for Disclosing the Documents and Announcing Affiliation of Bulgarian Citizens to the State Security and the Intelligence Services of the Bulgarian National Army is retractable: http://www.comdos.bg [accessed 20 April 2019].
14. The last discussion on this issue was held at the Channel One of the Bulgarian National Television, Program *Vyara i obshtestvo*, 30 March 2019, at https://www.bnt.bg/bg/a/prodlzhava-li-bpts-da-boykotira-komisiyata-po-dosietata-30032019 [accessed 20 April 2019].
15. Daniela Kalkandjieva, *Balgarskata pravoslavna tsarkva i darzhvata, 1944–1953* [The Bulgarian Orthodox Church and the State, 1944–1953] (Sofia: Albatros, 1997); Stoyan Gruychev, *Cherna kniga za prestapleniyata i zhertvite na komunizma v Balgariya, 1917–1990 g.* [Black Book on the Crimes and Victims of Communism in Bulgaria]

(Sofia: Zornitsa, 2001); Momchil Metodiev, *Mezhdu vyarata i kompromisa: Balgarskata pravoslava tsarkva i komunizma (1944–1989 g.)* [Between Faith and Compromise: The Bulgarian Orthodox Church and Communism (1944–1989)] (Sofia Ciela, 2010); and Ivan Denev, *Cheda na sotsializma: Dokumentalno Chetivo* [Children of Socialism: Documents] (Sofia: Fondatsiya za regionalno razvitie, 2012).
16. Metodiev, *Mezhdu vyarata i kompromisa*, pp. 345–368.
17. "Protokol za kanonizatsiyata na novobalgarskite machenitsi" [Proceedings of the Alternative Synod on the Canonization of the New Martyrs of the Bulgarian Orthodox Church], 24 October 2002, at http://sourteardrop.blog.bg/izkustvo/2014/07/08/protokol-ot-kanonizaciiata-na-novobylgarskite-mychenici.1279423 [accessed 20 April 2019].
18. "Reshenie na Sv. Sinod ot 31.03.2016 g.: Zapochva protsedura po kanonizatsiyata na prisnopamentniya Nevrokopski mitropolit Boris" [Decision of the Holy Synod of 31 March 2016 on the Canonization of the Late Metropolitan Boris of Nevrokop], *Bulgarian Patriarchate*, 1 April 2016, at http://www.bg-patriarshia.bg/news.php?id=200038 [accessed 20 April 2019].
19. Andrey Kostryukov, *Zhizneopisanie Arkhiepiskopa Serafima (Soboleva)* (Sofia: Sinodal'noe izdatel'stvo, Podvorie Patriarkha Moskovskogo i vseya Rusi v Sofii, 2011), p. 42.
20. "Doklad mitropolita Volokolamskogo Ilariona na Arkhiereyskom Sobore Russkoy Pravoslavnoy Tserkvi, 2–3 fevralya 2016 goda" [Report by Metropolitan Hilarion of Volokolamsk at the Council of Bishops of the Russian Orthodox Church held on 2–3 February 2016], 3 February 2016, at www.patriarchia.ru/db/print/4367084.html [accessed 20 April 2019].
21. Ol'ga Nikolaeva Reshetnikova, *Russkaya tserkov' v Sofii* [The Russian Church in Sofia] (Sofia: Podvor'e Russkoy Pravoslavnoy tserkvi v Sofii, Moskovskiy kul'turno-delovoy tsentr MKDTs "Dom Moskvy v Sofii," 2010).
22. Kostryukov, *Zhizneopisanie Arkhiepiskopa Serafima (Soboleva)*.
23. "V Sofii nachala rabotu komissiya pokanonizatsii arkhiepiskopa Serafima (Soboleva)" [The Commission on the Canonization of Archbishop Serafim (Sobolev) Opened Its Working Session in Sofia], *Sedmitsa.ru*, 4 December 2014, at https://www.sedmitza.ru/text/6039617.html [accessed 20 April 2019].
24. "Sveteyshiyat balgarski patriarch Neofit izrazi podkrepata na BPTs-BP za kanoniziraneto na arhiep. Serafim Sobolev" [The Holy Patriarch Neofit of Bulgaria Expressed the Support of the Bulgarian Orthodox Church—Bulgarian Patriarchate for the Canonization of Archbishop Serafim (Sobolev)], *Bulgarian Patriarchate*, 5 December 2014, at http://www.bg-patriarshia.bg/news.php?id=158119 [accessed 20 April 2019].

25. "Bishops' Council Glorifies Archbishop Seraphim (Sobolev)," *Department for External Church Relations of the Moscow Patriarchate*, 3 February 2016, at https://mospat.ru/en/2016/02/03/news127756/ [accessed 20 April 2019].
26. "Solemn Celebrations Held in Sofia on Commemoration Day of St. Seraphim the Archbishop of Boguchar," *Moscow Patriarchate*, 27 February 2016, at http://www.patriarchia.ru/en/db/text/5381967.html [accessed 20 April 2019].
27. Peter Bouteneff, "The Orthodox Churches, the WCC, and the Upcoming Assembly," *World Council of Churches*, 1 October 1998, at https://www.oikoumene.org/en/resources/documents/wcc-programmes/ecumenical-movement-in-the-21st-century/member-churches/special-commission-on-participation-of-orthodox-churches/first-plenary-meeting-documents-december-1999/the-orthodox-churches-the-wcc-and-the-upcoming-assembly [accessed 20 April 2019].
28. Metodiev, "The Ecumenical Activities of the Bulgarian Orthodox Church: Reasons, Motivations, Consequences," *Occasional Papers on Religion in Eastern Europe*, Vol. 32, No. 3, Article 3 [pp. 1–12], p. 12, at https://digitalcommons.georgefox.edu/ree/vol32/iss3/3 [accessed 20 April 2019].
29. Kalkandjieva, *The Russian Orthodox Church, 1917–1948: From Decline to Resurrection* (London: Routledge, 2014), pp. 314–315.
30. "Reshenie na Sv. Sinod ot 21.04.2016 g. s predlozhenie za promeni v predsaborniya dokument za otnoshenieto kam ostanalite hristiyani" [Decision of the Holy Synod from 21 April 2016, proposing amendments in the Pre-Conciliar document on the "Relations of the Orthodox Church with the Rest of the Christian World"], *Bulgarian Patriarchate*, 21 April 2016, at http://www.bg-patriarshia.bg/news.php?id=201851 [accessed 20 April 2019].
31. "Relations of the Orthodox Church with the Rest of the Christian World" (Chambésy, 10–17 October 2015), *Holy and the Great Council*, 2016, at https://www.holycouncil.org/-/rest-of-christian-world [accessed 20 April 2019].
32. Jolyon Naegele, "Bulgaria: Pope's Visit Will Attempt to Heal Rift with Orthodox Church," *Radio Free Europe/Radio Liberty*, 22 May 2002, at https://www.rferl.org/a/1099784.html [accessed 20 April 2019].
33. "Apostolic Voyage of His Holiness John Paul II in Azerbaijan and Bulgaria, 22–26 May 2002, Program," Vatican, 2002, at https://w2.vatican.va/content/john-paul-ii/en/travels/2002/documents/trav_azerbaijan-bulgaria_program_20020522.html [accessed 20 April 2019].

34. "Reshenie na Sv. Sinod ot 02.04.2019 г. otnosno poseshtenieto na papa Frantsisk u nas" [Decision of the Holy Synod from 2 April 2019 Concerning the Visit of Pope Francis to Bulgaria], *Bulgarian Patriarchate*, 3 April 2019, at http://bg-patriarshia.bg/news.php?id=286989 [accessed 20 April 2019].
35. "Apostolic Trip of His Holiness Francis to Bulgaria and the Republic of North Macedonia, 5 to 7 May 2019," *Vatican*, 2019, at http://www.popeinbulgaria.gov.bg/en/apostolic-journey/program/program [accessed 20 April 2019].
36. Yanko Dimov, *Kiril--'Patriarch Balgarski'* [Kiril – 'Bulgarian Patriarch'] (Sofia: Sofia University Press, 2005), pp. 208–209.
37. Petya Vladimirova, "Za parvi pat ot 70 godini na groba na tsar Boris III shte zastane pocheten voenen karaul" [For the First Time a Military Guard of Honor Will Stand at the Grave of Tsar Boris III], at https://www.dnevnik.bg/bulgaria/2013/08/23/2128171_za_purvi_put_ot_70_godini_na_groba_na_car_boris_shte/ [accessed 20 April 2019].
38. "Slovo-privetstvie na Plovdivskiya mitropolit Nikolay pri poseshtenieto nap patriarch Neofit i Sv. Sinod na BPTs v m-ra "Sv. sv. Kirik i Yulita" [Welcome Address of Metropolitan Nikolay of Plovdiv to Patriarch Neofit and the Holy Synod of the Bulgarian Orthodox Church During Their Visit to Sts Kirik and Yulita Monastery]," *Bulgarian Patriarchate*, 15 December 2014, at http://bg-patriarshia.bg/news.php?id=159004 [accessed 20 April 2019].
39. "Reshenie na Sv. Sinod ot 29.04.2015 g. za bogosluzhebno spomenavane na NV Simeon II, Tsar na balgarite" [Decision of the Holy Synod for the Liturgical Mentioning of the Name of His Majesty Simeon II, Tsar of Bulgarians], *Bulgarian Patriarchate*, 29 April 2015, at http://bg-patriarshia.bg/news.php?id=172424; "Bulgarian Orthodox Church Includes Blessing for Saxe-Coburg as 'Tsar of Bulgarians' in liturgies," *The Sofia Globe*, 30 April 2015, at http://sofiaglobe.com/2015/04/30/bulgarian-orthodox-church-includes-blessing-for-saxe-coburg-as-tsar-of-bulgarians-in-liturgies/ [accessed 20 April 2019].
40. On the special request of Tsar Boris III, his son Simeon Saxe-Coburg-Gotha received his royal anointment together with his baptism on 12 June 1937. Bulgaria's Tsentral State Archives, fund 791k, opis [inventory] 1, a.e. [archival unit] 59, Proceedings of the Extended Holy Synod No. 17, 13 July 1937.
41. On 2 May, the Bulgarian Church commemorates the memory of Tsar Boris I, who baptized Bulgarians in 865.
42. The liturgy is defined as "pan-Orthodox" in the Web site of the Serbian Orthodox Church. See "Pan-Orthodox Liturgy on the Occasion of 1150th Anniversary of the Baptism of Bulgarians," 6 May 2015, at

http://www.spc.rs/eng/panorthodox_liturgy_occasion_1150th_anniversary_baptism_bulgarians [accessed 20 April 2019].

43. "Tarzhestvena sveta liturgiya za 1150 godini ot Pokrastvaneto" [Holy Divine Liturgy on the Occasion of the 1150th Anniversary of the Baptism of Bulgarians], *Bulgarian National Television*, 2 May 2015, at http://news.bnt.bg/bg/a/476773-bozhestvena-sveta-liturgiya-za-1150-godini-ot-pokra-stvaneto; Nikolay Krastev, Rositsa Arabadzhieva, "Otbelyazvame 1150 godini ot Pokrastvaneto na balgarskiya narod" [We Celebrate the 1150th Anniversary from the Baptism of the Bulgarian People], *Bulgarian National Radio*, 2 May 2015, at http://bnr.bg/post/100552341/dnes-otbelazvame-1150-godini-ot-pokrastvaneto-na-balgarskia-narod [accessed 20 April 2019].

44. "Vsepravoslavna liturgiya za 1150 godini ot Pokrastvaneto na balgaskiya narod" [All-Orthodox Liturgy on the Occasion of the 1150th Anniversary from the Baptism of Bulgarians], *Bulgarian Patriarchate*, 3 May 2015, at http://bg-patriarshia.bg/news.php?id=172589 [accessed 20 April 2019].

45. "Presidentat: Sinodat da ne tituluva Simeon kato tsar" [The President: The Synod Should Not Refer to Simeon as Tsar]," *Plovdiv Online*, 3 May 2015, at https://plovdiv-online.com/koi-kakvo-kaza/item/67129-prezidentaat-sinodaat-d%D0%B0-ne-tituluv%D0%B0-simeon-tz%D0%B0r [accessed 20 April 2019].

46. Evelina Kelbecheva, "The Short History for Bulgaria for Export," in Jø Nielsen (ed.), *Religion, Ethnicity and Contested Nationhood in the Former Ottoman Space* (Leiden, Boston: Brill, 2012), pp. 242–247.

47. Martina Baleva, "Koy (po)kaza istinata za Batak?" [Who Has Shown/Tell the Truth About Batak?], *Kultura*, Sofia, No. 17 (2412), 5 May 2006, at http://www.kultura.bg/bg/print_article/view/11756 [accessed 20 April 2019].

48. Naum Kaychev, "Kak Batak vleze v balgarskiya natsionalen razkaz" [How Did Batak Enter in the Bulgarian National Narrative], *Kultura*, No. 24 (2419), 23 June 2006, at http://www.kultura.bg/bg/article/view/11928 [accessed 20 April 2019].

49. Baleva, "Hiatusat Batak" [The Hiatus Batak], *Kultura*, No. 29 (2424), 8 September 2006, at http://www.kultura.bg/bg/article/view/12049 [accessed 20 April 2019].

50. Alexander Vezenkov, "Proektat i skandalat 'Batak'," [The Project and the Sacandal "Batak"], *Liberalen Pregled* [Bulgarian Online Journal], 25 February 2013, at http://www.librev.com/prospects-bulgaria-publisher/1963-batak-2 (Part 1) and http://www.librev.com/index.php/2013-03-30-08-56-39/prospects/bulgaria/1970-2013-03-29-11-00-22 (Part 2) [accessed 20 April 2019].

51. Desislava Panayotova, "Balgariya ochakva kanonizatsiyata na svoite machenitsi ot Batak i Novo selo" [Bulgaria Is Expecting the Canonization of Its Martyrs from Batak and Novo Selo], *Bulgarian Patriarchate*, 31 March 2011, at http://www.bg-patriarshia.bg/news.php?id=42326) [accessed 20 April 2019].
52. "Veselin Stankov: Tsarkva-kostnitsa i muzey Sv. Nedelya v Batak – vaztorzhen pametnik na svobodata" [An Interview of Radio "Focis" on the church-ossuary St. Nedelya in Batak with Veselin Stankov, the Chairman of the Cultural and Historical Society "Buditel"], 3 March 2014, Radio "Focus" - Pazardhzhik, at http://m.focus-news.net/?action=opinion&id=27485) [accessed 20 April 2019].
53. Ibid.
54. "Batak s nova podpiska sreshtu mitropolit Nikolay" [New Petition of the Citizens of Batak Against Metropolitan Nikolay], *Duma* (Sofia), No. 137, 20 June 2016, at https://duma.bg/batak-s-nova-podpiska-sreshtu-mitropolit-nikolay-n125997?go=news&p=list&categoryId=3) [accessed 20 April 2019].
55. Atanas Slavov, "The Macedonian Orthodox Church: Ecclesiastical and Geopolitical Stakes in the Western Balkans," *Bulgaria Analytica*, 21 November 2017, at http://bulgariaanalytica.org/en/2017/11/21/the-macedonian-orthodox-church-ecclesiastical-and-geopolitical-stakes-in-the-western-balkans/ [accessed 20 April 2019].
56. Angel Karadakov, "Za balgarskata i makedonskata tsarkva: Barzite resheniya nikoga ne sa dobri" [Concerning the Bulgarian and the Macedonian Church: The Speedy Decisions Are Always Bad], *Standart* (Sofia), 27 November 2017, at http://standartnews.com/mneniya-analizi/za_balgarskata_i_makedonskata_tsarkva_barzite_resheniya_nikoga_ne_sa_dobri-365463.html [accessed 20 April 2019].
57. Goran Blagoev, "Svetite bratya Kiril i Metodiy sa i vashi, i nashi" [The Holy Brothers Cyril and Methodius as Ours as Well as Yours], *Dveri.bg* [Bulgarian Orthodox Portal], 13 May 2015, at https://dveri.bg/94qqw [accessed 20 April 2019].
58. Blagoev, "Bulgarian Patriarchate and Church Problem in the Republic of Macedonia—Meetings and Talking at Cross-Purposes After 1989," *Macedonian Review* (Sofia), Vol. XXXIX, No. 4 (2016), p. 41.
59. "Pismo do Negovo Prevazhoditelstvo g-n Petro Poroshenko, President of Ukraine" [Letter to His Excellency Mr. Petro Poroshenko, President of Ukraine], *Bulgarian Patriarchate*, 12 June 2017, at http://www.bg-patriarshia.bg/news.php?id=237118 [accessed 20 April 2019].
60. Slavov, "The Macedonian Orthodox Church: Ecclesiastical and Geopolitical Stakes in the Western Balkans."
61. Ibid.

62. "Reshenie na Sv. Sinod po povod otpraveno pismo ot Makedonskata pravoslavna tsarkva" [Decision of the Holy Synod Concerning a Letter Received from the Macedonian Orthodox Church], *Bulgarian Patriarchate*, 27 November 2017, at http://bg-patriarshia.bg/news.php?id=249763 [accessed 20 April 2019].
63. "Bulgarian Orthodox Church and Schismatic Macedonian Church Hold Joint Meeting," *Orthodox Christianity*, 22 December 2017, at http://orthochristian.com/109439.html [accessed 20 April 2019].
64. "Orthodox Easter 2018: Bulgarian Orthodox Church Could Face Issue with Macedonian Church Over 'Holy Fire'," *Sofia Globe*, 16 April 2018, at https://sofiaglobe.com/2018/04/06/orthodox-easter-2018-bulgarian-orthodox-church-could-face-issue-with-macedonian-church-over-holy-fire/ [accessed 20 April 2019].
65. "Orthodox Easter 2018: For the First Time, Bulgarian Church Delegation Passes 'Holy Fire' to Macedonian Church," *Sofia Globe*, 7 April 2018, at https://sofiaglobe.com/2018/04/07/orthodox-easter-2018-for-the-first-time-bulgarian-church-delegation-passes-holy-fire-to-macedonian-church/; "Orthodox Easter 2019: N Macedonia Bishop to Go with Bulgarian Delegation to Jerusalem to Fetch 'Holy Fire'," *Sofia Globe*, 4 April 2019, at https://sofiaglobe.com/2019/04/04/orthodox-easter-2019-n-macedonia-bishop-to-go-with-bulgarian-delegation-to-jerusalem-to-fetch-holy-fire/ [accessed 20 April 2019].
66. "Concept of the Holy Synod of the Bulgarian Orthodox Church on the Statute of the Discipline 'Religion' in the Bulgarian Public School," *Bulgarian Patriarchate* [Spring] 2008, at http://bg-patriarshia.bg/index.php?file=concepts_1.xml [accessed 20 April 2019].
67. Kalkandjieva and Maria Schnitter, "Teaching Religion in Bulgarian Schools: Historical Experience and Post-Atheist Development," in Adam Seligman (ed.), *Religious Education and the Challenge of Pluralism* (Oxford and New York: Oxford University Press, 2014), pp. 70–95.
68. "Strategiya na BPTs—BP za duhovna prosveta, katehizatsiya i kultura" [Strategy of Bulgarian Orthodox Church—Bulgarian Patriarchate the for Spiritual Enlightenment, Catechism and Culture], *Bulgarian Patriarchate*, 6 October 2012, at http://www.bg-patriarshia.bg/index.php?file=strategies_1.xml; "Osnovni nasoki za prilagane na Strategiyata za duhovna prosveta, katehizatsiya i kultura na BPTs--BP" [Main Directions for the Implementation of the Strategy of Bulgarian Orthodox Church—Bulgarian Patriarchate the for Spiritual Enlightenment, Catechism and Culture], at http://bg-patriarshia.bg/index.php?file=strategies_2.xml [accessed 20 April 2019].

69. "Stanovishte na Sv. Sinod na BPTs—BP otnosno metodite na assistirana reproduktsiya i zamestvashtoto maychnstvo" [Statement of the Holy Synod of the Bulgarian Orthodox Church—Bulgarian Patriarchate on the Assisted Reproduction and Surrogate Motherhood], *Bulgarian Patriarchate*, 30 December 2011, at http://www.bg-patriarshia.bg/index.php?file=attitude_6.xml [accessed 20 April 2019].
70. "Izyavlenie na Svetiya Sinod na BPC po povod na organiziraniya na 27 yuni gey parad" [Statement of the Holy Synod of the Bulgarian Orthodox Church on the Occasion of the Gay Parade Scheduled for 27 June], *Bulgarian Patriarchate*, 25 June 2015, at http://bg-patriarshia.bg/news.php?id=177455 [accessed 20 April 2019].
71. "Stanovishte na Sv. Sinod na BPTs—BP ot 28.11.2014 g. za deystvashtiya meditsinski standart "Akusherstvo i ginekologiya" otnosno nedonosenite detsa [Statement of the Holy Synod of the Bulgaria Orthodox Church—Bulgarian Patriarchate on the Medical Normative Documents on Premature Babies]." *Bulgarian Patriarchate*, 9 December 2014, at http://www.bg-patriarshia.bg/news.php?id=158486 [accessed 20 April 2019].
72. "Special Address of the Holy Synod of the Bulgarian Orthodox Church—Bulgarian Patriarchate with Reference to the Migration Crisis," *Bulgarian Patriarchate*, 25 September 2015, at http://bg-patriarshia.bg/news.php?id=184530 [accessed 20 April 2019].
73. "Patriarch Neofit: Dobriyat zakon lezhi na traditsionnite tsennosti" [Patriarch Neofit: Good Law Steps on Traditional Values], *BTV News*, 12 July 2016, at https://btvnovinite.bg/bulgaria/obshtestvo/patriarh-neofit-dobrijat-zakon-lezhi-na-tradicionnite-cennosti.html [accessed 20 April 2019].
74. Alicja Curanović, *The Guardians of Traditional Values: Russian and the Russian Orthodox Church in the Quest for Status*, 2014–2015 Paper Series, No. 1 (Washington: Transatlantic Academy, 2015), pp. 8–10. See also "Bazisnyye tsennosti — osnova obshchenatsional'noy identichnosti" [Basic Values—Fundaments of All-National Identity], *Moscow Patriarchate*, 26 May 2011, at http://www.patriarchia.ru/db/text/1496038.html [accessed 20 April 2019].
75. Curanović, *The Guardians of Traditional Values*, pp. 8–9.
76. Aleksandra Karamihaleva, "Tsarkva i obshtestvo v konteksta na usiliyata za sahranenie na traditsionnite tsennosti v savremenna Evropa" [Church and Society in the Context of the Efforts for Preserving Traditional Values in Contemporary Europe], *Orthodox Youth*, 7 December 2017, at http://www.pravmladeji.org/print/2912 (Part 1) & http://www.pravmladeji.org/print/2913 6/ (Part 2) [accessed 20 April 2019].
77. Ibid.

78. "Stanovishte na Svetiya Sinod po povod na Istanbulskata konventisya" [Statement of the Holy Synod on the Istanbul Convention], 22 January 2018, at http://www.bg-patriarshia.bg/news.php?id=254101 [accessed 20 April 2019].
79. Constitutional Court of the Republic of Bulgaria, Judgment No. 13/2018, at http://www.constcourt.bg/bg/Acts/GetHtmlContent/f278a156-9d25-412d-a064-6ffd6f997310 [accessed 20 April 2019].
80. "Stanovishte na Svetiya Sinod na Balgarskata pravoslavna tsarkva – Balgarska patriarshiya otnosno proekt za Natsionalna starategiya za deteto 2019-2013 g." [Statement of the Holy Synod of the Bulgarian Orthodox Church—Bulgarian Patriarchate on the Draft of the National Child Strategy 2019–2030], 7 February 2019, at http://www.strategy.bg/PublicConsultations/View.aspx?lang=bg-BG&Id=4012 [accessed 20 April 2019].
81. "Stanovishte na Svetiya Sinod na Balgarskata pravoslavna tsarkva – Balgarska patriarshiya otnosno proekt za Natsionalna starategiya za deteto" [Statement of the Holy Synod of the Bulgarian Orthodox Church—Bulgarian Patriarchate on the Draft of the National Child Strategy], 2 April 2019, at www.bg-patriarshia.bg/news.php?id=286900 [accessed 20 April 2019].

CHAPTER 5

The Church, the Nation, and the State: The Serbian Orthodox Church After Communism

Jelena Subotić

Abstract My chapter focuses on the role the Serbian Orthodox Church has played in Serbian politics since 1989, but especially since 2000, with the end of the authoritarian rule of Slobodan Milošević. Centering the discussion on four principal dimensions that capture the Serbian Church's influence in this period—nationalism, conservatism, homophobia, and religious intolerance—this chapter pays special attention to two main social and political fault lines in post-2000 Serbia and the Church's central role in them: the status of its LGBTQ community and the continuing contention over Kosovo's secession. The chapter concludes that the SOC continues to serve as a political force in Serbian society—a foundational source of Serbian national identity and an organization deeply immersed in contemporary Serbian politics. It is a Church that is deeply conservative, opposed to change, and primarily interested in preserving its status and privilege in Serbian society.

J. Subotić (✉)
Georgia State University, Atlanta, GA, USA
e-mail: jsubotic@gsu.edu

The Serbian Orthodox Church (SOC) emerged from World War Two devastated economically, physically, culturally, and with no clear role to play in communist Yugoslavia. The new regime was hostile to religion, and with a series of laws marginalized and further weakened all religious organizations in the country, including the Orthodox Church, dramatically limiting the Church's role in society.[1] The SOC was, for all intents and purposes, placed under the control and authority of the state.[2] The relationship between the Church and the communist state improved somewhat in the 1960s with the general liberalization of Yugoslav society, which also brought a period of renewed cooperation on the part of the Church in official matters.[3] The Church was run by the pragmatic Patriarch German who attempted to compromise with the communist order.[4]

Ideologically, and not in the least bit surprisingly, the SOC remained fundamentally anti-communist and nationalist. The episcopate had a hostile view of communism, perceiving it—correctly—as anti-religious. Instead, historically it supported Serbian nationalists and anti-communists, most directly—the Yugoslav Homeland Army (specifically the Chetniks of Draža Mihailović) during World War Two.[5] This would become important in the run-up to the wars of Yugoslav succession, when the Church came to fully support the Serbian nationalist project and link it, ideologically, to its historical support of the Yugoslav Homeland Army.

Nationalism

The Role of the Church in Nationalist Mobilization

The Church became more politically assertive in the 1980s, when the radical anti-communist and anti-Western current started to gain strength within the SOC leadership. A precipitating event for this new Church activism was a series of student demonstrations in Kosovo in 1981, when Kosovar Albanians organized to demand stronger autonomy within the Serbian republic. Specifically, the protesters demanded that Kosovo be elevated to the status of one of the constituent republics instead of remaining an autonomous province within Serbia and asked for improvement of general social conditions in the province.[6] The demonstrations in Kosovo shook the Serbian political leadership, emboldened Serbian nationalists within the communist ranks and also opened up the space for the SOC to assert itself in the political arena.[7]

An important marker in this overt politicization of the SOC was the publication of the *Appeal for the Protection of the Serbian Populace and Its Holy Sites in Kosovo* in 1982, in which 21 leading priests and theologians expressed their concern about the "necessity of protecting the spiritual and biological being of the Serbian people in Kosovo and Metohija."[8] In this open letter to the Presidency of the Socialist Federated Republic of Yugoslavia (SFRY) and other high state institutions, the priests declared, "For Serbs the Kosovo issue is not only a biological one or about 'region,' 'province' or 'republics' [...] it is about the spiritual, cultural or historic identity of the Serbian people," and warned that "Kosovo is our memory, our hearth, the focus of our being. And to take away from a nation its memories means to kill it and destroy it spiritually." The *Appeal* advanced the idea—which has since become a regular trope in Serbian nationalist discourse on Kosovo—that Kosovo is for Serbs what Jerusalem is for the Jewish people who, "because of necessity of survival among the living and the miracle of their unremitting memory, even despite the logic of history, return, after two thousand years, in suffering, to their Jerusalem. Likewise, the Serbian nation continues to fight its Kosovo battle, thus fighting for such a memory of its identity, for a meaningful life and survival on this land, ever since 1389 until this day."[9] Although the state media called the *Appeal* a "dangerous step" and a "nationalist challenge," Atanasije Jevtić, one of the SOC leaders behind the document (who later went on to be consecrated as Bishop), disclosed that it was very well received by the Serbian government.[10]

From 1982 on, the SOC took on the care of the remaining Serbian population in Kosovo, but also in Croatia and Bosnia–Herzegovina, as its primary responsibility.[11] Throughout the mid-/to the late 1980s, the Serbian Church press focused relentlessly on the issue of Kosovo and what it argued was the neglect and abuse of the Serbian minority at the hands of the Albanian majority. The key Orthodox Church leader in the construction of this narrative was Atanasije Jevtić, whose articles, published between 1982 and 1984 in the SOC's main publication, *Pravoslavlje*, included increasingly graphic and gruesome imagery of alleged crimes committed against the Serbs by Albanians in Kosovo.[12] Two central themes of these highly influential articles were the suffering of the Serbian nation and the sacred land of Kosovo, represented as "the cradle and the tomb" of the Serbian people.[13]

Throughout the 1980s, this SOC rhetoric intensified. In 1987, the official statement from the session of the Holy Synod of the Serbian

Orthodox Church for the first time used the term "genocide" for the plight of Serbs in Kosovo.[14] It is at this time that the SOC truly incorporated the narrative of the "victim" (for the Serbs generally, but also for the SOC itself) of various foreign nations, religions, and movements, most often the Vatican, the USA or, more generally "the West." The SOC began to frequently recall Serbia's difficult past and warn against future threats and misfortunes, including, ultimately, a new genocide against the Serbian nation looming on the horizon. To make these threats and challenges appear truly existential, the looming disaster to befall the Serbian people was often compared to the destiny of Christ himself.[15]

The SOC also conflated Orthodoxy with Serbian national identity. In 1991, the Church's official publication *Glas crkve* published a statement that "Serbhood grew on Orthodoxy and without it there could be no Serbhood. Serbs who stopped being Orthodox stopped being Serb."[16]

The SOC and the Serbs in Croatia and Bosnia–Herzegovina

The nationalism pushed by the Serbian Orthodox Church was, however, not only related to Kosovo. An equally significant part of the Church's nationalist project was the construction of Serbian victimization in Croatia and mobilization of their protection.

As early as 1984, Church publications began to write about the catastrophe that had befallen the Serbian population in the Independent State of Croatia (Nezavisna Država Hrvatska—NDH) during World War Two. In 1990, the SOC issued two statements on the difficult, "almost occupation-like conditions" the Serbian Orthodox Church had faced in Croatia and Slovenia.[17] This was followed by a campaign of exhumations of Serbian victims of the NDH regime in the republics of Croatia and Bosnia and Herzegovina, and their official, SOC-led, reburials throughout 1990 and 1991.[18]

On the eve of the Croatian war in 1991, the SOC intensified its public presence as well as its international activism. In October 1991, the newly enthroned Patriarch Pavle wrote a letter to Lord Carrington, president of the International Conference on Yugoslavia (and a similar one to all participants in the Peace Conference in the Hague), in which he claimed that, due to the past genocide against the Serbs in Croatia, as well as current problems, Serbs cannot remain in any future independent Croatia, but must live in Serbia, across Serb lands as "the victims of genocide cannot live together with their past, and perhaps also their future perpetrators."[19]

In this period, World War Two-era Croatian death camp Jasenovac—the site of the murder of some 86,000 Croatian Serbs, Jews, and Roma[20]—became newly sacralized, with the Serbian Church beginning to treat it as a religious heritage site, a site of Orthodox mourning. What the SOC did with this move, however, was to memorialize wartime atrocities, especially atrocities committed by the Croatian fascist Ustasha, as primarily atrocities against the Serbs.

But many members of the SOC establishment did more than just give speeches. They visited soldiers in barracks, as well as Serbian paramilitary troops, including a group of paramilitaries led by the notorious organized crime boss turned war criminal Željko Ražnatović Arkan.[21] The most notorious example, however, was the blessing Serbian Orthodox hieromonk Gavrilo gave to the brutal Serbian paramilitary group "Scorpions" right as they were about to go to Potočari, outside Srebrenica,[22] and embark on the preplanned and systematic genocidal extermination of Bosniac boys and men in July 1995.[23]

The SOC also officially encouraged Serbs in Croatia (as well as Bosnia–Herzegovina) to leave the territories no longer under Serbian military control.[24] At the same time, it directly asserted its authority over all Serbs, everywhere, as in this official May 1996 Holy Synod of Bishops statement: "Notwithstanding the dissolution of Versailles Yugoslavia, i.e., the Socialist Federated Republic of Yugoslavia, the jurisdiction of the Serbian Orthodox Church still extends to all the Orthodox on that territory."[25]

The SOC clearly understood its role to extend far beyond the pastoral care of the Orthodox population within Serbia. As the next section indicates, this expansive view of the Church's spiritual jurisdiction had direct consequences on the political negotiations of the disputed sovereignty of Kosovo since 2008.

The Role of the SOC in Kosovo Negotiations

In addition to their teachings, sermons, and publications, SOC leaders often made directly political claims related to the status of Kosovo.[26] In 1992, Bishop Irinej of Bačka famously said that Kosovo is "the most precious Serbian word," and as such, presumably, non-negotiable.[27] This sacralization of Kosovo was part of the larger objective of the Serbian

Orthodox Church to extend its control over all Orthodox Serbs, regardless of whether they lived in Serbia or in the independent states that emerged from the breakup of socialist Yugoslavia.[28] But the claim that Kosovo is non-negotiable is an extension of the Church's position that Kosovo's independence is not only politically, but morally unacceptable. In his inaugural speech, Serbian Patriarch Irinej warned political actors not to commit a "sin" of denying the Serbian people their right to Kosovo[29] and in a later statement claimed that "we should suffer for Kosovo if need be."[30]

This SOC position on Kosovo's non-negotiability has continued throughout the diplomatic crisis in the aftermath of Kosovo's 2008 declaration of independence. While Serbian political elites have de facto—but not rhetorically—accepted the reality of Kosovo's independence,[31] as the political negotiations were underway, the Patriarch proclaimed, "Kosovo is, will be and will remain Serbian as long as it is in our thoughts." Once again, the Patriarch brought up the Kosovo/Jerusalem comparison, as in this statement: "If some audacious power makes us lose Kosovo and Metohija, we will always have an example of the Jewish people who waited for Jerusalem for 2000 years and finally got ahold of it."[32] All of these proclamations further institutionalized the notion of Kosovo as "sacred" and as lying under the purview of the SOC, first, and the Serbian state, second.[33]

The Church's policy on Kosovo continues to be one of the biggest purveyors of Serbian nationalism. Its stance on Kosovo has remained rigid. The SOC continues to present Kosovo as the sacred land of the Serbian people: "What Jerusalem is for the Jewish people, Kosovo is for the Serbs. Like Jerusalem, Kosovo is not only about geography or demography. It is about national, spiritual, cultural, Christian and human identity [...]."[34] The SOC also requested that the new Serbian constitution stipulates, "nobody ever has the right to relinquish Kosovo and Metohija as it is the inseparable territory of the Serbian nation, Serbian state and Serbian Saint Sava's Church."[35] In the words of Bishop Artemije of Raška-Prizren, "Kosovo is not about geography, but about ideology, it is an ideal [...] whoever thinks differently is only biologically a Serb, but not [a Serb] in the spirit."[36]

In the view of the Church, Kosovo is not simply a part of Serbia's (desired) territory; it is, above all else, its sacred covenant.[37] In their 2008 Easter message bishops called upon all Orthodox Serbs to implement the Kosovo covenant: "If we fulfill this covenant," bishops reassured their flock, "no one can take Kosovo and Metohija from us, not in this or in any other century, just as nobody could take away from the Jewish people their holy Jerusalem."[38]

More directly, the Synod—the Church's governing council—has consistently urged Kosovo's Serbs to abstain from participation in Kosovar political institutions and consider loyalty only to Serbia's political institutions.[39] In 2004, Bishop Artemije appealed to the US Congress not to support the independence of Kosovo: "The independence of Kosovo, in a situation where most elementary standards of rule-of-law simply do not exist, would lead directly to the final eradication of the Serbian Christian presence in the historic heart of its nation. It would further destabilize the region which is so desperately in need of peace and stability."[40]

In 2008, the Serbian Patriarchate issued its Easter message in which Kosovo was again portrayed as the heart of Serbia that mighty powers wished to take away from the Serbian people and thus spiritually destroy it. The message states: "Kosovo and Metohija is not only about Serbian territory. Above all, it is about our spiritual being, because we used to be born with Kosovo and Metohija, we used to grow and live with it as individuals and as a people, we lived and died with the Kosovo covenant […] this is why the question of Kosovo and Metohija is so vitally, psychologically, spiritually and mystically important for each and every one of us."[41]

The Serbian Orthodox Church has made it a centerpiece of its public role to oppose any Serbian compromise on the status of Kosovo. Church officials, from the Patriarch on down, issue almost daily statements, speeches, and public calls to Serbian political authorities to "never give in" on Kosovo, to keep the territory under Serbian control at all cost.[42] In fact, the SOC continues to organize Kosovar Serbs, especially in the north, to set up independent Serbian political institutions and not participate in Kosovo elections at all.[43] Even during the intense March 2013 negotiations between Serbian and Kosovar leaderships on the final status of Kosovo, the Patriarch issued a stern statement opposing any such deal.[44] The SOC has, therefore, become the principal political backer of Kosovo Serbs in the ongoing Kosovo–Serbia negotiations and as such one of the principal obstacles to the Kosovo problem's resolution.

Conservatism

While initially offering enthusiastic support for Milošević's nationalist program, as the wars of the 1990s went on, however, the SOC increasingly distanced itself from the Milošević regime, mostly on account of

Milošević's willingness to cut loose the Serbs in Croatia and Bosnia in exchange for a peace deal. After almost a decade of full support of Milošević and his policies, this renewed opposition was then recast as being consistent with the Church's deep anticommunism. This break with Milošević on nationalist grounds—the SOC felt Milošević had lost his commitment to the nationalist cause—then allowed it to assert itself directly, and with great authority, into the post-Milošević political life after 2000.

Although the SOC had supported the efforts of the Milošević regime's nationalist program in the early 1990s, and, as outlined above, had been the principal purveyor of nationalist mobilization around the Kosovo myth, it turned against it when it became clear that the project had in fact failed. Moreover, Milošević was increasingly seen as "an ugly remnant of communism."[45] This rejection of Milošević, however, coincided with the increasing clericalization of Serbian state and society, which encompassed not only a much more pronounced presence and influence of religion in society, but also a much more direct SOC involvement in state affairs.[46]

While the Serbian Orthodox Church played an instrumental role in Milošević's rise to power by aligning its national priorities with those of Milošević's state-building project,[47] the true hold of the SOC over Serbian society became even more visible after the 5 October 2000 revolution, when Milošević was overthrown by a popular revolt over fraudulent elections. Many leaders of the anti-Milošević opposition who came to power in 2000 built their careers as anti-communist dissidents. Their problem with Milošević, therefore, was primarily that he was a communist autocrat. His nationalism was much less of a problem for the new leadership, who in fact absorbed much of Milošević era nationalist rhetoric throughout the post-2000 period including, especially on the issue of Kosovo.[48]

In many ways, it was the fall of Milošević and the seeming "democratization" of Serbia that truly revitalized the SOC and gave it a renewed and extremely dominant position in Serbian society. This re-establishment of the Church's social presence has to do in part with the fact that post-Milošević elites (especially the first post-2000 president, Vojislav Koštunica and, to a somewhat lesser degree, first post-2000 Prime Minister Zoran Đinđić) delegitimized Milošević primarily as a "communist" and brandished their own nationalist, anti-communist and correspondingly, devout believer, credentials. It was, therefore, important for the post-Milošević government to demonstrate its reverence for the SOC. In fact, the introduction of religious classes in schools was one of the new government's first orders of business in 2001.[49]

The SOC allied with the conservative political parties, primarily the Democratic Party of Serbia (DSS), which formed the government in 2004. The new post-Milošević democratic elites restored the Church's nationalized property and granted the SOC privileged status among Serbian religious communities. Orthodox priests became omnipresent at many official state public events. Moreover, for the first time the SOC established a strong presence in the universities through clerical-nationalist student organizations, such as Dignity Patriotic Movement (*Otačastveni Pokret Obraz*), the St. Justin the Philosopher Student Association (*Udruženje Studenata Sveti Justin Filozof*), the "Doorway" Serbian Assembly (*Srpski Sabor "Dveri"*), and the Serbian Orthodox Youth (*Srpska Pravoslavna Omladina*).

All Serbian military units now have designated chaplains and their own patron saints, and the SOC has also organized collective baptisms for the soldiers and pilgrimage journeys of military brass to Serbian religious sites, such as the Hilandar monastery in northern Greece.[50] Members of the Orthodox far right, such as the organization *Obraz*, have infiltrated the ranks of the army, which is increasingly seeing its mission in religious, and not secular terms.[51]

Most Serbian political parties now also have patron saints—a practice that is quite new and is now increasingly accompanied by a Serbian Orthodox priest's blessing the party on its Saint's Day. Many politicians have adopted the habit of traveling abroad on official state visits accompanied by a religious figure. Priests are routinely appointed to executive boards of public companies, inaugurations of local political leaders are accompanied by religious ceremonies, a new chapel was opened at the main dormitory of the University of Belgrade, and celebrations of patron saints (*slava*) are now akin to public holidays where various public as well as private offices now observe them.[52] The Serbian state has also provided financial support for the extraordinary expansion of new church construction throughout Serbia.[53]

This neo-conservative revival and clericalization of public life have been expressed quite clearly by the army leadership, as editorialized in the army magazine *Vojska*: "The SOC has outlived numerous states and remained one and the same, while society changes all the time. There is now an awareness that democratic society has to recognize the SOC as a constant. It is an organism which is permanent and a guidepost for the state."[54] The SOC, therefore, has become what Radmila Radić and Milan Vukomanović referred to as the cultural and ideological "flag keeper" of the state.[55]

Serbia, as a country, has become much more religious than it has ever been—measured less by church-going and more by religious holidays observance.[56] There is an increasing conflation of Serbian national identity and Orthodox Christianity.[57] This relationship, however, is complicated and not straightforward. According to Radić and Vukomanović, "religiosity is on the rise in Serbia, even though the majority of its citizens link this notion to their belonging to the nation or tradition, and not to God,"[58] which means that increasing religiosity is really nationalism expressed through religious symbols. Serbia, in other words, has undergone profound social desecularization, which is clear in the increasing importance and influence of religion in everyday life, but more significantly in much greater participation of the SOC in the affairs of the state.[59]

The introduction of religious teaching into public education has also brought a particular nationalist construction of gender, with a very strong Orthodox view of the role of women in society which revolves around "unconditional love and sacrifice for others; subservience and modesty; and biological and spiritual motherhood."[60]

Since the 1990s, the SOC has also led a campaign to ban access to abortion. While during the 1990s, the anti-abortion movement was couched in the larger pro-natalist policies, which understood women's reproduction as part of building the nation,[61] since 2000 the anti-abortion movement is best understood within the Church's increasingly active role in re-traditionalization of Serbian society.[62] In 2006, the first single-issue pro-life group was formed in Serbia—the Movement for Life, established by the SOC-affiliated student organization *Dveri*.[63]

This revival of the Church's significant role in Serbian society has been exclusively along extremely conservative lines. The SOC has directly inserted itself in the social life in Serbia by, for example, in 2009 lobbying for the overturning of the antidiscrimination laws because they provide protection to sexual minorities. The SOC has also embarked on a full-on campaign against atheism, birth control, and women's equality and has opposed Serbia's European Union bid, on account of European liberal values, which are deemed incompatible with the teachings of the SOC.[64]

More disturbingly, the SOC has largely sanctioned or condoned routine violence and discrimination against various minority groups—religious minorities, the Roma, civil society leaders, dissident intellectuals and, increasingly, the LGBTQ population—all human rights abuses largely tolerated by the state. There are a number of extremely violent right-wing groups associated with the Serbian Orthodox Church (*Obraz, Dveri, Pokret 1389*), which attack minorities and political opponents with criminal impunity.[65] For example, one of the leaders of *Obraz* issued a statement confirming that "not one of his organization's activities was carried out without the support and blessing of the Church."[66]

These far-right Christian groups—especially *Obraz*—are also openly anti-Western and frequently anti-Semitic.[67] They base their manifestos and activities on the teachings of Nikolaj Velimirović, the celebrated Serbian bishop of the interwar period and an overt racist and anti-Semite, whose strong anti-Western positions also provide these groups some of their political inspiration.[68] They have also maintained their legitimacy by tying themselves to the SOC, which often grants them access to its premises to hold meetings or public presentations.[69]

Homophobia

Perhaps the most socially visible campaign in which the SOC has been central is the regulation of the private sphere, most notably the regulation of sexuality. To the extent that the SOC has a coherent view of homosexuality, it begins with the argument that it is a sinful, degrading behavior imported from the "decadent" West—and not indigenous to Orthodoxy or to Serbia.[70] The SOC and SOC-affiliated extremist groups have been dominating the public discourse over LGBTQ rights, an issue that regularly comes up every year around the time of efforts to stage a Gay Pride Parade.[71]

The story of the Pride Parade is a difficult one, and it begins in 2001 when the first ever parade was held in Belgrade.[72] This event ended quite brutally when SOC-affiliated thugs and extremist soccer hooligans attacked the parade participants and beat them up.[73] Nine years later, in 2010, LGBTQ activists tried again, and with the same result—a brutal attack by the clerical right.[74] In fact, while the SOC nominally opposed any violence, by so clearly aligning itself with the extreme right, it provided institutional and moral legitimacy for homophobic violence.[75]

One of the many paradoxes here, of course, is that these violent attacks were all carried out during the ostensibly "reformist" government of the Democratic Party (DS). In fact, it is precisely the more "pro-European" rhetoric of the DS government that allowed LGBTQ activism to develop important international linkages with activists abroad and open up more of a domestic political space for the fight against institutional discrimination.[76] Ironically, then, the various Serbian governments since 2000 onward have used declared "pro-European" policies to rhetorically accept international norms of sexual equality, but then effectively resist these norms by couching the Pride Parade as an issue of "security," over which domestic police, not European overlords, have control.[77] The Pride Parade has repeatedly been canceled by the Serbian government in 2011, 2012, and 2013, always under the pretext of "protecting the safety and security of Serbian citizens."[78] In 2014, the small Parade was finally held, but it was restricted to a very short itinerary pre-approved by the government, and was completely cordoned off by an excessive level of police security, which included water cannons and military transportation vehicles. The heavy police presence prohibited any citizen or passer-by to either see the Parade or join it at any point.

The SOC has been an active instigator of all of this violence. In 2010, influential Archbishop Amfilohije Radović compared the Pride Parade to Sodom and Gomorrah.[79] In 2011, the Patriarch of the Serbian Orthodox Church Irinej weighed in, calling for the cancelation of what he called "The Shame Parade."[80] He also stated that, "[w]e have had enough of humiliation and meeting external expectations. This unnatural freedom offered to us by 'gay pride' is foreign to our history, tradition and culture."[81] Amfilohije Radović, the powerful Metropolitan of Montenegro and the Littoral, has similarly argued, from the position of the Church's deep conservatism, that homosexuality is something imposed by modernity. In 2010, he said after the small Gay Parade followed by anti-LGBTQ violence, "yesterday we saw what kind of stench, worse than uranium, poisoned and polluted the capital Belgrade. The worst sodomite stench this modern civilization elevated to the pedestal of deity. And, you see, one violence, the violence of these ungodly and degenerate people provoked the other violence."[82]

On the eve of the 2011 Parade, the Serbian Patriarch called for ignoring the Parade and stopped short of advocating anti-LGBTQ action. However, a leaflet calling for an Orthodox rally against a "shame parade" was distributed to all Belgrade's churches.[83] In fact, so prominent to contemporary Serbian Orthodox practice is this extreme and often physically violent xenophobia that homosexuality has become the principal demarcation point on how the SOC defines who is and is not Orthodox.[84]

Throughout 2010, the main SOC publication *Pravoslavlje* continued to publish a series of articles on the threat posed by homosexuality. Various Orthodox scholars wrote articles in this publication with titles such as "The Circle of Death on the Streets of Belgrade," "Homosexuality is Unnatural and Sinful," and "The Violence of Infidels Provokes More Violence."[85]

This attitude on the part of the Serbian Orthodox Church finds a lot of support among the general public, which continues to display an extremely high level of homophobic prejudice. A survey in 2008 found that 70% of Serbian citizens view homosexuality as a disease.[86] In 2012, an updated survey discovered that Serbs feel the greatest social distance toward the LGBTQ population. As many as 79.5% would prefer not to have an LGBTQ person in their family, 58.8% as a teacher, 46.2% as a friend, and 30.02% not even as a neighbor.[87] And while homophobia is often understood as a generational issue that will "go away" as the society ages and liberalizes, the opposite trend has been the case in Serbia. A comprehensive study of Serbian high-school students showed that more than 70% of them held strongly homophobic views, 41% thought the LGBTQ population was "sick," and as many as 22% agreed that LGBTQ persons "deserve a beating."[88] A 2014 report, while noting some improvements in the treatment of LGBTQ population, especially the now relatively peaceful holding of annual Pride Parades, also emphasized that the "LGBT population remains one of the social groups that are most exposed to violence and intolerance in society."[89]

The Church's attitude toward homosexuality has also been tied quite directly to its attitude toward the continuing crisis in Kosovo. In 2011, Patriarch Irinej accused the organizers of the Gay Pride Parade of diverting the people's attention from the Kosovo crisis: "Bearing in mind the announced parade in Belgrade, we come to the conclusion that one wants to cover up and obscure the tragic position of Serbian people in mournful Kosovo and Metohija."[90]

But it is not just Kosovo. The Serbian Church has tied any misfortune—real or perceived—to befall the Serbian nation to the rise in acceptance of homosexuality. In 2014, Patriarch Irinej blamed homosexuality for the catastrophic flooding, as it occurred at the same time the Gay Pride Parade was being planned—a gathering which, Irinej said, "represents great lawlessness and a despicable vice, in which they declare pride and assert their dignity and democracy, yet which entirely opposes god and the law of life."[91]

While the SOC has taken a hard stand against homosexuality, it has at the same time completely ignored and covered up a series of pedophilia scandals in its own ranks. Bishop Pahomije Gačić of Vranje, Bishop Vasilije Kačavenda of Zvornik-Tuzla, and the Abbot of Novo Hopovo monastery Ilarion Mišić were all accused of sexual abuse of children, accusations denied and never investigated by the SOC.[92]

It is worth noting, however, that since 2015, there has been evident progress in the guarantees of physical rights of LGBTQ population, at least as far as the Pride Parade is concerned, which has been held under much tighter police security. This meant that the number of people participating has gone down (as participation is more tightly controlled), but episodes of violence have become much less frequent. In 2017, Ana Brnabić was appointed Serbia's Prime Minister, becoming the first ever openly gay person to hold such a high office. While Brnabić has shown very little distance between herself and Serbia's quite conservative government on matters of policy, she has made overt gestures of support of the LGBTQ community, such as walking in the Pride Parade alongside other participants.[93]

The Church's position on homosexuality, however, remains unchanged.[94] Most of the mainstream media have continued to report uncritically on the Church's position on homosexuality and have perpetuated the reverence with which the general population views the SOC and trusts it to be the principal moral arbiter in Serbian society.[95] Instead of the SOC reflecting the changing norms in society, the SOC has actively worked to reverse any progress in social values, and make Serbian society more conservative, more intolerant, and more exclusionary.

Religious Intolerance

The SOC continues to have fraught relationships with religious minorities, and the issue of anti-Semitism is analyzed in depth by Francine Friedman in this volume. In this section of the chapter, I instead focus on the continuing problem of the SOC ethnophyletism as it relates to the SOC relations with other regional Orthodox Churches.

While the SOC continued to assert its authority over the entire Serbian Orthodox world—inside as well as outside Serbia—it has also engaged in ongoing conflict with canonically unrecognized Churches in Montenegro and Macedonia. The Serbian Church has made a tremendous effort to prevent these Churches from having their autocephaly recognized.

In the case of Montenegro, an Autocephalous Church was proclaimed in 1993, as a result of a civic initiative.[96] This move was broadly rejected by the SOC which accused the Montenegrin Church of creating a new schism. This split, however, needs to be understood within the political context of Yugoslav succession and increasing desire of Montenegro for its own statehood. It is also an example of the Church's political nationalism, as the argument that Montenegro should not have its own Church followed directly from the argument—widespread among Serbian nationalists to this day—that no such nation as "Montenegro" exists that can be distinguished from the Serbs. The opposition to the Montenegrin Church, therefore, was based primarily on nationalist grounds. One of the leading SOC leaders, the aforementioned Metropolitan Amfilohije Radović, led this charge, at times referring to the Montenegrin Church as a "so-called Church" or a "pseudo-Church."[97]

It is important to note, however, that the position of the Montenegrin Church is especially tenuous because, unlike the Macedonian Church which is a hierarchy (episcopate) in schism, the Montenegrin Church has not met some of the key requirements for asking for recognition of its autocephaly, such as a clear hierarchy which can persuasively claim apostolic succession. Further, it is a minority denomination even within Montenegro, where the majority of self-identified Montenegrins decided to remain within the Serbian Orthodox Church.[98]

But this conflict was not only rhetorical, it also included violent clashes over church property through the late 1990s and early 2000s. The Serbian Orthodox Church has continued to deny the Montenegrin claim to autocephaly and in doing so, it seems to have a majority of Montenegrin believers on its side. In a March 2018 opinion poll, the Montenegrin Orthodox Church has the lowest level of public trust in the country of any public institution (22.4%), while the Serbian Orthodox Church had the highest (62.3%).[99]

The relationship with the Macedonian Orthodox Church is equally fraught, and the conflict is even longer-standing. Unlike Montenegro, Macedonia had an established (autonomous) Church even during the socialist period (the Macedonian Church declared autocephaly in 1967), but one that was still unrecognized by the SOC. As Yugoslavia collapsed, the Serbian Church was anxious to take the Macedonian Church under its wing, but a proposed canonical unity between the two Churches was rejected by the Macedonian Church in 2002.[100]

The conflict between the Churches escalated in 2002, when the SOC initiated an internal schism within the Macedonian Orthodox Church, by consecrating Jovan (Vraniškovski) as Archbishop of Ohrid. Tensions further increased in 2003, when the SOC issued an ultimatum to the Macedonian Church, threatening demotion of its metropolitans unless the Macedonian Church would recognize SOC authority. In 2003, the SOC denied access to the Prohor Pčinjski monastery to a Macedonian delegation on the Macedonian national holiday, the 100th anniversary of *Ilinden* uprising, even though this has been the long-standing location of Macedonian national holiday celebrations. Since then, the SOC continues to deny Macedonian official celebrations to be held at the monastery, which it manages (because it is on the territory of the Republic of Serbia). In response, Macedonia built a memorial center on its side of the border.[101]

While the SOC remains steadfast in its refusal to recognize Macedonian autocephaly, the Macedonian Church turned to the Bulgarian Church in search of a sponsor.[102] The Macedonian Orthodox Church was hoping that by recognizing the Bulgarian Church as a "mother Church" it would gain recognition of its autocephaly and lobby for its recognition internationally. However, this has not happened.

This has, then, further fueled the Serbian Orthodox Church's intransigence and anger at the Macedonian Church.[103] In 2018, Serbian Patriarch Irinej sent a letter of protest to the Ecumenical Patriarch Bartholomew of Constantinople over his interference in what he considers a question to be dealt with by the Serbian Patriarchate alone. In the letter, Irinej complains, "The heresy of ethnophyletism is one of the essential misfortunes of contemporary Orthodoxy,"[104] completely ignoring the fact that this very "misfortune" of ethnophyletism (the conflation of Church and nation)[105] has been one of the guiding principles of the SOC as it relates to its own understanding of what it means to constitute a Serbian nation.

Patriarch Irinej did not only go after the Macedonian Church, but also placed the conflict over autocephaly within his larger set of grievances about increasing secularism and atheism: "The States, population and 'peoples', among which autocephaly is requested today, actually foster 'political schisms' and openly justify their disastrous activity by invoking state and national interest (Ukraine, 'North Macedonia', Montenegro). These states, he argued, were created by the communists, and most of them are allegedly led today by atheists, as is the case of the non-baptized and atheistic ruler of Montenegro."[106] These rulers do not ask for an Autocephalous Church as alleged loyal members of it, "but [act] with an opportunistic or rather untimely purpose, using it to consolidate a secular ideology, in fact an atheist one, as well as their petty interests. It is ultimately a maltreatment of the Church and of faith."[107]

Conclusion

The Serbian Orthodox Church has developed its political identity as inseparable from the Serbian nation and, since the collapse of the socialist Yugoslavia, from the Serbian state.[108] It has long seen itself as a national and not only religious institution.[109] This idea that being Serb means being Orthodox is deeply ingrained in SOC doctrine, which makes its criticisms of other Churches' ethnophyletism that much more hypocritical. It is a Church that is deeply conservative, opposed to change, and primarily interested in maintaining a political role in Serbian society, especially since the democratic transformation, or the hopes of democratic transformation in 2000.

The SOC has built its legitimacy on the foundation of its strong nationalism and has maintained a form of veto power over any negotiated solution to the Kosovo sovereignty dispute. It has chosen not to play a constructive role, but one that is intransigent and extreme. Its refusal to compromise has, in fact, made the political future of the remaining Serbs in Kosovo that much more difficult. In fact, the Church's rigid position on Kosovo has created a rare rift between the SOC and the Serbian government. In 2018, Metropolitan Amfilohije accused Serbian President Aleksandar Vučić's Kosovo policy (which includes negotiations over territory and sovereignty of Kosovo) as "leading to the betrayal of Serbia and Kosovo."[110] Vučić then reminded the SOC that "Serbia is a secular country… in which the most important political decisions should not be made by the Church."[111] A few months later, in a possible effort to silence the Church's criticism, the Serbian government approved a 10 million euro grant to the Church for reconstruction of the St. Sava Church in Belgrade.[112]

But the Serbian Orthodox Church has reserved its strongest stance for the regulation of the private sphere, especially sexuality. It has placed LGBTQ issues front and center to its entire social agenda. It has promoted violence, fostered intolerance, and made it impossible for LGBTQ Orthodox Serbs to feel like they could, also, belong to their Church. It is this violent and intolerant legacy of the Church's post-2000 activism that will remain one of its longest lasting stains.

Notes

1. Srđan Barišić (2018), "Srpska pravoslavna crkva i Jugoslavija," *YU Historija*, http://www.yuhistorija.com/serbian/kultura_religija_txt00c5.html [last accessed 20 April 2019]. Some 25% of the churches and monasteries have been destroyed and about half of all churches were severely damaged by the end of the war. Sabrina P. Ramet, "The Serbian Orthodox Church," in Ramet (ed.), *Eastern Christianity and Politics in the Twentieth Century* (Durham, NC: Duke University Press, 1988), pp. 232, 238.
2. Mirko Blagojević, *Religija i crkva u transformacijama društva: sociološko-istorijska analiza religijske situacije u srpsko-crnogorskom i ruskom (post) komunističkom društvu* (Beograd: Institut za filozofiju i društvenu teoriju, 2005).
3. Radmila Radić, "Odnosi između Srpske pravoslavne crkve i Katoličke crkve u poslednjim decenijama pred raspad jugoslovenske države," in Mile Bjelajac (ed.), *Pisati istoriju Jugoslavije: Viđenje srpskog faktora* (Beograd: Institut za noviju istoriju Srbije, 2007).
4. Klaus Buchenau, "Orthodox Values and Modern Necessities: Serbian Orthodox Clergy and Laypeople on Democracy, Human Rights, Transition and Globalization," in Ola Listhaug, Sabrina P. Ramet, and Dragana Dulić (eds.), *Civic and Uncivic Values: Serbia in the Post-Milošević Era* (Budapest and New York: Central European University Press, 2011), p. 118.
5. Barišić, "Srpska pravoslavna crkva i Jugoslavija."
6. Dejan Jović, *Yugoslavia: A State That Withered Away* (West Lafayette, IN: Purdue University Press, 2009), pp. 184–186.
7. Filip Ejdus and Jelena Subotić, "Kosovo as Serbia's Sacred Space: Governmentality, Pastoral Power and Sacralization of Territories," in Gorana Ognjenović and Jasna Jozelić (eds.), *Politicization of Religion, the Power of Symbolism: The Case of Former Yugoslavia and Its Successor States* (Basingstoke: Palgrave, 2014), pp. 159–184.

8. Apel za zaštitu srpskog življa i njegovih svetinja na Kosovu (15 May 1982), http://www.rastko.rs/kosovo/istorija/stradanje_srba/atanasije_3deo.html#_Toc485531500 [last accessed 20 April 2019].
9. Ibid.
10. Atanasije Jevtić, "Kosovo u znaku krsta," *Pravoslavlje*, no. 445 (1985).
11. Barišić, "Srpska pravoslavna crkva i Jugoslavija."
12. These travelogues have later been published as a book, Atanasije Jevtić, *Od Kosova do Jadovna: putni zapisi* (Beograd: Hrišćanska misao, 2002).
13. Atanasije Jevtić, "Kosovsko stradanje sprskog naroda danas," *Hilandar*, 12 (1983/1984).
14. Barišić, "Srpska pravoslavna crkva i Jugoslavija."
15. Radmila Radić and Milan Vukomanović, "Religion and Democracy in Serbia Since 1989: The Case of the Serbian Orthodox Church," in Sabrina P. Ramet (ed.), *Religion and Politics in Post-Socialist Central and Southeastern Europe: Challenges Since 1989* (Basingstoke: Palgrave Macmillan, 2014), pp. 180–211, at 181.
16. *Glas crkve*, 1/1991, as quoted in Barišić, "Srpska pravoslavna crkva i Jugoslavija." *Glas crkve* was the publication of the Šabac-Valjevo eparchy.
17. Barišić, "Srpska pravoslavna crkva."
18. See ibid.
19. As quoted in ibid.
20. The exact number of those killed in Jasenovac has been an issue of intense debate in both Serbian and Croatian historiography. Other than the tendentiously small number (10,000) offered by Croatian nationalists, or the unreasonably high number (600,000) insisted on by Serbian nationalists, the scholarly consensus today sits at around 85,000 killed, 50,000 of whom were Serbs, 13,000 Jews, 16,000 Roma (almost the entire Croatian Roma population), and the remainder communists and enemies or perceived enemies of the Ustasha regime. The numbers listed here are the confirmed identified victims by the Jasenovac Memorial Site, which is a database in progress. Since this number includes only identified victims, the actual death toll is likely higher http://www.jusp-jasenovac.hr/Default.aspx?sid=6711 [last accessed 20 April 2019].
21. Barišić, "Srpska pravoslavna crkva i Jugoslavija."
22. Milan Vukomanović, "The Serbian Orthodox Church as a Political Actor in the Aftermath of October 5, 2000," in *Politics and Religion*, Vol. 1, No. 2 (2008), pp. 237–269.
23. International Criminal Tribunal for the former Yugoslavia, "Facts About Srebrenica," at http://www.icty.org/x/file/Outreach/view_from_hague/jit_srebrenica_en.pdf [accessed 26 April 2019].

24. Radić and Vukomanović, "Religion and Democracy in Serbia Since 1989," p. 182.
25. *Glasnik*, no. 6 (June 1996).
26. The following five paragraphs build on Ejdus and Subotić, "Kosovo as Serbia's Sacred Space."
27. *NIN* (20 March 1992).
28. Ejdus and Subotić, "Kosovo as Serbia's Sacred Space."
29. *Radio Slobodna Evropa*, "Ustoličen patrijarh Irinej" (3 October 2010), at https://www.slobodnaevropa.org/a/ustolicenje_patrijarha_irineja_pecka_patrijarsija/2175117.html [last accessed 20 April 2019].
30. Srpska pravoslavna crkva, "Vidovdan na Kosovu i Metohiji" (29 June 2011), at http://spc.rs/sr/vidovdan_na_kosovu_metohiji_1 [last accessed 20 April 2019].
31. Jelena Subotić, "Narrative, Ontological Security, and Foreign Policy Change," in *Foreign Policy Analysis*, Vol. 12, No. 4 (2016), pp. 610–627.
32. *B92* (17 March 2013).
33. Ejdus and Subotić, "Kosovo as Serbia's Sacred Space."
34. Srpska pravoslavna crkva, "Memorandum o Kosovu i Metohiji Svetog Arhijerejskog Sabora Srpske Pravoslavne Crkve" (Beograd: Sveti Arhijerejski Sinod, 2003), p. 5.
35. Ibid., p. 87.
36. Artemije Radosavljević, Kosovo i Vidovdan (Kosovska gračanica: Eparhija Raško prizrenska, 2007), pp. 7, 12.
37. Ejdus and Subotić, "Kosovo as Serbia's Sacred Space."
38. Srpska pravoslavna crkva, "Vaskršnja poslanica 2008. godine" (18 April 2008), at http://www.spc.rs/sr/vaskrsnja_poslanica_2008_godine [last accessed 20 April 2019].
39. Ejdus and Subotić, "Kosovo as Serbia's Sacred Space."
40. Quoted in Radić and Vukomanović, "Religion and Democracy in Serbia Since 1989," p. 184.
41. Srpska pravoslavna crkva, "Vaskršnja poslanica 2008. Godine."
42. Ejdus and Subotić, "Kosovo as Serbia's Sacred Space."
43. Vukomanović, "The Serbian Orthodox Church as a Political Actor," p. 248.
44. *B92* (17 March 2013).
45. Buchenau, "Orthodox Values and Modern Necessities," p. 119.
46. Jelena Subotic, "Building Democracy in Serbia: One Step Forward, Three Steps Back," in Sabrina P. Ramet, Christine M. Hssenstab, and Ola Listhaug (eds.), *Building Democracy in the Yugoslav Successor States: Accomplishments, Setbacks, Challenges Since 1990* (Cambridge and New York: Cambridge University Press, 2017).

47. Radmila Radić, "The Church and the Serbian Question," in Nebojša Popov (ed.), *The Road to War in Serbia: Trauma and Catharsis* (Budapest and New York: Central European University Press, 2000), pp. 247–273.
48. Hilde Katrine Haug, "Kosovo in Serbian Politics Since Milošević," in Listhaug, Ramet, and Dulić (eds.), *Civic and Uncivic Values*, pp. 329–368.
49. For the full text of the decree, see "Uredba o organizovanju i ostvarivanju verske nastave i nastave alternativnog predmeta u osnovnoj i srednjoj školi," in *Službeni glasnik Republike Srbije 46/2001*, at http://www.pravno-informacioni-sistem.rs/SlGlasnikPortal/eli/rep/sgrs/vlada/uredba/2001/46/1/reg [last accessed on 25 April 2019].
50. Radić and Vukomanović, "Religion and Democracy in Serbia Since 1989," p. 197.
51. Jovan Byford, "Christian Right-Wing Organisations and the Spreading of Anti-Semitic Prejudice in Post-Milošević Serbia: The Case of the Dignity Patriotic Movement," in *East European Jewish Affairs*, Vol. 32, No. 2 (2002), pp. 43–60.
52. Rada Drezgić, "Religion, Politics and Gender in the Context of Nation-State Formation: The Case of Serbia," in *Third World Quarterly*, Vol. 31, No. 6 (2010), pp. 955–970.
53. Radić and Vukomanović, "Religion and Democracy in Serbia Since 1989," p. 194.
54. Quoted in Vukomanović, "The Serbian Orthodox Church as a Political Actor," p. 259.
55. Radić and Vukomanović, "Religion and Democracy in Serbia Since 1989," p. 182.
56. Mirko Blagojevic, "Desecularization of Contemporary Serbian Society," in *Occasional Papers on Religion in Eastern Europe*, Vol. 28, No. 1 (2008), pp. 37–50.
57. Ivan Čolović, "Nationalism as a Religion: Examples from Contemporary Serbia," in Listhaug, Ramet, and Dulić (eds.), *Civic and Uncivic Values*, pp. 241–252.
58. Radić and Vukomanović, "Religion and Democracy in Serbia Since 1989," p. 199.
59. Vukomanović, "The Serbian Orthodox Church as a Political Actor," p. 239.
60. Drezgić, "Religion, Politics and Gender," p. 964.
61. Jeremy Shiffman, Marina Skrabalo, and Jelena Subotic, "Reproductive Rights and the State in Croatia and Serbia," in *Social Science and Medicine*, Vol. 54, No. 4 (2002), pp. 625–642.

62. Rada Drezgić, "Orthodox Christianity and Gender Equality in Serbia: On Reproductive and Sexual Rights," in Christine M. Hassenstab and Sabrina P. Ramet (eds.), *Gender (In)Equality and Gender Politics in Southeastern Europe: A Question of Justice* (Basingstoke and New York: Palgrave Macmillan, 2015), pp. 297–317.
63. Ibid.
64. Radić and Vukomanović, "Religion and Democracy in Serbia Since 1989," p. 193.
65. Subotic, "Building democracy in Serbia." For the list of major far right and neo-Nazi groups in Serbia, see "Prvi zvaničan spisak neonacista," *B92* (10 December 2005), at https://www.b92.net/info/vesti/index.php?yyyy=2005&mm=12&dd=10&nav_id=182260 [last accessed 20 April 2019].
66. Jelena Dzombic, "Rightwing Extremism in Serbia," in *Race & Class*, Vol. 55, No. 4 (2014), pp. 106–110, at 108–109. *Obraz* was officially banned by the Constitutional Court of Serbia on 12 June 2012 as an extremist proto-fascist organization, and its leader Mladen Obradović was sentenced to ten months in prison for incitement of hateful violence against LGBT population. *B92* (12 June 2012), https://www.b92.net/info/vesti/index.php?yyyy=2012&mm=06&dd=12&nav_category=12&nav_id=617788 [last accessed 20 April 2019].
67. The first version of the *Obraz* Web site included a section on "Zionists-Jewish racists," who *Obraz* blamed for NATO bombing of Serbia. This language has since been removed. Byford, "Christian Right-wing Organisations," pp. 44–45.
68. Jovan Byford, "Distinguishing 'Anti-Judaism' from 'Antisemitism': Recent Championing of Serbian Bishop Nikolaj Velimirović," in *Religion, State & Society*, Vol. 34, No. 1 (March 2006), pp. 7–31; Byford, "Christian Right-wing Organisations"; and Julia Anna Lis, "Anti-Western Theology in Greece and Serbia Today," in Andrii Krawchuk and Thomas Bremer (eds.), *Eastern Orthodox Encounters of Identity and Otherness* (New York: Springer, 2014), pp. 159–168.
69. Byford, "Christian Right-Wing Organisations," p. 51.
70. Miloš Jovanović, "Silence or Condemnation: The Orthodox Church on Homosexuality in Serbia," in *Družboslovne razprave*, Vol. 29, No. 73 (2013), pp. 79–95.
71. Gay Straight Alliance, "Sloboda se ne dobija, sloboda se osvaja: Izveštaj o stanju ljudskih prava LGBT osoba u Srbiji 2011" (Belgrade: GSA, May 2011).
72. The subsequent paragraphs build on Subotic, "Building Democracy in Serbia."

73. Christian Axboe Nielsen, "Stronger Than the State? Football Hooliganism, Political Extremism and the Gay Pride Parades in Serbia," in *Sport in Society*, Vol. 16, No. 8 (2013), pp. 1038–1053.
74. Helsinki Committee for Human Rights in Serbia, *Human Rights in Serbia 2011: European Option Obstructed* (Belgrade: HCHRS, 2012); Marek Mikuš, "'State Pride': Politics of LGBT Rights and Democratisation in 'European Serbia'," in *East European Politics & Societies*, Vol. 25, No. 4 (November 2011), pp. 834–851.
75. Tamara Pavasovic Trost and Nikola Kovacevic, "Football, Hooliganism and Nationalism: The Reaction to Serbia's Gay Parade in Reader Commentary Online," in *Sport in Society*, Vol. 16, No. 8 (2013), pp. 1054–1076.
76. John A. Gould and Edward Moe, "Nationalism and the Struggle for LGBTQ Rights in Serbia, 1991–2014," in *Problems of Post-Communism*, Vol. 62, No. 5 (2015), pp. 273–286.
77. Filip Ejdus and Mina Božović, "Europeanisation and Indirect Resistance: Serbian Police and Pride Parades," *International Journal of Human Rights* (2016), http://dx.doi.org/10.1080/13642987.2016.1161212, [online only].
78. Ibid.
79. *Blic* (9 October 2010).
80. *B92* (30 September 2011).
81. Srpska pravoslavna crkva, "Poruka Njegove Svetosti Patrijarha srpskog G. Irineja" (30 September 2011), http://www.spc.rs/sr/poruka_njegove_svetosti_patrijarha_srpskog_g_irineja [last accessed 20 April 2019].
82. *B92* (14 October 2010).
83. Zorica Mršević, "Homophobia in Serbia and LGBT Rights," in *Southeastern Europe*, Vol. 37, No. 1 (2013), pp. 60–87, at 70.
84. Danica Igrutinović, Srdjan Sremac, and Mariecke van den Berg, "Pride Parades and/or Prayer Processions: Contested Public Space in Serbia #Belgrade Pride 2014," in *Journal of Empirical Theology*, Vol. 28, No. 2 (2015), pp. 204–225.
85. Jovanović, "Silence or Condemnation."
86. Research conducted for Gay Straight Alliance by Centre for Free Elections and Democracy (CeSID). "Prejudices Exposed—Homophobia in Serbia: Public Opinion Research Report on LGBT Population," Gay Straight Alliance, http://en.gsa.org.rs/wp-content/uploads/2012/07/Research-Prejudices-Exposed-2008-GSA.pdf [last accessed 25 April 2019].

87. CESID (2012), Izveštaj sa istraživanja javnog mnenja: Odnos građana prema diskriminaciji u Srbiji, http://www.mc.rs/upload/documents/saopstenja_izvestaji/2012/121012_Poverenik_za_zastitu_ravnopravnosti-istrazivanje.pdf.
88. Marija Radoman, *Stavovi i vrednosne orijentacije srednjoškolaca u Srbiji* (Belgrade: Helsinki Committee for Human Rights in Serbia, 2011).
89. Gay Straight Alliance (25 March 2015), "Annual Report on the Status of Human Rights of LGBT Persons in Serbia For 2014," http://en.gsa.org.rs/wp-content/uploads/2015/03/2014-GSA-Annual-Report-Summary.pdf [last accessed 20 April 2019].
90. Srpska pravoslavna crkva (30 September 2011), "Poruka Njegove Svetosti Patrijarha srpskog G. Irineja," http://www.spc.rs/sr/poruka_njegove_svetosti_patrijarha_srpskog_g_irineja [last accessed 20 April 2019].
91. Tanjug (15 May 2014), "Patrijarh Irinej: Ovo je Božja opomena zbog pripreme skupa bezakonja i mrskog poroka," http://www.pressonline.rs/info/drustvo/311579/patrijarh-irinej-ova-kisa-nije-kazna-vec-bozja-opomena-zbog-gej-parade.html [last accessed 20 April 2019].
92. Vasilije Kačavenda was prematurely retired and officially demoted after an explicit piece of evidence of his homosexual affairs (but not pedophilia charges, which were never properly investigated) was presented to the Bishops' Assembly of the Serbian Orthodox Church. Pahomije Gačić evaded prosecution after a number of cases against him were declared past the statute of limitations, and others were dismissed for lack of evidence. For more context, see Srđan Sremac, Zlatiborka Popov-Momčinović, Miloš Jovanović, and Martina Topić, "For the Sake of the Nations: Media, Homosexuality and Religio-Sexual Nationalisms in the Post-Yugoslav Space," in Srđan Sremac and R. Ruard Ganzevoort (eds.), *Religious and Sexual Nationalisms in Central and Eastern Europe: Gods, Gays, and Governments* (Leiden and Boston: Brill, 2015), pp. 52–73.
93. "Parada ponosa u Beogradu održana bez incidenata," *Radio Televizija Srbije* (17 September 2017), http://www.rts.rs/page/stories/ci/story/124/drustvo/2872928/parada-ponosa-u-beogradu.html [last accessed 20 April 2019].
94. For example, the Church routinely disseminates messages against LGBT families, such as placing anti-LGBT leaflets on its doors. "Plakati protiv LGBT zajednice na vratima crkve," in *Insajder* (13 September 2016), at https://insajder.net/sr/sajt/tema/1478 [last accessed 20 April 2019].
95. Tamara Pavasovic Trost and Koen Slootmaeckers, "Religion, Homosexuality and Nationalism in the Western Balkans: The Role of Religious Institutions in Defining the Nation," in Sremac and

Ganzevoort (eds.), *Religious and Sexual Nationalisms in Central and Eastern Europe*, pp. 154–180.
96. Crnogorska Pravoslavna Crkva, "Kratki osvrt na istorijat Crnogorske Pravoslavne Crkve," http://www.cpc.org.me/latinica/istorija_crkva.php?id=1 [last accessed 20 April 2019].
97. Sabrina P. Ramet, "The Politics of the Serbian Orthodox Church," in Sabrina P. Ramet and Vjeran Pavlaković (eds.), *Serbia Since 1989: Politics and Society Under Milošević and After* (Seattle: University of Washington Press, 2005), pp. 255–285.
98. I thank an anonymous reviewer for pointing out these complex issues.
99. Center for Democracy and Human Rights (CEDEM), Političko javno mnjenje Crne Gore (March 2018), at http://www.cedem.me/programi/istrazivanja/politicko-javno-mnjenje/send/29-politicko-javno-mnjenje/1900-cedem-objavio-rezultate-istrazivanja-politickog-javnog-mnjenja-crne-gore [last accessed 20 April 2019].
100. Daniel P. Payne, "Nationalism and the Local Church: The Source of Ecclesiastical Conflict in the Orthodox Commonwealth," in *Nationalities Papers*, Vol. 35, No. 5 (2007), pp. 831–852, at 839.
101. Marija Nikolovska (24 July 2017), "Serbia Bans Macedonia from Celebrating Ilinden at Prohor Pcinski," *MINA Report*, http://www.minareport.com/2017/07/24/serbia-bans-macedonia-from-celebrating-ilinden-at-prohor-pcinski [last accessed 20 April 2019].
102. Mariya Cheresheva and Sinisa Jakov Marusic, "Macedonia's Lonely Church Seeks Bulgarian 'Parent'," *Balkan Insight*, 20 November 2017, at https://balkaninsight.com/2017/11/20/macedonian-church-asks-bulgarian-brethren-for-backing-11-20-2017/ [accessed 20 April 2019].
103. I thank Andreja Bogdanovski for clarifying these points.
104. Emma Cazabonne (31 August 2018), "Patriarch Irinej of Serbia Addressed a Letter of Protest to Patriarch Bartholomew of Constantinople about the Ukrainian 'Autocephaly' and Other Similar Schismatic Entities," Orthodoxie.com, at https://orthodoxie.com/en/patriarch-irinej-of-serbia-addressed-a-letter-of-protest-to-patriarch-bartholomew-of-constantinople-about-the-ukrainian-autocephaly-and-other-similar-schismatic-entities [last accessed 20 April 2019].
105. More specifically, ethnophyletism represents the idea that a local, autocephalous Church should be organized on a national, not an ecclesial foundation.
106. This is a reference to Milo Đukanović.
107. Cazabonne, "Patriarch Irinej."
108. Barišić, "Srpska pravoslavna crkva i Jugoslavija."
109. Milan Vukomanović, *Sveto i mnoštvo* (Beograd: Čigoja štampa, 2001).

110. *Radio Slobodna Evropa* (8 January 2018), "Amfilohije: Strahujem da Vučić vodi politiku izdaje Srbije i Kosova," https://www.slobodnaevropa.org/a/28962447.html [last accessed 20 April 2019].
111. Branka Trivić (23 May 2018), "Kosovo udaljava Vučića od Crkve," *Radio Slobodna Evropa*, at https://www.slobodnaevropa.org/a/kosovo-udaljava-vucica-od-crkve/29244992.html [last accessed 20 April 2019].
112. Ljudmila Cvetković (28 March 2019), "Kupuje li država lojalnost Srpske pravoslavne crkve?" *Radio Slobodna Evropa*, at https://www.slobodnaevropa.org/a/srbija-spc-kupovina-lojalnost/29845816.html [last accessed 21 April 2019].

CHAPTER 6

Orthodoxy and Antisemitism: The Relationship Between the Serbian Orthodox Church and the Jews

Francine Friedman

Abstract This chapter explores conflicting claims about the relationship between the Serbian Orthodox Church and the Yugoslav/post-Yugoslav Jewish community. It focuses particularly on complaints about, and incidents suggesting, that there are antisemitic tendencies in contemporary Serbia, also briefly considering Republika Srpska's record with regard to Jewish-Orthodox relations.

The dynamic of antisemitism has been characterized by Charles Y. Glock and Rodney Stark as movement along a continuum—from belief (concealed animosity) to feeling (openly demonstrated animosity) to action (ideologically based discrimination eventually manifested in violence against Jews).[1] Individuals with a propensity to resent Jews (belief) may or may not proceed to feeling and action. However, individuals are less likely to be able to move to action; that usually takes a group. This chapter examines allegations that an influential faction within the

F. Friedman (✉)
Ball State University, Muncie, IN, USA

© The Author(s) 2019
S. P. Ramet (ed.), *Orthodox Churches and Politics in Southeastern Europe*, Palgrave Studies in Religion, Politics, and Policy, https://doi.org/10.1007/978-3-030-24139-1_6

Serbian Orthodox Church is complicit in provoking antisemitic action by encouraging violence against Jews.

Laslo Sekelj identified three stages of antisemitism in Yugoslavia.[2] The first stage, from 1945 to 1967, was characterized by only rare displays of antisemitism. From 1967 to 1988, antisemitism was manifested as "anti-Zionism." The years 1988–1991 as Yugoslavia collapsed recorded a process of what Sekelj called "republicanization" and "functionalization" of the Jews.

Contrary to Sekelj's analysis of the existence of Yugoslav antisemitism, some claim that "Serbs never hated the Jews." A 1994 research project, "The Pulse of Yugoslavia 94," showed that 46% of Serbs (excluding those living in Kosovo) had a positive view about Jews, while 21% had a negative view. The rest had neither a positive nor a negative view.[3] However, others point to such iconic Church leaders as (now canonized) Bishop Nikolaj Velimirović (1881–1956) as "the true face of the Serbian Orthodox Church" in his expressions of fascism and antisemitism. I examine here the contemporary responses of the Serbian Orthodox Church to the Jewish community in Serbia and in Republika Srpska seeking to determine if the Church continues to display a fractured response to its Jewish neighbors or if it has resolved that tension into one universal reaction.

The Relationship Between Judaism and Orthodoxy

Antisemitic rhetoric peddled by the Christian right over the past century consists of themes originating in the medieval demonology of Jews. Nineteenth-century antisemitic conspiracy theories and racial antisemitism are ideas that have been assimilated into the discourse of anti-Judaism.

One Russian scholar of Christian Orthodoxy has offered a description of the complex relationship between the Orthodox Christian and Jewish religions. Since the New Testament is undoubtedly grounded in the Hebrew Bible, Orthodox Christians believe that Judaism before Jesus Christ "is also the religion of the Orthodox Church."[4] However, because the Jews did not accept Jesus as the messiah, they unilaterally dissolved their covenant with God, even though God did not forsake His eternal bond with them. The advent of Jesus Christ meant that God made a new covenant with humanity, which included Jews but also "spiritual Jews," i.e., Christians.[5] The fact that the Jews denied that Jesus was the messiah was not a crime, and they should not be persecuted for it. In fact, they should be honored for having transmitted the "holy religion" over the centuries. Therefore, antisemitism "is not compatible with Christianity," and a racist/antisemite "dissolves his side of the covenant with God."[6]

While Orthodox leaders contend that "Jews are often suspicious and sense antisemitism where there is none,"[7] Christians are, indeed, among those responsible for attacks against the Jews, which contradict the teaching of the Church.[8] On the other hand, Church leaders mitigate this somewhat by saying that past vocal and written hostility by Church leaders, such as St. John Chrysostom and others, was a product of historical conditions or a particular situation during a particular period.[9]

The above description of Orthodoxy is rather general. However, the Orthodox religion is not centralized like the Roman Catholic Church is. That is, the Orthodox Churches are autocephalous and, as such, have no figure like the pope, who speaks for the entire Catholic religious hierarchy.

Having said this, it is acknowledged that, while efforts of the Catholic Church have been slow and, in many ways, inadequate, the Vatican has taken significant steps toward improving Catholic-Jewish relations. However, the Orthodox world has not moved as far along that road as the Catholic Church. Both the doctrinal and the ecclesiastical perspectives of the Eastern Churches continue to maintain an implicit view of Christian anti-Judaism, which persistently assures the continuance of "medieval preconceptions" of Jews in contemporary Orthodox culture. While the Orthodox faithful do not reflect on a daily basis on Jews as Christ-killers, Orthodox Christianity's official religious doctrine and liturgy do seem to allow for the perpetuation of this view.

THE SERBIAN ORTHODOX CHURCH AND THE JEWS

Ethnic and religious tolerance over the past decades has been prevalent in the relationship between the Jewish community and the Serbian Orthodox Church, continuing a long tradition of amiable Christian-Jewish relations there (aside, of course, from the Holocaust).[10] While the Orthodox Church leadership has not revised its official position on Jews and Judaism, the Serbian Orthodox Church has distanced itself from the occasional overt expression of antisemitism within its ranks, usually in response to public pressure.

On the other hand, antisemitic expression does have a long history in Serbia. After the 1804 Serbian insurrection against Ottoman rule, Jews were expelled from the Serbian interior and could live only in Belgrade. Because it was believed that Jews were secret agents of the Turks, Jewish merchants could not travel freely for commercial purposes.

However, one of the conditions for granting full independence to Serbia at the Congress of Berlin in 1878 was the guarantee of legal equality for all people without regard to nationality or religion. Thus, Article 23 of the Serbian Constitution granted equality to all citizens, including Jewish citizens. This was the first time that Serbian Jews were equal before the law. But antisemitic propaganda was encountered in Serbia up to, and including, the period between the Congress of Berlin and the issuance of the Constitution of 1888. In fact, Article 132 of the Serbian Constitution denied Jews the right of domicile. The Serbian Parliament took eleven years to remove those restrictive decrees from Serbian law. In 1879, Nikola Jovanović complained that Europe was trying to force Serbia to grant its Jews, who were a non-Serbian element, all the rights that native Serbs had acquired.[11]

In the interwar period, the Serbian Orthodox Church was relegated to being the representative of only one of the recognized religions, according to the 1921 Vidovdan Constitution (Paragraph 12). This challenge to its position as Yugoslavia's leading spiritual force may have been one of the reasons why its clergy became so involved in the state's politics,[12] often to the detriment of other religious groups. For example, there was resistance to the change in the status of Serbian Jews.

One of the roots of interwar Yugoslav antisemitism was economic competition. However, in the Serbian Orthodox area of Yugoslavia, the economic role of the (mostly Sephardic) Jewish community was secondary. Thus, Jews were mostly tolerated and well established in Serbian society. The same could have been said of Bosnia's Sephardic Jews, although its Ashkenazic population worked mostly in commerce and the professions.

There was a lack of explicit antisemitism in everyday life in the early years of interwar Yugoslavia. In fact, political antisemitism was not nearly as important as the conflicts among the South Slav nations. On the other hand, antisemitism was at least implicitly present in interwar Yugoslav politics. For example, in the Yugoslav Kingdom, the media outlets of the rightist Serbian nationalist groups (e.g., *Balkan* and *Vreme*) regularly published antisemitic articles. There was also some state-sponsored antisemitism, encouraged by German and Italian pressure on Yugoslavia, which, as World War Two drew near, accused the Jews and the Freemasons of causing all of the troubles of the world, especially in Serbia.

Nikolaj Velimirović

Representing the ideology of interwar Serbian fascism was the Orthodox Bishop of Ohrid and Žiča, Nikolaj Velimirović. From the 1920s, his religious writing expressed a clerical nationalist, anti-modernist, anti-democratic, and antisemitic strain. Regarding the Serbian nation as messianic, he claimed that it had its own mission in world history, based on the link between Orthodoxy and Serbian-ness.[13] His writings helped to formulate the Serbian populism of the 1930s upon which several notable fascist movements were based. In 1934, pro-Nazi politician, Dimitrije Ljotić, utilizing elements of Velimirović's ideology, founded Zbor, which became a collaborationist Serbian organization during the fascist occupation.[14]

Velimirović's xenophobic political outlook negated many of the principles of the Enlightenment, including individualism, parliamentary democracy, and science. His clerical nationalism considered Orthodox values to be spiritually superior and antithetical to those of the West.[15] Admiring Hitler's regime, he noted in 1935 that the Nazi leader "realized that nationalism without religion is an anomaly, a cold and insecure mechanism."[16] Not surprisingly, Velimirović's writings portrayed Jews in the most negative light: as Christ-killers and satanic conspirators against Christian Europe. But he also considered the Jews responsible for the worst ills of society, including both socialism and capitalism, as well as atheism. Serbia's Church authorities never officially condemned Velimirović's antisemitic tendencies, and, in fact, continue to regard him as one of the Church's most respected national religious figures.[17]

Although Velimirović had demonstrable ideological links with, and "significant intellectual influence" on, Ljotić in the pre-World War Two years,[18] unlike Ljotić, the bishop refused to collaborate with the Nazis during the occupation. Suspected of supporting the Chetnik resistance, he was placed under house arrest in July 1941 and incarcerated in a Serbian monastery. When the Partisans were making significant inroads against the Germans, in September 1944 Velimirović, along with Serbian Patriarch Gavrilo Dozić, was transferred for almost three months to the

Dachau concentration camp, where they were designated "honorary prisoners." Their release in December 1944 appears to have been part of a political deal struck between the Serbian collaborationist government of Milan Nedić and the German envoy for the Balkans, Hermann Neubacher.[19]

In recent decades, Velimirović's supporters have published biographical accounts of his brief imprisonment at Dachau portraying him as enduring "enormous suffering and torture," despite the fact that he was an "honorary prisoner." However, this account ignores the fact that, at Dachau, Velimirović wrote some of his most antisemitic material, even while Germans and Serbian collaborators were murdering Serbian Jews for alleged anti-Serbian crimes.[20]

Velimirović's notes from Dachau, which he is said to have written surreptitiously on scraps of toilet paper, were collected and edited only in the 1980s. The principal message of the book assembled on the basis of those notes is that World War Two was the "inevitable consequence of the secularisation of 'godless Europe'." Velimirović castigated the Serbs, who suffered so much during the war, for their "betrayal of God and Christian traditions" for "secular European culture."[21] The latter phrase seems to have been a code for malign Jewish influence, for Velimirović claimed that "all modern ideas including democracy, and strikes, and socialism, and atheism, and religious tolerance, and pacifism, and global revolution, and capitalism, and communism are the inventions of Jews, or rather their father, the Devil."[22] Thus, Jewish suffering during World War Two might be seen as divine retribution for the murder of Christ. Velimirović also called for the establishment of an Orthodox Christian society, based on a uniquely Serbian form of religious nationalism and monarchism, which rejected Western traditions, such as individualism, equality, religious tolerance, and democracy.

Velimirović died in 1956 in the United States, to which country he had immigrated. In Yugoslavia, the communist authorities had revoked his citizenship, calling him a traitor and a "clerical-nationalist." Because the Yugoslav authorities considered him a fascist and even a war criminal, his work could not be openly published in the country.[23]

Velimirović's rehabilitation began in the late 1980s when Serbian nationalism gained traction. Nationalist theologians within the Serbian Orthodox Church—Amfilohije Radović, Artemije Radosavljević, and Atanasije Jevtić—who were ordained as bishops by 1991, along with the Serbian Academy of Arts and Sciences and the Serbian Union of

Writers, represented the voice of Serbian chauvinistic nationalism. The bishops began an intensive public program to restore Velimirović's reputation, which included publications by him and about him, as well as commemorations dedicated to him. There was also a campaign to canonize him, preceded by the transport of his remains from the United States to Serbia in May 1991. This flurry of activity on Velimirović's behalf was meant to portray a groundswell of popularity and adoration, which would bolster the progress toward his canonization, even though, in reality, only a relatively small proportion of the population attended the various functions.[24]

Nevertheless, in 1990, the commission appointed to investigate the issue of Velimirović's canonization, headed by the newly elected Patriarch Pavle, rejected that request—at least temporarily. Patriarch Pavle argued that Velimirović's reputation of sanctity was not quite as faultless as a saint's should be. He cited, for example, Velimirović's well-known smoking habit. What he did not mention as working against his sainthood, however, was Velimirović's antisemitic political opinions.

Despite the previously cited concerns and controversies surrounding the bishop, in 2003, the Council of Bishops of the Serbian Orthodox Church finally announced its decision to canonize Velimirović. This placed his memory as a "martyr" during World War Two and his writings, including his antisemitic tracts, in a position to be utilized by adherents of the Serbian right wing. They parroted his contempt for Jews, citing his prophetic assertion that the Holocaust was God's retribution against their rejection of Christian teachings, which rendered them, in effect, "godless."[25]

In spite of the controversy surrounding his life and work, many Orthodox Serbs regard Velimirović as "one of the most important national religious figures since medieval times" and approve of his religious philosophy. For example, Serbian right-wing antisemitic literature finds its ideological roots in his writings and directly invokes Velimirović's power of prophecy to support the assertion that the Holocaust represented divine retribution against the "godless" and "treacherous" Jews.

However, the canonization drew, in response, attacks on Velimirović's reputation, because of the blatant antisemitism of his writings from Dachau. The Serbian Orthodox Church responded with the typical Christian claim that Velimirović was only reiterating the age-old Christian theological stance toward the Jews that they repent and return to the path of Christ, drawing on the traditional Christian antisemitic premise that the Jews killed Christ and have drawn upon themselves eternal damnation until they begin to pursue the correct (i.e., Christian) path.

The Serbian Orthodox Church and the Jewish Community Today

A formal interfaith dialogue between Jews and Orthodox Christians began in 1972, although Lavoslav Kadelburg, a prominent leader of the Yugoslav Jewish community until his death in 1994, did remark that "the Orthodox Church's dogma against the Jews is 'still on the books'." He further commented that "where there is indoctrination there is also collusion between the state and the Church."[26] But, later, after the collapse of Yugoslavia and during the Wars of Yugoslav Succession, there were occasions when the Serbian Orthodox Church made special efforts to engage with the Jewish community. For example, in the January 1992 edition of its newspaper *Pravoslavlje*, the official publication of the Serbian Orthodox Patriarchate, there was a decidedly antisemitic article entitled "Jews Are Crucifying Christ Again!", which claimed that Jews in Israel were persecuting Christians there. The article maintained that the intolerance of outsiders displayed by certain ultra-Orthodox Jews in Jerusalem's Mea Shearim quarter was "endemic to Israelis and that Jews generally are anti-Christian."[27]

Following protests from the country's Jewish community, the Synod of the Serbian Church dismissed the newspaper's editor-in-chief. The Serbian Orthodox Church Patriarchate approached the president of the Serbian Jewish community, Jaša Almuli, with an apology. Furthermore, at a conference following the incident, Patriarch Pavle, the head of the Serbian Orthodox Church, assured the Jewish leadership that the Church Synod was not antisemitic. The Church representatives offered to establish a joint committee to cleanse Serbian religious educational textbooks of any material that might elicit intolerance and antisemitism. Finally, the Serbian Orthodox Church expressed its willingness to support the establishment of a branch of the International Council of Christians and Jews in Serbia.[28]

On 5 October 2000, Slobodan Milošević was forced to resign as president of the Federal Republic of Yugoslavia. The aftermath was supposed to signal the introduction of a democratic and civil society ending the bloody ultra-nationalist and ethno-national trajectory that the state had pursued for the previous ten years. Indeed, Serbia appeared to be liberalizing, which made it all the more puzzling to observe a rise in the number of antisemitic vandalism, graffiti, and the like, despite the modest number of Jews remaining in the country and their inconspicuous economic and political profile there.

It is interesting to note that post-World War Two antisemitic hate crime had been an infrequent occurrence in Serbia. Even during the 1990s, which were fraught with xenophobia and ethnic intolerance there, anti-Jewish prejudice was on display only with far-right groups. Criminal acts against Jews were almost nonexistent.[29] Therefore, it is likely that Serbian antisemitism may be found "in the interplay between the conspiratorial character of anti-Semitism and the specific features of the ideological and political milieu in post-Milošević Serbia."[30]

On the other hand, in certain respects, the upsurge in Serbian antisemitism parallels the above-mentioned phenomenon of antisemitism without Jews being experienced in Western Europe, as well as other locales.[31] Yet, recent developments in Serbia cannot be explained simply as part of this broader, pan-European political trend. Britain's Chief Rabbi, Professor Jonathan Sacks, identified three sources of the "new antisemitism":

> Once Jews were hated because of their religion. Then they were hated because of their race. Now they are hated because of their nation state. The second difference is that the epicenter of the old antisemitism was Europe. Today it's the Middle East and it is communicated globally by the new electronic media.

> The third is particularly disturbing.... Throughout history, when people have sought to justify anti-Semitism, they have done so by recourse to the highest source of authority available within the culture. In the Middle Ages, it was religion. So we had religious anti-Judaism. In post-Enlightenment Europe it was science. So we had the twin foundations of Nazi ideology, Social Darwinism and the so-called Scientific Study of Race. Today the highest source of authority worldwide is human rights. That is why Israel—the only fully functioning democracy in the Middle East with a free press and independent judiciary—is regularly accused of the five cardinal sins against human rights: racism, apartheid, crimes against humanity, ethnic cleansing and attempted genocide.

The new antisemitism has mutated so that any practitioner of it can deny that he or she is an antisemite. After all, they'll say, I'm not a racist. I have no problem with Jews or Judaism. I only have a problem with the State of Israel. But in a world of 56 Muslim nations and 103 Christian ones, there is only one Jewish state, Israel, which constitutes one-quarter of one per cent of the land mass of the Middle East. Israel is the only one of the 193 member nations of the United Nations that has its right to exist regularly challenged, with one state, Iran, and many, many other groups, committed to its destruction.[32]

Rabbi Sacks' remarks, however, do not necessarily reflect conditions in Serbia. First, radical Islamists from the Middle East are relatively absent in Serbia. Second, Serbian antisemitic rhetoric does not usually mention Israel or Middle Eastern conditions, and, therefore, does not share an ideological tradition with left-wing antisemitism. Third, Serbian antisemites do not call for the elimination of Israel or publicly support the Palestinian cause. In contrast to the contemporary European or Middle Eastern antisemitism, Serbian antisemitic verbiage is entirely focused on how the international Jewish conspiracy is victimizing Serbs, harking back to the tradition of Serbian right-wing ideology of the 1930s.[33]

The NATO bombing of Yugoslavia was particularly invoked to illustrate the belief in a Jewish conspiracy. Byford described the abstract quality of antisemitism at this stage,[34] when the proliferation of conspiracy theories did not, yet, lead to anti-Jewish hate crimes.[35] However, after Milošević's ouster, when the belief in a Jewish conspiracy became more concrete and less abstract, the local Jewish population began to suffer antisemitic violence.[36]

In 2001, Serbian bookstores stocked an edition of the Tsarist-era forgery, *Protocols of the Elders of Zion*, prefaced by an introduction that alleged that Jews had masterminded the NATO bombing of Yugoslavia; the document had been previously published in *Greater Serbia* (No. 16) in 1994.[37] The Federation of Jewish Communities filed a lawsuit against the publishers, alleging incitement of ethnic hatred. The lawsuit failed because the district public prosecutor, Milija Milovanović, declared that neither the book nor its introduction "contain elements of the stated criminal offence."[38] This decision failed to make the connection between the conspiracies supposedly being perpetrated by the Jewish elite mentioned in the *Protocols* and the damages being suffered by the contemporary Serbian Jewish community at the hands of those who bought the book and interpreted it as the truth.

Until the turn of the century, post-communist Serbia had suffered relatively little institutionally backed antisemitism.[39] Those who fostered antisemitism were a relatively small number of activists, found on the margins of political expression. Their nationalist and religious publications, such as *Logos, Pravoslavni Misionar* (Orthodox missionary), *Kruna* (The Crown), *Glas Srpske* (The Voice of Srpska), *Ovde* (Here), and *Velika Srbija* (Greater Serbia), as well as magazines with a more mystical orientation, such as *Treće Oko* (Third eye) and *Nostradamus,* had only limited impact on Serbian public opinion.[40]

However, the NATO bombing in the spring of 1999 brought anti-Jewish themes, which had been largely absent from the mainstream press until then, to the fore. Surprisingly, *Politika,* Serbia's oldest and most trusted daily newspaper until becoming a vehicle for Milošević's propaganda, which had not published antisemitic political ideas, suddenly in June 1999, in the final days of the NATO bombing campaign, published articles that accused David Rockefeller, alleged to be Jewish, of orchestrating a Satanic conspiracy against Serbia.[41] Known antisemites were given a platform in the same publication, demonstrating that the antisemitism that had been kept on the margins of Serbian society, by the spring of 1999 had penetrated the country's mainstream political and media culture, becoming an acceptable and plausible explanation of Serbia's predicament.[42]

Thus, Byford correctly situates this Serbian antisemitic discourse, not as a result of a turn to the right by the Milošević regime, which actively promoted Serbian nationalism, but as part of a re-emergence of right-wing conspiratorial myths in the late 1990s that harkened back to Serbia's conspiracy culture dating from the mid-nineteenth century until the end of World War Two. This conspiracy myth was traditionally, anywhere it surfaced, dominated by the notion of a Jewish plot to rule the world, and Serbia, always believing itself to be the subject of anti-Serbian plots, was fertile ground for the connection between anti-Serbian conspiracies and antisemitic conspiracy theories. Thus, says Byford, "a conspiracy theorist, even if not overtly antisemitic, operates in an ideological space with an antisemitic legacy that cannot be easily discarded…[and cannot easily evade] the legacy of the conspiratorial cultural tradition."[43]

Formerly marginal conspiracy-minded ideologues now gained regular access to the mainstream media. For example, Ratibor Đurđević, who has been called "Serbia's most virulent antisemitic author,"[44] gained an audience despite his admitted World War Two engagement in "national service of General Milan Nedić" and as a "transmitter of missionary-ideological work" on Draža Mihailović's staff.[45] For example, he was able to write a piece for *Pravoslavlje*. Despite the more open expressions of antisemitism in print, the Serbian Jewish community did not, at least initially, suffer increased violence. In fact, it is likely that conspiratorial antisemitism served as an indirect way to criticize Western values, as it did for Velimirović in the 1930s and 1940s, rather than precisely call for antisemitic actions.

An abstract usage of "Jew" without all of the racial inflection showed up, for example, in an interesting quotation by Đurđević in 1999: "We do not blame all Italians for the crimes of the Mafia, or all Irish Catholics for the crazy bombings and murders committed by the IRA. In the same way, ordinary Jews must not be blamed for the crimes of Judeo-bankers."[46] In this way, he drew a distinction between "ordinary Jews" and those Jews who were part of the evil conspiracy to create a new world order.

Similarly, in 1997, Đurđević had referred to Serbia's Jewish community as "our Jews, adapted to life in the Balkans [who] do not pose a threat to Serbs, or any other people on Yugoslav territory" in contrast to "Judaists," upon whose heads he heaped numerous calumnies.[47] The latter were those who personified for Serbian society the popular anti-Western sentiment that prevailed in Serbian society at the time, which meant that Serbian antisemites were not expressing hatred of all Jews, only the "evil Judaists."

While Milošević remained in power, defying the Western powers and values and claiming that he was defending Serbia against the whole world, "Judaists" (meaning simply "the West") were an external enemy being kept at bay. As a matter of fact, Aca Singer, president of Yugoslavia's Federation of Jewish Communities, described meetings he held with Milošević, who promised to try to stop sporadic antisemitic incidents in Serbia, although he did not publicly denounce them.[48] But when Milošević was overthrown and the external enemy remained undefeated, conspiracy theorists turned to a quest for the internal enemy. At this point, the distinction between Jews and "Judaists" began to break down for them, as it became difficult for the antisemitic press to separate imagined characteristics of "the Jewish people" from those of "the evil Judaists" in a conspiracy to create an anti-Christian "New World Order." Thus, "the good" Serbian Jews, whose ancestors had fought side-by-side with other Serbian patriots during World War One and World War Two, now were seen as linked to "the Judaists," at least through their religious and ethnic characteristics. Serbian Jews began to be looked at askance as potential enemies of Serbian Christian values—as possibly part of the global Jewish conspiracy.

This formulation did not appear in the mainstream media after Milošević's departure, as the press began to write about the new Serbian conditions in the post-Milošević era. There was a greater focus on Serbia's external relations, not internal conspiracies, which, again, placed Orthodox Christian right-wing ideology at the margins of society. Thus, the promoters of antisemitic conspiracy theories were no longer welcome in the public press and interpreted the change of regime and its new focus on promoting good relations with the West as a win for Serbia's enemies, including "the Judaists" in their quest for world domination. And these "Judaists" now were not only external, but also lived within Serbia—all the better to undermine the country and its values with the assistance of the new political elite, the media, secular educational organizations, and even parts of the Serbian Orthodox Church.[49]

The response to the perceived threat posed to the Serbian people by these now-deposed radicals was the increased activity of several ultra-right organizations, such as Obraz (Dignity) (founded in 1997), St. Justin, and Dveri (Doors). These groups shifted their focus from "Judaists" to individual members of Serbia's Jewish community. And their activity morphed from verbal and written to physical. Belgrade's Jewish cemetery and a synagogue were plastered with swastikas. Similar manifestations appeared in northern Serbia. While Obraz denied involvement in the cemetery and synagogue vandalism, its rhetoric, especially an online "Letter to Our Enemies," supports antisemitic, anti-Roma, and anti-gay violence. These activities increasingly appeal to Serbia's youth, who see their future as hopeless in the wake of the ruin of Serbia during the Milošević era. It is easy to be led to blame "the Roma, the Jews, the Croats or the Albanians" for the bad economic and political situation.[50] The Christian right's antisemitic graffiti ("Death to Jews," "Jews out," etc.) reflects a shift to a concrete internal enemy who can be blamed for Serbia's current ills.

The authorities appear to have found little concrete proof that any of the Christian right-wing groups, which propagate a Velimirović-type religious ideology, were directly implicated in the aforementioned instances of antisemitic violence. Nonetheless, Obraz, St. Justin, and Dveri are widely recognized as the principal purveyors of anti-Jewish prejudice in post-Milošević Serbia. Most importantly, representatives of the local Jewish community perceive the continuing presence of the Christian right as the greatest threat to the peaceful existence of Serbia's Jews. Abusive graffiti, threatening phone calls, and antisemitic remarks in the media have increased. Singer noted that "we are so insignificant in the social and political life of the country that it is surprising that we are under great pressure and attacks."[51] This is partly because state authorities continue to treat Obraz and similar organizations as legitimate patriotic political movements, while the representatives of these groups consistently deny that they engage in religious and racial hatred. Singer suggested that, while the leaders of the Serbian Orthodox Church have condemned antisemitism, "perhaps they did not do so as vigorously as they could."[52] Thus, Christian right-wing groups seem to maintain close organizational and ideological links with influential mainstream Serbian institutions, including the Serbian Orthodox Church and the right-wing element of the new Serbian political establishment. This connection fosters an environment for acts of anti-Jewish violence and intimidation.

In 2005, in reaction to antisemitic posters and graffiti that appeared on 22 March in Belgrade, the Holy Synod of Bishops of the Serbian Orthodox Church issued a statement condemning "every manifestation of antisemitism," calling it theologically and morally unacceptable. They called on state authorities to take proper measures to ensure that such actions were not repeated. The statement also reiterated that the Serbian people, of all people, should be able to understand how devastating the Holocaust was to the Jewish people and rejected any attempt to minimize it, even by members of its own clergy.[53] Nor did the Holy Synod accept the calumny that Jews were all psychologically criminal.

In 2015, outside Athens, Greece, 38 leading Jewish and Orthodox Christian scholars engaged in a discussion on relations between the two religions. This was the eighth round of discussions since 1972. However, demonstrating how much more work on inter-religious relations there is to do, while the rapport was reportedly warm and friendly throughout most of the meeting, the atmosphere changed when the head of the Jewish delegation, Rabbi David Rosen, called on the Orthodox leadership to deny that God had rejected the Jews. The Orthodox response was only to call for greater people-to-people contacts and more engagement with youth. Thus, the Orthodox Church was as yet unwilling to go as far as the Catholic Church had in rejecting collective Jewish guilt for the killing of Christ.

Republika Srpska and the Jews

While Republika Srpska maintains very close relations with Serbia, its religious establishment follows a more independent path. As relations between Republika Srpska and Israel have developed, Jewish centers (including synagogues in Banja Luka and Doboj) have been reopened in recent years.[54]

Contrary to the rather subdued response of the Federation government to Holocaust commemorations, Republika Srpska has taken several recent initiatives. For example, on 22 April 2007 (the anniversary of the liberation of Jasenovac), in Banja Luka, capital of Republika Srpska, a monument called "Poplar of Horror" was erected to the victims of Jasenovac. The inscription is in Serbian, English, and Hebrew. Furthermore, the workers' collective of a local factory in the District of Brčko, a special area outside the jurisdiction of the Federation or of Republika Srpska, although claimed by both, erected a monument near the site of the World War Two shooting of around three hundred Jewish refugees from Austria. Also, the Federation of Soldiers, in cooperation with the local government, raised a memorial on the bridge on the Sava where, in December 1941, around 130 Brčko Jews were killed by the Ustaše and thrown into the river. When the Jewish cemetery was destroyed as part of the town's urbanization plan, an Orthodox parish priest requested permission from the Sarajevo Jewish community to rescue four tombstones that he turned into a Holocaust memorial, which is now located in the Bosnian Serb cemetery.

Conclusion

The antisemitism discussed in this chapter is not an example of "routine bias," linked throughout the ages to Jewish economic or cultural competition.[55] Instead, contemporary Serbian Orthodox antisemitism goes a step further. It claims that powerful Jews are supposedly plotting a vast international conspiracy to destroy the contemporary international order to be replaced by a new world order hearkening back to the roots of the Enlightenment that would unite all of the enemies of Christianity, including communism, capitalism, freemasonry, the Catholic Church, and Islam.

Contradicting Pierre-André Taguieff's three-part description of racism in his study of prejudice,[56] Zygmunt Bauman has contended that the persistence of anti-Jewish hatred, such as manifested by influential Serbian Orthodox leaders, requires an explanation that goes beyond the notion of intergroup relations and resentment and that distinguishes between antisemitism and everyday prejudice or "heterophobia." In Bauman's view, anti-Jewish hatred may be hard to distinguish, either ideologically or psychologically, from a belief in a Jewish conspiracy and the omnipotence of Jewish economic and political power. Therefore, Jews must be isolated and/or annihilated to "render them harmless."[57]

The Jewish minority may be the only ethno-religious group in the world that has been continually accused of planning world domination. Such conspiratorial charges occur even where there are no Jews present in the culture, particularly, but not exclusively, in Eastern and Central Europe.[58]

In contemporary Serbia, too, this conspiratorial type of antisemitism has been reflected in an increasing number of anti-Jewish hate crimes in the aftermath of the ousting of Slobodan Milošević in the autumn of 2000, despite some liberalizing tendencies. Thus, after the collapse of Yugoslavia, there was a re-emergence of traditional antisemitism in Serbia as that society utilized (or "mis-used") its Jewish population in the promotion of the Serbian nationalistic agenda.[59]

In conclusion, post-Yugoslav Serbia entertains a mixture of appreciation of its Jewish population with a reluctance by the Serbian Orthodox Church to travel too far down the road of full acceptance of the Jewish religion as anything other than "the wrong road to God." The Serbian Orthodox Church has within its ranks both the most welcoming and the most exclusionary visions. Thus, its relations with its domestic Jewish population are likely to vacillate with respect to external, but also to internal, factors and pressures.

Notes

1. Charles Y. Glock and Rodney Stark, *Christian Beliefs and Anti-Semitism* (New York: Harper Torchbooks, 1969), pp. 102–106.
2. Laslo Sekelj, "Antisemitism and Jewish Identity in Serbia After the 1991 Collapse of the Yugoslav State," in *Analysis of Current Trends in Antisemitism Acta*, No. 12 (Vidal Sassoon International Center for the Study of Antisemitism, 1997), at http://sicsa/huji.ac.il/12sekel.html [accessed 13 October 2017].

3. Milica Mihailović and Srećko Mihailović, "Anti-Semitism in the Nineties," in Stefano Bianchini and Dušan Janjić (eds.), *Ethnicity in Postcommunism* (Belgrade: Institute of Social Sciences, 1996), p. 254.
4. Aleksandr Gurevich, "The Orthodox View of the Jews and Judaism," in *Religion, State and Society*, Vol. 23, No. 1 (1995), p. 53.
5. Ibid.
6. Ibid., p. 54.
7. Ibid. On the other hand, Aca Singer, former head of the Yugoslav Federation of Jewish Communities, noted that antisemitic actions are "evaluated as 'unimportant' by the non-Jewish population, although experience shows that what at first glance seems to be an insignificant event can be the basis for developments with tragic consequences." Aca Singer, "Položaj jevrejske zajednice u Jugoslaviji," *Saopštenje na Međunarodnoj konferenciji položaja manjina u Saveznoj republici Jugoslavije*. Belgrade, 11–13 January 1995.
8. Gurevich, "The Orthodox View of the Jews and Judaism," p. 55.
9. Ibid., 54.
10. Harriet Pass Freidenreich, *Jews of Yugoslavia: A Quest for Community* (Philadelphia: Jewish Publication Society, 1979), p. 179.
11. Nikola Jovanović, *O jevrejskom pitanju u Srbiji* (Belgrade: Stefanović, 1879).
12. Maria Falina, "Between 'Clerical Fascism' and Political Orthodoxy: Orthodox Christianity and Nationalism in Interwar Serbia," in *Totalitarian Movements and Political Religions*, Vol. 8, No. 2 (June 2007), p. 252.
13. Ibid., p. 253.
14. For the program of the Zbor movement, see Istorijski arhiv Sarajeva, Zbirke varia, Box 21, ZV-598.
15. Jovan Byford, "Anti-Semitism and the Christian Right in Post-Milošević Serbia." https://www.academia.edu/3147437/Anti-Semitism_and_the_Christian_right_in_post-Milošević_Serbia [accessed 22 March 2019].
16. *Nacionalizam Svetog Save: Predavanje održano na proslavi nedelje pravoslavlja u Beogradu 1935* (Belgrade: Udruženje srpskog pravoslavnog sveštenstva Arhiepiskopije beogradsko-karlovačke, 1935), p. 21, as cited in Falina, "Between 'Clerical Fascism' and Political Orthodoxy," p. 253.
17. Jovan Byford, "Distinguishing 'Anti-Judaism' from 'Antisemitism': Recent Championing of Serbian Bishop Nikolaj Velimirović," in *Religion, State & Society*, Vol. 34, No. 1 (March 2006), p. 10.
18. Falina, "Between 'Clerical Fascism' and Political Orthodoxy," p. 48.
19. Byford, "Distinguishing 'Anti-Judaism' from 'Antisemitism'," p. 11.
20. See, for example, the Grand Anti-Masonic Exhibition that opened in Belgrade on 22 October 1941, which expressed the Nedić regime's

canard that Masons, communists, and Jews were conspiring against Serbia on their road to world domination. *Antimasonski plakati 1941–1942*, Sarajevo, 2013.
21. As quoted in Byford, "Distinguishing 'Anti-Judaism' from 'Antisemitism'," p. 12.
22. Bishop Nikolaj Velimirović, *Poruka Srpskom Narodu kroz tamnički prozor* (Hilmünster, Germany: Himmelstuer, 1985), as cited in Jovan Byford, "Canonizing the 'Prophet' of Anti-Semitism: The Apotheosis of Bishop Nikolaj Velimirović and the Legitimization of Religious Antisemitism in Contemporary Serbian Society (Part 1)," in *Radio Free Europe/Radio Liberty, East European Perspectives*, Vol. 6, No. 4 (18 February 2004), pp. 5–6 of 14, at https://www.rferl.org/a/1342451.html [last accessed 19 March 2019].
23. Byford, "Canonizing the 'Prophet'", p. 6 of 14.
24. Byford characterized this as attempting to project that Velimirović was so popular that he had a "living cult." Ibid., p. 9 of 14.
25. Ibid.
26. Paul Gordiejew, "The Yugoslav Experiment in Secular Jewishness," in *European Judaism*, Vol. 40, No. 2 (Autumn 2007), p. 64.
27. "Serbian Orthodox Church Reaches out to Jewish Community," *Jewish Telegraphic Agency*, 7 February 1992, at https://www.jta.org/1992/02/07/archive/serbian-orthodox-church-reaches-out-to-jewish-community [last accessed 24 March 2019].
28. Ibid.
29. Sekelj, "Antisemitism and Jewish Identity in Serbia," p. 7.
30. Byford, "Anti-Semitism and the Christian Right."
31. The Office of Rabbi Sacks, "The Mutating Virus: Understanding Antisemitism," at http://rabbisacks.org/mutating-virus-understanding-antisemitism/ [last accessed 19 March 2019].
32. Ibid.
33. Byford, "Anti-Semitism and the Christian Right."
34. Ibid.
35. Andrija Gams and Aleksandar Levi wrote that antisemitism was not a widespread phenomenon in Serbia. "However, due to the difficult situation in which Serbia and the Serbs outside Serbia are finding themselves, due to unjust sanctions and the slandering of Serbs in the world media, there are some examples of anti-Semite feelings among the Serbs. Up to now these have been only sporadic cases, but they do deserve concern." *The Truth About "Serbian Anti-Semitism"* (Belgrade: Ministry of Information of the Republic of Serbia, 1994), pp. 86–87.
36. Byford, "Anti-Semitism and the Christian Right."

37. Mihailović and Mihailović, "Anti-Semitism in the Nineties" [note 3], p. 253.
38. Morning News, Radio B-92, 28 July 2001.
39. Sekelj, "Antisemitism and Jewish Identity in Serbia," p. 6.
40. Byford, "Anti-Semitism and the Christian Right."
41. Gordana Knezević, "Invisible Clique Rules the Planet," in *Politika* (Belgrade, English-language edition), 4–6 June 1999, p. 15.
42. Byford, "Anti-Semitism and the Christian Right."
43. Ibid.
44. Ibid.
45. A.L.L., "Rasizam, nacizam, antisemitizam: Dva aršina," in *Jevrejski pregled*, Vol. 5 (September 1997), p. 17.
46. Ratibor M. Đurđević, *Pet krvavih revolucija Judeo-bankara i njihove Judeo-masonerije* (Belgrade: Ihtus Hrišćanska knjiga, 1999), p. 22.
47. Ratibor M. Đurđević, *Idejni i duhovni trovači sa zapada* (Belgrade: Ihtus Hrišćanska knjiga, 1997), p. 30.
48. "Racism Defies Serbian Democracy/Violence Grows Despite Change in Leadership," *San Francisco Chronicle*, 18 April 2001, at https://www.sfgate.com/news/article/Racism-defies-Serbian-democracy-Violence-grows-2930563.php [accessed 31 January 2019].
49. Byford, "Anti-Semitism and the Christian Right."
50. "Racism Defies Serbian Democracy."
51. Branko Bjelajac, "Yugoslav Jews Targeted," Institute for War & Peace Reporting, 3 August 2001, at https://iwpr.net/global-voices/yugoslav-jews-targeted [accessed 31 January 2019].
52. Ibid.
53. From Milan Bulajić (ed.), *Jasenovac – 1945-2005/06. 60/61. godišnjica herojskog proboja zatočenika 22. aprila 1945.: Dani sećanja na žrtve genocida nad jermenskim, grčkim, srpskim, jevrejskim i romskim narodima* (Belgrade: Pešić i sinovi, 2006), p. 85.
54. Boris Vukićević, "Jewish Communities in the Political and Legal Systems of Post-Yugoslav Countries," in *Trames* (Tallinn), Vol. 21, No. 3 (2017), p. 259.
55. Byford, "Anti-Semitism and the Christian Right."
56. Pierre-André Taguieff, *La force du préjugé: essai sur le racism et ses doubles* (Paris: Editions La Découverte, 1988), pp. 69–70.
57. Zygmunt Bauman, *Modernity and the Holocaust* (Oxford: Polity Press, 1991), pp. 62–66.
58. See, for example, Paul Lendvai, *Anti-Semitism Without Jews: Communist Eastern Europe* (Garden City, NY: Doubleday, 1971).
59. Sekelj, "Antisemitism and Jewish Identity in Serbia," p. 8.

CHAPTER 7

The Orthodox Church of Greece

Altuğ Günal and Zeynep Selin Balcı

Abstract The Greek Orthodox Church has a crucial role in identifying "Greekness" in a quite exclusionary manner. Today the Church combats secularization by using a religious discourse, and Westernization by using a nationalist discourse, viewing itself as the guardian of Greek identity. Aligning itself with the right and extreme right wing's policies, it has come into conflict with leftist governments from time to time—the dispute on the removal of the religion section in the identity cards being the most serious one, there has never been a hostile stance toward the Church from any Greek political party. Having said that, the adherents of the other faiths in Greece are still deprived of many of their rights and even though tolerant voices can be heard from clergymen from time to time, the Church of Greece does not differ considerably from other Orthodox Churches in its negative approach toward LGBTQ rights.

A. Günal (✉) · Z. S. Balcı
Ege University, Bornova, Turkey

Z. S. Balcı
e-mail: zeynep.selin.balci@ege.edu.tr

© The Author(s) 2019
S. P. Ramet (ed.), *Orthodox Churches and Politics in Southeastern Europe*, Palgrave Studies in Religion, Politics, and Policy,
https://doi.org/10.1007/978-3-030-24139-1_7

In 1833, shortly after the Greek independence from the Ottoman Empire, the Orthodox Church of Greece (OCG) proclaimed its autocephalous status. Even though the Phanar Patriarchate in İstanbul did not concede this until 1850, since then, it has been ruled by its own Holy Synod under the de jure presidency of the Archbishop of Athens and all Greece. Today not only is it regarded as the sole state church, but it also has a great amount of influence on all segments of life, culture, and politics in Greece.[1] Maintaining a belief that it is authorized by God to speak on his behalf, the Church nonetheless delivers binding messages to a lesser extent than political ones.[2]

For some, while the OCG is seen as the sole protector of Hellenism against the hostile or at least the unfriendly West,[3] many other Greeks believe in secularization and see the Church as the source of backward tradition that holds Greece back from a "globalised secular modern state identified with the West, Europe or the EU."[4] (The latter usually projects the Church as a fundamental and traditional nationalist institution, conservative and hostile to minorities and other denominations as well as intolerant of sexual minorities.)[5] For advocates of European modernity and cosmopolitanism, the OCG does not have the will to adapt to the changing world and new global political and cultural reality.[6]

In the newborn Greek state which was largely governed by foreign interests and a foreign imported king, the Church became subordinated to the State while popular Byzantine culture constituted a central element of the Greek ethnic identity.[7] However invented Helleno-Orthodox identity may be, it represented cultural continuity and provided a bond between ancient Greece, Byzantium, and Modern Greece, but also created a source of confusion as to where to place Greece in the minds of Europeans. At the time of Greece's accession to the EU, Prime Minister Constantinos Caramanlis had said: "at last the belonging of Greece to Europe, with which it shared a classical Greek and Christian heritage, was realized."[8] Archbishop Christodoulos of Athens and all Greece was more assertive: "Europe would not exist without us. Not only is its name Greek, but its civilization too."[9] From 1981 until 2004, Greece remained the only Orthodox member of the EU and tried to be a bridge between the EU countries and the other Orthodox countries of Southeastern Europe.[10]

However, since Greece started its EU integration process in the 1970s, the state has faced with numerous challenges in implementing the required EU reforms. Mainly because of the OCG's influence and resistance, Greece still has difficulties in adopting and enforcing laws that are fundamental for the protection of human rights and freedoms above all. The Church does its best to counter the effects of the "Westernization" of Greece, among other ways by appealing to nationalism. It portrays itself as the guardian of the "Greek identity" and feels justified in intervening in Greek political affairs. It has directly opposed the spirit of secularization and left/center-left parties of Greece such as PASOK. As summarized by *The Economist* "Intelligence Unit," the Church has been criticizing the socialists' adoption of an increasingly secular stance in order to achieve European and international acceptance for many years, which the Church says has undermined the unique Greek cultural heritage which has been protected by the Church for centuries.[11]

Samuel Huntington's famous work, *The Clash of Civilizations*, gave a stimulus to studies on the Church of Greece. According to Huntington, even though Greece was situated in the Western camp during the Cold War, and was an EU member as well, in the new post-Cold War context the lines of division run along civilizations rather than between competing ideologies. Accordingly, as an Orthodox country, Greece now belongs not to the Western Bloc but to the Eastern Slavic Orthodox one. Huntington's identification of Greece as an "anomaly" because of its religious background stirred great controversy in Greece.[12] In a word, the civilizations approach attributes the problems Greece faces on EU reforms to its belonging to a different civilization.

In the light of the aforementioned evaluations, this chapter will examine the OCG's influence over Greek politics, identity, culture, and society from the past to the present. More weight will be given to the post-1974 period which began with the end of the traumatic Junta rule. Moreover, starting with a discussion of nationalism and identity, this chapter will also try to reveal the Church's attitude toward conservatism, religious freedoms, homophobia, and contemporary challenges.

On Nationalism and Identity

The "nation is an imagined political community"[13] and collective memories and narratives of a future destiny are its most important buttresses. No doubt, religion plays one of the fundamental roles in nation- and state building, not only for interpreting the communion but also in determining the criteria for being an insider or outsider. In this respect, Christianity played a very important role in the founding process of the

European nation-state system. National Churches had become an essential element in cementing and mobilizing the nation around a particular religion.[14] In this context, broad discussions in the literature have taken place about the roles of various actors in the construction of the Greek national identity. In spite of a few objections from some authors such as Anna Koumandaraki, who highlights the Greek state's role in consolidating Greek nationalism and identity while undervaluing the Church's,[15] there is a broad agreement that the Greek Church played a vital role in the construction of Greek identity and the fomenting of Greek nationalism.

Orthodox populations under Ottoman rule, as well as ethnically diverse citizens of the Byzantine Empire, were defined by their faith. The Ottoman Sultan had recognized or indeed put the Orthodox Church in charge of representing the Orthodox Millet in both secular and religious terms. So the Church, while acting as a civil authority over the Orthodox millet, also had the spiritual responsibility for the preservation of the collective identity of Orthodox believers.[16]

The creation of the autocephalous Church of Greece and the independent Greek state coincided in time. In the process of nation-building and identity formation, different discourses competed to acquire a hegemonic position.[17] However, when the idea of independence from the Ottomans emerged, an important question emerged: in what way was the new Greek nation-state ancient, and how was its Byzantine and Ottoman past going to be defined? The Christian New Testament was written in Greek and the language of Orthodox rites and liturgy was and is also in Greek. As an answer, an endeavor to merge classical Hellenism and Byzantine Christianity produced the notion of *Helleno-Christianity*. With this ethno-religious invention, historical continuity starting from ancient Greece was asserted. The term Helleno-Christianity/Orthodoxy, not only excluded the Ottoman past and interdigitated Hellenism, Christianity, and contemporary Greece, but also embraced the cultural, historical, and spiritual heritage which have together constructed the modern Greek identity and acted as "an adhesive body holding together the national unity of Greece."[18] In Anthony D. Smith's words, "it attempted to incorporate classical antiquity, along with the Byzantine Empire, in a single coherent narrative of 'the Greek nation' from the Mycenaeans to modern Greece."[19]

Orthodoxy was recognized as an integral part of Greek identity, socially and culturally. Thus, it could be seen in official and unofficial public discourse, with historiography, education, folklore, literature, art, and architecture, as well as in everyday practices and customs.[20] As expected, Helleno-Orthodox nationalism was successful in creating a durable segregation between insiders and outsiders, or more precisely Greeks and non-Greeks, and thus "provid[ing] the newborn nation with a solid collective identity." Associating the identity with only the religious component would not be enough to distinguish Greeks from other Orthodox populations with an Ottoman past. On the other hand, relying on Hellenism only would not encompass the ethnically, linguistically, and culturally fragmented Christians that together constituted the Greek nation.[21] This fusion of religion, ethnicity, and nation made the designation of Greek identity's domestic and foreign enemies more relaxed as well. For Greeks, this enemy has come to be known as Islam and the Ottomans, Islam's former strongest flagship. Even today's political disputes related to Islam, Turkey, or Muslims in Greece are heavily under the influence of this Ottoman past and interpretation of it.[22]

In the late Archbishop Christodoulos' words, "our people easily and naturally accept that their physiognomy in history was shaped by our religion i.e., Orthodoxy and its conjunction with Hellenism for twenty centuries."[23] This narrative of a long history that connects ancient Greece and modern times via the Byzantine Empire was backed and sustained by the Orthodox Church of Greece. On the other hand, the Greek state legitimised these historical claims and the religious connection to Greek identity with the 1822, 1823, and 1827 constitutions adopted after the 1821 revolution.[24] In all, a Greek citizen was defined as an autochthone who believed in Christ so that there was "no clear distinction" between a Greek citizen and a Greek Orthodox Christian.[25] Since then, close ties between the OCG and the Greek nation have been strongly preserved. In the words of former Prime Minister Constantinos Caramanlis, "The nation and Orthodoxy…have become in the Greek conscience virtually synonymous concepts, which together constitute our Helleno-Christian civilization."[26]

As Elisabeth Diamantopoulou points out, Orthodoxy remains deeply nationalistic in orientation and is rooted in nineteenth-century interpretation and the construction of Greek national identity. This process has made Orthodoxy and Greece and, by the same virtue, being Greek and Orthodox, inseparable.[27] Münir Yıldırım claims that there is no other country where nation and religion are so tightly intertwined.[28] As Teuvo Laitila points out, for nation-building reasons, it turned out that one could not be a Greek, without being a member of the Greek Church.[29] In May 2000, Archbishop Christodoulos reinforced this view, claiming that "For Greeks, to be an Orthodox Christian [is] a defining attribute of their identity."[30] The historical interpretation that the OCG served as the protector not only of the Greeks but also of the Greek identity and language has been sown deeply in the collective consciousness of Greeks.[31] The OCG seized the opportunity to remind Greeks whenever possible of this diachronic role.[32]

Being the leading factor for identity, the OCG re-emerged as a powerful social and political institution, with strong influence on Greek society and politics. Furthermore, it has also undertaken the duty of legitimating nationalist projects. In Nikolaos Chrysoloras' words, "the presence of a national religion in Greece made Greek nationalism a moral as well as a political project."[33] Besides the Church's religious monopoly on a substantially homogeneous population, its Byzantine ideal, especially after politician Ioannis Kolettis' speech in the National Assembly in 1844, paved the way for the reinterpretation of Greek history and the birth of irredentist Greek ideology, which is to say the radical program of regaining once Greek Orthodox lands, from the Aegean Sea to the Mediterranean, including the western part of today's Turkey. After 1859, the Orthodox Church of Greece endorsed this irredentist vision of the Megali Idea or in other words the restoration of the Byzantine Empire, in order to underline the so-called organic continuation of ancient Greece.[34] After they were united with the political aspirations of the Megali Idea, the OCG and the Greek State struggled through the political turmoil of the twentieth century together.[35]

In 1923, after the Greek defeat in the Turkish War of Independence, religion and nationality were equated or substituted once more. Under the compulsory population exchange agreement signed in Lausanne in 1923, the Christian Orthodox population of Turkey was considered Greek and was sent to Greece. In exchange, the Muslim population in Greece was counted as Turkish and sent to Turkey.[36]

Koumandaraki, however, argues that it was only after the Civil War (waged during 1946–1949) that national homogeneity was achieved, that the Left was defeated, and that the power of the "nationally-thinking" Greeks became unquestionable. Communists who could oppose or question this program were deported and an extensive state educational mechanism reconstructed national history on the glorious past and inspired strong nationalist feelings in the educated. The political regime accepted the national rhetoric as it was set free and unchallenged. "The construction of a rigid national identity did not leave any room for the ethnic variety within the Greek borders to be acknowledged either by the Right or [by] the Left."[37]

It is clear that Orthodox Christianity is not simply a religion for Greeks but rather an integral part of Greek identity. National holidays overlap with religious days and state celebrations with particular religious feasts. Their association is appearing in religious feasts such as Easter or other symbolic events such as marriage, funeral, and baptism.[38] However, this close relationship of nationhood and nationalism experienced periods of cracks over the time.

In the beginning, the OCG enjoyed privileges granted by the constitution. During the dictatorship of 1967–1974, the Church was rewarded by the junta with the motto "Greece of Christian Greeks." For instance, attendance at church services on Sundays became compulsory for children and their teachers. However, the OCG had failed to assume its historical role of protecting fellow Greeks, who were actually being tortured, imprisoned, and persecuted by the regime. This was a breaking point for the Church's decline in the eyes of Greek people. For them, it was the Church that supported the junta and sided with the oppressors. In reality, the OCG was used as a pawn, although some members sympathized with the junta. Meanwhile, the Metaxas regime exploited the OCG through its doctrines and religious practices.[39] The Zoe Brotherhood, a movement of theologians founded in 1907 and following the doctrines of the excommunicated nineteenth-century religious personality Apostolos Makrides, was an important tool for the colonels to infiltrate OCG ranks. With the indoctrination of the Church, the Zoe Brotherhood and the Junta were able to damage the OCG's reputation as a trustworthy institution, which would protect the Greeks in any eventuality.[40]

The destructive effects of the junta period can be recognized from the church-going ratio of Greeks, which used to be 63% in 1960 but declined to 29% by 1980. Attendance at liturgy and interest in the missionary movements of "Zoe" and its successor "Soter" (*Saviour*) declined as well.[41] In addition, priests lost their popularity and the "organic" link of Church with national identity of people was attenuated.[42]

In the post-junta era, the Church wanted to regain its old position, though it was not easy. Nevertheless, the OCG could have a chance to regain its constitutional position thanks to democratization.[43] With the 1975 constitution, which is still in force today with considerable amendments in 1986, 2001, and 2008, the Church regained some rights and lost others. The constitution reaffirmed Orthodoxy as the "prevailing religion" in its 3rd article.[44] That fact notwithstanding, the clause devoted to the "prohibition of proselytism" was removed from Article 3 where it used to mean "proselytism by other religions," to Article 13, which is about human rights, changing the meaning to refer to proselytism at the expense of any faith. In this way, Article 13 guaranteed religious freedom and equality for all faiths. In Article 14, offense against not only the prevailing religion but also any other religion in media was punishable by imprisonment.[45] Article 16 of the constitution was, on the other hand, more of an accomplishment for the OCG because it sets the goal of developing religious consciousness for youth in national education. Additionally, it was settled again, as it had been after 1945, for the state to pay the salaries and pensions of clergy, pastors, and lay employees—which gave clergymen the status of civil servants. Furthermore, the Church gained tax exemptions, with state holidays to be based on the religious calendar; the Archbishop of Athens and all Greece would preside over opening sessions of the Parliament, blessing members of Parliaments with Holy Water and presiding over state events and national holidays jointly with the head of state.[46]

Besides adopting constitutional amendments, the state lost its former interest in controlling the Church and tried to downgrade its influence. Despite being in favor of the separatism of Church and state, both Prime Minister Karamanlis[47] and major political parties emphasized the importance of the Church's role in Greek society. Moreover, even the decision of the Highest Administrative Court of Greece (hereafter the Council of State) in favor of separation remained incomplete.[48]

The 1975 Constitution granted suitable rights to the OCG to safeguard society's traditions. The OCG also plays a dynamic role in Greece's international affairs that was strengthened with the country's accession to the European Community in 1981. By the Church Charter of 1977, the Church's independence was guaranteed in the name of democratization. Thus, the state emancipated the Orthodox Church internally while keeping it accountable. However, due to globalization, states were no longer the only masters in their home, and this would weaken Church too because the state was also the protector of the Church. The new actors in internal matters, which could come into conflict the Church as well, were the European Community (later the European Union) and its human rights principles, with the EC starting to blame the Church for violations.[49]

As a part of the accession procedure in 1981, the newly elected Socialist Government (PASOK) initiated reforms and legal amendments. PASOK adopted its election manifesto for an "administrative separation of Church and state" with the pledge nonetheless to preserve the Church's bonds with the nation. In addition, there was pressure from the EU on secularization. However, it would not be as peacefully manifested due to the inextricability of religious culture, ethnicity, morality, identity, and even civil code.[50]

Following EC accession and the spreading effects of globalization, Greece became more of an immigrant society than a source of emigrants. This resulted in a change in the composition of Greek society, in addition to religious minorities recognized in the constitution, such as the Muslims of Thrace, Jews, and the recognized religions of Roman Catholics, Protestants, and Jehovah's Witnesses. By hosting immigrants in the country, the Church's importance in its traditional role of preserving the linkage of Greek national identity with Orthodox Christianity increased in the eyes of the Church hierarchy.[51]

EC membership was a part of the Westernization and modernization of Greece as well as democratization. However, as the evolution of Greek national identity depended upon Eastern Orthodoxy, with modernization, it was the OCG that would simply lose its independence and evolve into a state mechanism. According to the OCG, Western Catholic influence had blinded Greek people and convinced them to apply Western traditions which led them gradually to abandon their own traditions. As the Eastern Orthodox Church is the inspiration of a communal life, unlike Western individuality, supporting the role of the Church that binds people with the state through rituals and public celebrations, became irrelevant. This change in society's expectations and the role of the Church, however, created a contrast in the traditional way of living for Greeks. With modernization, the religious character of the "new" imagined community started to weaken.[52]

The beginning of the 1990s, however, was the dawn of a new phase in Greece as well as around the globe. For the world at large, the collapse of socialism eased multiculturalism and pluralism. This, on the other hand, would challenge the relative homogeneity of Orthodoxy in Greece by allowing Orthodox believers from neighboring, formerly socialist countries, to move to Greece. In addition to high numbers of immigrants already before the 1990s, there were Orthodox immigrants coming from Bulgaria, Romania, Ukraine, and Georgia as well as non-Orthodox immigrants who comprised the majority among total immigrants. Adding the two up, where the OCG was responsible for protecting Orthodoxy as Greek national identity, the Orthodox immigrants created complexity for the equation of Orthodoxy with Greek identity in the society while the non-Orthodox immigrants, already changed the composition of society and altered the nationalistic image of the OCG.[53]

Having in mind that Orthodoxy was a component of Greek nationalism, the alliance with other Orthodox communities or pan-Orthodoxism was observed as a necessary understanding for every Greek citizen. During the War of Yugoslav Succession (1991–1995), the OCG publicly supported Serbia with the purpose of creating a Balkan Orthodox axis. The reason for this religious association can be traced to the times when the two nations lived under Ottoman rule. Without the title of Archbishop of Athens at that time in 1992, Christodoulos had defended this nationalistic and even irredentist alliance against Muslim communities who fought against Orthodox Serbian sisters. He also proposed a united bloc bringing together Greece, Serbia, and Russia to build an "Orthodox-Axis against Islamic fanaticism."[54] Another important issue came up with the dissolution of Yugoslavia. One of socialist Yugoslavia's six constituent republics had borne the official name "the Socialist Republic of Macedonia." When socialist Yugoslavia broke up and socialism was abolished, the erstwhile Socialist Republic of Macedonia thought it could simply drop the word "Socialist" from its name. However, both the Greek state and the Orthodox Church of Greece objected, insisting that the country adopt a new name. The OCG was and still is against the usage of the term "Macedonia," even within the compromise name "Republic of North Macedonia" (agreed in June 2018), because the Greeks lay *exclusive* claim to the Macedonian cultural heritage.[55]

In 1998, nationalism in Greece started to gain traction with the election of charismatic Archbishop Christodoulos as the head of the OCG. This post-1998 era is also known as "new-Orthodoxy" or "Orthodox revival," in which Greek national identity has once more been identified with Orthodoxy. Despite the fact that he was chosen as the spiritual leader of Orthodox Greeks and defender of faith and morality, his popularity was associated in the first place with his being an outspoken guardian of national identity which he claimed was threatened by Islamism, Westernization, globalization, and modernization. He reassumed the traditional position of Orthodox clergyman as a national leader. His belief in Orthodoxy depended on the Church being the indispensable factor in Greeks' national identity. His focus in his speeches was mainly on Greek national consciousness, which had been shaped in part by the trauma of 1204, when Constantinople, the Byzantine capital, fell to the crusaders of the Fourth Crusade, as well as by that of 1453, when this time Constantinople fell to the Ottomans. Recalling the first of these catastrophes, Christodoulos demanded an apology, on behalf of the Greek people and the Orthodox Church of Greece, from the Papacy. In considering the latter context, he always insisted that Turkey had no place in Christian Europe.[56]

INFLUENCE ON POLITICS

We are not interfering in politics, we just care for the nation.[57] —Archbishop Christodoulos

The political engagement of the Church is not of recent vintage. Since the days of the Byzantine Empire, it has had an important political role in the Balkans and therefore acquired the status of the "state approved Church."[58] Its independence from the Ecumenical Patriarch in Istanbul established a type of state Orthodox Church functioning as an irreplaceable supplement to the state's authority and its ideological device.[59] Successive Greek governments thereafter benefited from the Church in order to realize their projects and consolidate their power.[60] After all, it is hard to deny the legitimating power of the "will of God" which is supposedly identified with the Church. It claims to carry a divine legitimation, which, it asserts, places it above positive law and supposedly renders it immune to criticism.[61]

In a broad sense and in conformity with its historical role, the Orthodox Church of Greece has developed both nationalist and conservative discourses and allied itself with right-wing governments.[62] As the government became more nationalist, its practices became even more authoritarian.[63] In 1916, the Church excommunicated and anathematised reform-oriented Prime Minister Eleftherios Venizelos in an act of support for the King. As an institution supporting the nationalists against the communists during the Civil War of 1947–1949, the Church acted in harmony with the "Greece of Christian Greeks" motto of the brutal military Junta that ruled Greece between 1967 and 1974.[64]

However, while the state depends on the OCG as a homogenizing, legitimating, and unifying force, the Church in turn expects patronage and legal and financial protection from the state. Many Archbishops had close relations with the state in order to enhance the Church's interests, such as exemption from taxation or priests' salaries and so forth.[65] Moreover, Orthodox clergy are frequently invited to officiate at military parades, national celebrations, and prisons and during high-level statesmen's inaugurations.[66] However, it is necessary to stress that the political role of the Church is also associated with the political ambitions of the higher clergy.[67]

On Conservatism and Confrontations with State

The question of Greek Church-state relations, and of the future separation of Church and state, is a highly polarized subject in Greece.[68] The main areas of conflicting interest between the Church and the state involve the articles of the Civil Code governing the family, education, freedom of religion, tolerance, cultural pluralism, Church lands and property, the financial affairs related to the Church, democratisation, and secularization. The Church typically believes that these areas should fall within its own jurisdiction or interest area and accuses the state of unjustly intervening in the Church's legitimate sphere of activity.[69]

The 1980s were delicate times for the Greek state to complete its transition to democracy after the end of the Junta regime and the country's accession to the EC. In this respect, political leaders had to seek compromises with the Church, while in the meantime trying to pass reforms aiming, at least to a degree, at achieving the separation of the Church from the state. Even though full separation started to be discussed as early as 1975, no government has pursued this goal to the conclusion. However, there have always been confrontations between Church and State on this matter.

In 1982, with the passage of the law regarding civil marriage, although its real purpose was to replace the religious marriage with a civil one or at least make it a prerequisite to a Church-conducted marriage, the state could achieve civil marriage only as an alternative to a church marriage.[70]

Further reform proposals, which followed in 1985, were met with hostility. The PASOK government claimed that using its funds to cover the Church's expenses was becoming more and more of a burden to the state budget and demanded that, in compensation, the Church cede part of its vast ecclesiastical property to the state. Antonis Tritsis, the Minister of Education and Religious Affairs, introduced a law on the Regulation of the Issue of Church Estate (law 1700/1988) "yielding forest and agricultural estates of monasteries of [the] Church of Greece to [the] public."[71] Following this, the Church took the issue to the Council of State. After the decision was in favor of the government's decision, Archbishop Seraphim threatened the government with declaring publicly that the Church was held under prosecution. After a series of negotiations between the Church and state officials, the law was defeated and as a result of this defeat, Tritsis resigned.[72]

In the meantime, a law permitting abortion up to the 12th week of pregnancy was finally introduced in 1986, although it was not coming on the initiative of women's organizations at that time. Meanwhile, the risks of illegal abortion were high. The Justice Minister pointed out that, even though there had been a legal ban on abortion, abortions had continued "under unsuitable medical conditions," leading to health complications and eventually impacting the country's demographics in a negative way. By law, the costs would be covered by state or private insurance plans. In addition to demographic and health-related problems, illegal abortion has also drained the economy due to the fact that the physicians do not report that they have performed illegal abortions and, therefore, do not pay tax on their abortion-related fees. Speaking from a conservative perspective, the Minister of Justice accused women of citing the ban in order "to blackmail their partners into marriage."[73] The OCG opposed any relaxation of the ban and, together with the support of conservative political parties, managed to postpone the decision for five years. The Orthodox Church equates abortion with murder, in other words a mortal sin. Nonetheless, the OCG has expressed itself as obdurately as the Catholic Church has done. When the OCG lost some support on the issue from conservatives, PASOK was able to pass the law liberalizing restrictions on abortion.[74] The change to the law notwithstanding and in spite of the passage of some years, many clergymen still think abortion is unacceptable. Some still consider it murder while others have started to think that legal abortion is the reason for the decline of Greek morality and more importantly paves the way for a more flexible and tolerant society vis-à-vis other challenging issues such as homosexuality.[75]

After the 1980s, the popularity of the OCG increased thanks to the private efforts of Archbishop Christodoulos. When there were proposals for constitutional revisions aimed at secularization, the position of Christodoulos as a conservative charismatic leader of the Church became prominent. Before the reform packages, he did not pursue antagonistic attitudes toward the state, acknowledging that it would only harm the people of Greece, whose values he was responsible to protect.[76] The dangers he identified were Islamism, alienation due to EU membership, Panturkism, Panslavism, and papal [i.e., Catholic] expansionism.[77]

The reform packages issue started when Foreign Minister George Papandreou appointed an advisory group on religious issues regarding Church-state relations, religious instruction in the schools, and the identification of a person's religious affiliation on ID cards; the listing of religious affiliation on ID cards reminded some people of the Nazi requirement that Jews wear the six-pointed Star of David.[78] Other controversial issues included proselytism, oaths, and the preconditions for the construction of houses of worship. Not all of these points were under the jurisdiction of the foreign minister, according to the Archbishop. However, Papandreou defended his position by referring to the requirements of the EU and the European Court of Human Rights. Trials against Greece or the OCG were internationalizing the issues, and therefore putting these issues under his jurisdiction. Nevertheless, the OCG kept up its objections and parliament decided not to proceed with the separation of Church and state. As it was, it seemed like the Archbishop won, but there were still some reforms to be made. In the schools, pupils could be exempted from compulsory religious instruction only if they or their families made an official request, declaring difference in faith. In addition, the Council of State ruled that any reduction in the hours of religious instruction would be unconstitutional. On the issue of construction of religious buildings, with the exception of Thrace,[79] local communities could gather signatures in support of a request to build a new religious facility. Meanwhile, the OCG always reserves the authority to decide on the construction of Orthodox buildings without interference from civil authorities. The issue of cremation in Greece, on the other hand, is another symbol of intolerance vis-à-vis other religions. It was prohibited by law. However, as some people wanted to be cremated and the OCG strongly opposed, Greek officials had to find a solution. In the end, it became possible for non-Orthodox to be cremated if it was carried out outside Greece. Bringing the remains back to Greece, though, could be possible only on the condition that it was proved that the dead person was a non-Orthodox.[80]

There were public confrontations of Church and state on some of the aforementioned and other reforms. The first was the desire of Muslims to construct a mosque in Athens. In the neighborhood of Athens, there were 120,000 Muslims who demanded the right to construct a mosque. However, the local bishop responded by calling on people to struggle against the "…establishment of foreign, dangerous and heretic elements" in their region. Bishop Epifanios emphasized that, in his view, the Greek Orthodox people were not ready to see minarets in their Orthodox state's capital, while Foreign Minister Papandreou admitted that Athens was the sole European capital lacking an operational mosque.[81] In the meantime, the Church had found a more valid excuse to oppose the construction of a mosque. The OCG and local bishops were against the location of the mosque, which was supposed to be built next to the Athens Airport. The OCG claimed that constructing it there would cause direct harm to Orthodoxy and irrationally contended that foreigners arriving at the airport and seeing a mosque might think that Greece was a Muslim country. Even the thought of this possibility was a way to "hurt Greeks' religious feelings."[82]

The second issue which stirred up controversy between the OCG and the state concerned the state identity cards. In April 2000, Prime Minister Costas Simitis appointed a non-parliamentarian, Michalis Stathopoulos, to head the Ministry of Justice. His reform ideas started with the abolition of the religious oath in court, followed by an option for secular funerals, and lastly the exclusion of religion from the identity cards. This was "naturally" unacceptable for the OCG even though the inclusion of religion on identity cards was in fact inherited from the times of Nazi occupation, in order to distinguish the Jews from non-Jews. Moreover, since 1993, Greece was already convicted by the European Court of Human Rights of discrimination against religious minorities because, although Article 13 of the Constitution already accepted religious equality before law, the law was applied in an unequal way, favoring the Orthodox.[83]

The issue became a crisis when the Hellenic Data Protection Authority convened and unanimously decided on the exclusion of religion together with other sensitive personal data, such as occupation, age, and sex which could lead to discrimination. After parliament announced that it would implement the decision, Christodoulos declared that this could not be merely an administrative decision because ID was the proof of one's selfhood which should not be differentiated from Greece's religious identity as Orthodox. It was an understandable reaction, considering that the OCG embraces the logic of ethnic nationalism and equates Greekness with being Orthodox.[84] This step was characterized by the Archbishop as a "coup d'état." He made public speeches declaring that "laws are not unchangeable" and asserting that "when the People do not want a law, it is not applied." He also initiated an attack on the liberal democratic foundation of the state. He also launched a signature campaign together with mass rallies in Thessaloniki and Athens. Through his appearances on mass media, his speeches had significant political impact.[85]

Although approximately 3 million signatures were collected against what was understood as the exclusion of religion, there was a legal fact which could not be undermined: Any referendum for change or opposition to the legal package could be decided only by parliament, according to the Constitution of Greece, and the OCG's petition was not legally sufficient.[86] As the Constitutional Court rejected the appeal, the President of Greece, Constantine Stephanopolous, held a meeting with the Archbishop and the Holy Synod, which ended with a declaration that the conditions for a referendum had not been met.[87] However, there were also some gains made by the OCG after this crisis. For instance, with law 2873/2000, the tax-free limit of donations to the Church was increased to €3000 from €300. Moreover, in 2004, right before the parliamentary elections, the agreement about the obligation of the Church to contribute 35% of its revenues to the state budget toward coverage of a part of the clergy's salaries paid by the state was abolished.[88]

On Other Religious Faiths and Entities

The Church is not ready to surrender its own rights in the name of the human rights of any other people. We don't care who likes us, We are Greek Orthodox Christians.[89] —Archbishop Christodoulos

Article 9 of the European Convention for the Protection of Human Rights and Fundamental Freedoms (1950) guarantees that freedom of religion is a basic human right and a fundamental freedom. All EU and Council of Europe member-states are signatories. Moreover, the protection of minority rights is also a fundamental component of democratic pluralistic societies.[90] However, Greece has clearly lower standards in religious freedoms, compared with other Western democracies.[91] There are a series of discriminatory and biased legal and administrative practices related to the rights of religious groups.[92] As a result of the sequential waves of mostly Muslim immigration in the last 20 years, the issues of religious minorities, freedom of religion, and implementation of human rights have become even more challenging for Greece.[93] The 9/11 attacks by radical Islamist terrorists on New York's Twin Towers and on the Pentagon, and ensuing radical Islamist terrorist attacks, have stirred Europe-wide concerns; but Greece has reacted even more strongly than most other European states. Indeed, there has been a climate of fear in Greece, both because some Greeks recall the centuries of Ottoman occupation and because of Greece's geographic position, making it relatively accessible for illegal immigrants. Right- and extreme right-wing circles have exploited the opportunity to stir fear of Islamic terrorism to their advantage.[94] Unfortunately, it is not easy to address the status of Muslims in Greece simply in terms of religious freedom, since most of the Muslim citizens are Turks who live close to the border with Turkey. For many Greeks, Turks and Turkey are the most dangerous enemies that constitute a permanent threat to Greece's sovereignty. Therefore, it is also a matter of foreign policy and indeed national security.[95] This irrational historical approach is inescapably reflected also in the state's policies toward its Muslim population particularly.[96]

Issues of religious freedom are interconnected with the Orthodox Church's anti-Western critique as well. The Church's criticism has specifically been expressed in regard to the European Union, since it has been considered a Western product, which serves Western objectives while discounting Orthodox sensitivities.[97] For instance, Archbishop Christodoulos (1939–2008) saw the West as "heretical" and as an "existential enemy" of Greek society.[98] In this context naturally, the state has opposed the Orthodox Church of Greece by introducing the necessary EU reforms on human rights. For Payne, "this conflict can be understood as a conflict between the Orthodox understanding of the identity of the human person deriving from the collective and the western liberal understanding of the human person as an autonomous individual."[99] He defends the view that, rather than individual human rights, group rights should come to the fore in Orthodox political culture and here, the group involves only Orthodox.[100]

From another perspective, the fact that Greece has one "prevailing religion" recognized by the constitution is highly controversial in terms of religious freedom and tolerance. It is often discussed whether having a recognized state religion leads to religious discrimination against others or does not represent an obstacle to religious tolerance. One position emphasizes that state religion would eventually create religious intolerance or even compulsory conversions.[101] Special Rapporteur of Sub-commission on Prevention of Discrimination and on the Protection of Minorities, Odio Benito underlines that, when there is an official state religion, the policies of the state might be affected or proceed in the same line with that religion, so that it could involve some violation of religious freedom.[102] Another position, on the other hand, supports the idea that the presence of an official state religion is not decisive by itself as the local culture is more determinant. Moreover, as long as the institutions of state religion do not act as a state agency, it is possible to maintain a high level of religious tolerance.[103] However, considering the fact that Greece is ranked first in the European Court of Human Rights for violations of religious freedoms, it is necessary to look at the OCG's attitude toward other religions. Although religious freedom is constitutionally guaranteed in Article 13, declaring Orthodox Christianity the prevailing religion in Article 3 makes it look like Orthodoxy is the sole truly free religion in the country. However, it should be noted that there are three officially recognized faiths of legal persons in public law: Orthodoxy, Islam, and Judaism. The Roman Catholic Church, the Jehovah's Witnesses, and Protestant Churches are considered to be "legal persons in private law."[104]

As the Archbishop started to face the realities of globalization and Westernization, his attitudes toward other religious institutions moderated. Since the biggest rival of the OCG in representing Orthodoxy in the international arena, the Patriarchate in İstanbul, had already opened offices in Brussels, Christodoulos decided to give up his efforts to prevent a planned papal visit and, in May 2001,[105] Pope John Paul II finally came to Athens. Moreover, despite some opposition from the Church, the Archbishop reciprocated the Pope's visit by visiting Rome, in order to show the OCG's readiness to represent the Greek nation in "inter-faith dialogue." Instead of fighting and alienating it, the OCG claimed to undertake the role of building a common European home.[106] Eventually, after opening a permanent representation office in Brussels, the OCG finally started to act as an independent actor, within the scope of European integration, with the purpose of restoring an emphasis on the Christian roots of Europe.[107]

ON INTOLERANCE AND CONTEMPORARY CHALLENGES

Apart from ID crisis, the OCG started to lose power in general terms with changes in "hot issues" such as the "prohibition of catechism, [the] public operation of mosques and denominational churches, [the] issue of cremation and the issue of burial rites and baptism for individuals who have chosen to have a civil wedding ceremony instead of a religious ceremony."[108] Additionally, as the OCG has weakened against the state and in terms of churchgoers, it has faced more challenges.

In 2005, some bishops, priests, and high-ranking clergymen were caught in criminal acts, revealing a decline in the Church's morality. Although being under oaths of chastity, an aged bishop and some bishops were caught initially in sexual relations with women and later in homosexual relationships. Considering the OCG's declaration of homosexuality as an "abomination" and "sin," the tapes were evidence that these clergymen had violated the Church's own ethical code. As if that was not bad enough, there were priests and even senior clerics arrested on drug dealing charges or linked in trial-fixing scandals and bribing judges. Furthermore, it was revealed that an archbishop had helped Apostolos Vasilis, who was arrested on drug smuggling, to elect a cleric to the post of patriarch of Jerusalem in 2001 and even Archbishop Christodoulos himself was on the list of suspects of drug smuggling. With these revelations coming out one after another, Archbishop Christodoulos made public apologies by guaranteeing the suspension of these clerics and the trial of criminals.[109]

After the crisis and the compulsory change of Archbishop, due to the death of Christodoulos, the relationship between the state, the OCG, and society softened. The new archbishop, Hieronymos II, adopted a "controlled compromise" strategy which earned him the sobriquet "sacred cow" among conservatives. Yet his purpose was to make the OCG more spiritual and less politicized. However, while he tried to bring the OCG closer to the Orthodox tradition of "humility and love," he also had to face some challenges.[110]

The first challenge he chose to address involved the Republic of Macedonia, as Greece's northern neighbor was still calling itself.

The OCG called this the "Skopje issue." As the OCG claims to protect the national identity and territorial integrity, it does not accept the use of "Macedonia" by a bordering country, which can lead to irredentist ambitions in the future. The Church therefore organized mass rallies against the Greek state because its leading clerics had not been consulted on the issue. Although in June 2018 the governments of Athens and Skopje agreed that the erstwhile Republic of Macedonia might call itself North Macedonia, with this agreement even ratified in the respective parliaments in early 2019, the OCG denounced the agreement as a betrayal of Orthodoxy. On the other hand, although the Church in now-North Macedonia gave up on "Macedonia" in order to be recognized, it has applied to the Ecumenical Patriarchate for recognition under the name "Archbishopric of Ohrid." Nonetheless, the Ecumenical Patriarch denied its application by forwarding it to the Serbian Orthodox Church from which the Church in what is now-North Macedonia had originally declared its autocephalous status.[111]

With the economic crisis starting in 2008 and subsequent austerity measures, the Holy Synod declared the creditors from EU and IMF foreign occupiers who should not be allowed to collect the debts owed to them. As a part of austerity measures, in 2010, Socialist Prime Minister George Papandreou wanted to tax the OCG and the issue on Church's ownership of property was brought to the agenda. Archbishop Hieronymos declared that, since 1821, the Church had lost many assets and was left with only 4% of its original properties; indeed, the state had already confiscated much of its property. Although the Church is known to be the second-largest landowner in Greece, after the state, the Holy Synod defended itself as having mostly forests. Explanations by the OCG closed the issue and, with support from conservative parties, the issue was resolved with the grant of an exemption to the Church from the austerity measures.[112]

Recovering from this challenge, the OCG, with its new moderate Archbishop Hieronymos II, decided to shed its image as a financial burden on the state. He disbanded NGO "Solidarity" which was caught in fraud scandals and established a "mission" for the rehabilitation of drug addicts, and care for homeless people and the elderly. Hieronymos II and the Ecumenical Patriarch, together, authorized the provision of charity meals for the needy, declaring that their obligation was to help the people who could not feed themselves, comprised mostly of Muslim immigrants. Meanwhile, the OCG criticized itself as well as politicians and admitted the Church's mistakes intervening in political matters and neglecting its original responsibility to lead people along the way of God, instead of leaving them to become mere consumers of products.[113]

Other than economic problems, the OCG had to deal with more state reforms. In spite of the opposition of the Orthodox Church, a cohabitation law, establishing civil partnership of same-sex couples, was adopted in 2015. In the course of protests on the part of clergy, Bishop Ambrosios, Metropolitan of Kalavryta and Aigialeia, posted a comment on his personal blog, emphasizing that politicians should have acted responsibly for their voters who had chosen them to "take the helm of the country." He condemned the politicians supporting the law and declared homosexuality a "diversion from the Laws of Nature" and "a social felony," excoriating homosexuals as "scums of society." He warned society not to approach or listen to them and even advised heterosexuals to "spit on them."[114] When the law passed anyway, the bishop declared two days of mourning, while a bishop at the Ecumenical Patriarchate supported him and pointed out that there were no gay marriages in any of the religions having only one Holy Book. On the other hand, he acknowledged that the law aimed to provide social security.[115]

Afterward, Greek Minister of Education Konstantinos Gavroglou changed the curriculum in order to prevent sexual prejudice, homophobia, and transphobia from being disseminated among youth, with instructions about "sexuality in adolescence." For the Church, this was to "distort [the] natural state of children" and "promote debauchery and perversion."[116] The bishop's concerns notwithstanding, the government passed a bill "On the Free Change of Sex" which provoked outrage in conservative sectors of society and the OCG alike. It let any 15 years old and older legally change his or her gender upon a written notification to the authorities, without the requirement of approval from family or medical experts. The Church declared that "sex is a sacred gift… gender is neither freely chosen nor altered at will," and said that all liberalization in matters of sexuality would bring the end of faith and of the spiritual integrity of Greeks. The OCG also feared that, at some point in the future, gay/lesbian couples might be granted permission to adopt children.[117]

Moreover, morning prayer in schools was canceled in 2016.[118] On October 2018, Greece's declared atheist prime minister Alexis Tsipras agreed in principle with Hieronymos II to end the government's salaries for 10,000 clergymen. In this way, the clergy of the OCG would no longer be civil servants and their salaries and pensions would be paid from a joint fund of €175 million, generated from the Church's properties. As clerics felt threatened and betrayed, they started to march and after a series of talks between the Archbishop and the government, it was agreed that clergymen would remain on the civil service payroll after all.[119] Furthermore, the Syriza government's attempt to revise the constitution by removing the clause on the country's "prevailing religion" (in Article 3) passed with the necessary vote of 151 in the second vote, if not at first. However, the final decision is left to the next parliament to be elected in October 2019. The OCG strongly opposes this measure, calling it a red line and, in this, was supported by the Ecumenical Patriarchate.[120]

Conclusion

As a historical institution which protected Hellenism for centuries and played a leading role in the nation-building process of Greece since the 1830s, the Orthodox Church of Greece has a deep, incontestable, and irreplaceable place in Greek identity, collective memory, culture and politics. However, even though it was subordinated to the state and has been used as a legitimizing mechanism for Greek governments, it would definitely be a misevaluation to see its role as simply a state puppet. Instead, Orthodoxy promotes a way of living for Greeks, and the Orthodox Church has been influential not only in the daily practices of the Greek people or in low politics but also in important national security and foreign policy matters. In the nineteenth century and early twentieth century, the Church was the leading actor that brought independence but later also catastrophe to the Greek nation due to its support for the Megali Idea of reviving the Byzantine Empire. Today, the Church can still be strongly influential in the Greek government's policies on Turkish/Muslim minority rights, the Cyprus Issue, relations with Turkey, the EU, the Vatican, (North) Macedonia, and so on. For many, charismatic ex-Archbishop Christodoulos had almost undertaken the role of an ethnarch. Furthermore, it was not only the high-ranking clergy who were influential or consequential in politics. For instance the priest of Kilimli/Kalymnos Island was among the protagonists who escalated the dangerous crisis with Turkey over the Kardak/Imia Islets, which brought the two states to the brink of war.[121]

The OCG believes that political issues, like much else, are related to religion, and therefore need the Church's guidance. In Olimpia Dragouni's words, maintaining a belief that it possesses God's authority to speak categorically, the Church delivers "divine" messages to a lesser extent than political ones.[122] However, for Christodoulos, this could not count as interfering in politics but rather as caring for the nation. Thus, the Church feels justified about reacting to or influencing political decisions of the government. In some cases, the OCG was able to dissuade the government as it was the case in the partial expropriation of the Church's properties which caused the responsible minister to resign in reaction to the government's retreat. In some other cases, like the law on compulsory civil marriage or on abortion, the OCG was able to partially change or postpone the government's decisions. On the other hand, there are also cases such as the cohabitation law and the law on gender change, in which the OCG's protests were not able to alter the result. The Church was defeated also in the identity cards issue; however, by being able to organize one of the biggest protests in Greek history against the government's decision, it proved its mobilization power.

Regarding religious and sexual tolerance, the OCG can be labeled neither completely intolerant nor tolerant of the other faiths in Greece. Since the OCG equates Greekness with Orthodoxy, it evaluates any improvement in the rights of other faiths' as a threat to national identity. After 9/11 and following religiously motivated terrorist attacks in Europe, the OCG has become firmer in its stance against granting Muslims more rights. Nonetheless, Roman Catholics, Protestants, and Jehovah's Witnesses and Jews are not given the rights they demanded as well. Homophobia, on the other hand, is openly manifested by the OCG's clergy. The Church sees homosexuality as a disease and a threat to society. In this regard, the clergy do not respect homosexuals and try to prevent the government from granting the rights gays and lesbians demand, like cohabitation and same-sex marriage. Unsurprisingly, the Church denounces the Gay Pride Parades in Greece and calls on Greek people not to attend them. On the other hand, the clergy is always represented in the protests against LGBTQ rights.

With the enthronement of moderate Archbishop Hieronymos II in 2008, the OCG admitted its mistakes, such as dealing too much with politics, and focused more on religious matters. Particularly since the 2009 economic crisis, the OCG has leaned more on its charity responsibility and has fed needy people, who are mostly Muslim immigrants.

Moreover, the OCG tried to lead people along God's path in order to alleviate the deterioration of the economic crisis as it defended its view that the crisis stemmed from caring only for earthly matters rather than for the ethereal life.

There is no reason to believe that the disagreement between the part of the society that sees the Church as the sole protector of Hellenism against Western or Eastern challengers and the other part that sees it as the source of backward and intolerant traditions which prevents Greece from Europeanizing will end in the near future. Due to the Church's objections, stemming from concerns about the nation's losing its distinct Greek identity which was constructed across the centuries, Greece still has difficulties in adopting and enforcing laws that are fundamental for the protection of human rights and freedoms, as expected from a respectable EU member. The Church will likely continue to counter the effects of the "Westernization" of Greece and globalization by appealing to nationalism and intervening in Greek political affairs. However, despite the conflict of civilization arguments, the Church's perpetual objections to EU reforms and the Helleno-Orthodox identity of Greece, there is no doubt in Europeans' minds as to where to position Greece anymore. Even though Greek-EU relations have had their ups and downs, Greece has been recognized as an equal member of this Western organization with high symbolic value. Furthermore, from 2004 onward, Greece is not the sole Orthodox country in the EU and other Orthodox sister Balkan states—Serbia, North Macedonia, and Montenegro—are in the queue. The Church is definitely aware that being a EU member strengthens the country's position vis-à-vis its historical and religious foe, Turkey. However, in addition to benefiting from the advantages, the Church should also come to terms with the responsibilities of being a respectable civilized European family member and should ease its reservations about the rights of other believers of different faiths and sexual minorities.

In the current situation, although still holding onto nationalism and conservatism and neglecting basic human rights such as religious freedom and sexual tolerance, the Orthodox Church of Greece is in a position that is becoming less effective in the decision-making process compared to its past. By turning more to its religious and spiritual responsibilities, the Orthodox Church of Greece can act more in compliance with its spiritual *raison d'être* and cope better with the challenges of the contemporary globalized world.

Notes

1. John Meyendorff, *Orthodox Church: Its Past and Its Role in the World Today*, 3 Rev. Sub edition (Crestwood, NY: St. Vladimir's Seminary Press, 1981), p. 155.
2. Olimpia Dragouni, "The Macedonian Dispute in the Activity of the Metropolitan of Thessalonica Anthimos," *Poznańskie Studia Slawistyczne*, No. 10 (4 June 2016), p. 73, https://doi.org/10.14746/pss.2016.10.5.
3. Even after 34 years of EU membership, in 2015, less than half (44%) of the Greeks declared that they felt European. In 2018 Eurobarometer results, the proportion of Greeks who feel like citizens of EU is 52%, which puts them second to last, even behind of UK which decided for Brexit. Eurobarometer, "Eurobarometer 40 Years: EU Citizenship" (European Commission, Spring 2015), at http://ec.europa.eu/commfrontoffice/publicopinion/topics/fs5_citizen_40_en.pdf; Eurobarometer, "Standard Eurobarometer 90: Public Opinion in the European Union" (European Commission, Autumn 2018), p. 33, at http://ec.europa.eu/commfrontoffice/publicopinion/index.cfm/ResultDoc/download/DocumentKy/84930 [last accessed 8 May 2019].
4. Gerasimos Makris and Vasilios Meichanetsidis, "The Church of Greece in Critical Times: Reflections Through Philanthropy," in *Journal of Contemporary Religion*, Vol. 33, No. 2 (May 2018), p. 248, https://doi.org/10.1080/13537903.2018.1469265.
5. Tassos Anastassiadis, "An Intriguing True–False Paradox: The Entanglement of Modernization and Intolerance in the Orthodox Church of Greece," in Vasilios N. Makrides and Victor Roudometof (eds.), *The Orthodox Church of Greece in the 21st Century* (London: Ashgate, 2010), p. 42.
6. Evangelos Karagiannis, "Secularism in Context: The Relations Between the Greek State and the Church of Greece in Crisis," in *European Journal of Sociology*, Vol. 50, No. 1 (April 2009), pp. 133–134, https://doi.org/10.1017/S0003975609000447.
7. Nikos Kokosalakis, "The Political Significance of Popular Religion in Greece," in *Archives de Sciences Sociales des Religions*, Vol. 64, No. 1 (1987), p. 41.
8. Anastassiadis, "An Intriguing True–False Paradox" [note 5], p. 117.
9. D. Oulis, G. Makris, and S. Roussos, "The Orthodox Church of Greece: Policies and Challenges Under Archbishop Christodoulos of Athens (1998–2008)," in *International Journal for the Study of the Christian Church*, Vol. 10, No. 2–3 (1 May 2010), p. 199, https://doi.org/10.1080/1474225X.2010.490123.

10. Lina Molokotos-Liederman, "The Religious Factor in the Construction of Europe: Greece, Orthodoxy and the European Union (Work in Progress)," n.d., p. 1, at http://www.lse.ac.uk/europeanInstitute/research/hellenicObservatory/pdf/1st_Symposium/Molokotos.pdf [last accessed 15 April 2019].
11. Chrysoloras, "Why Orthodoxy?" pp. 3–4.
12. Anastassiadis, "An Intriguing True–False Paradox" [note 5], p. 40; Anastassios Anastassiadis, "Religion and Politics in Greece: The Greek Church's 'Conservative Modernization' in the 1990s," SSRN Scholarly Paper (Rochester, NY: Social Science Research Network, 1 January 2004), p. 4, https://papers.ssrn.com/abstract=2290895.
13. Benedict Anderson, *Imagined Communities: Reflections on the Origin and Spread of Nationalism* (Brooklyn, NY: Verso, 1991), pp. 5–6.
14. Alexandros Sakellariou, "Anti-Islamic Public Discourse in Contemporary Greece: The Reproduction of Religious Panic," in Arolda Elbasani and Olivier Roy (eds.), *The Revival of Islam in the Balkans: From Identity to Religiosity*, The Islam and Nationalism Series (Basingstoke: Palgrave Macmillan, 2015), p. 513, https://doi.org/10.1057/9781137517845_3.
15. Anna Koumandaraki, "The Evolution of Greek National Identity," in *Studies in Ethnicity and Nationalism*, Vol. 2, No. 2 (September 2002), pp. 39–53, https://doi.org/10.1111/j.1754-9469.2002.tb00026.x.
16. Molokotos-Liederman, "The Religious Factor in the Construction of Europe: Greece, Orthodoxy and the European Union (Work in Progress)," pp. 2–3.
17. Chrysoloras, "Why Orthodoxy?" p. 5.
18. Molokotos-Liederman, "The Religious Factor in the Construction of Europe: Greece, Orthodoxy and the European Union (Work in Progress)," pp. 3–4.
19. Anthony D. Smith, *The Cultural Foundations of Nations: Hierarchy, Covenant, and Republic*, 1st edition (Malden, MA: Wiley-Blackwell, 2008), p. 163.
20. Chrysoloras, "Why Orthodoxy?" p. 5.
21. Ibid., p. 28.
22. Sakellariou, "Anti-Islamic Public Discourse in Contemporary Greece," pp. 513–514; Konstantinos Papastathis, "Religious Discourse and Radical Right Politics in Contemporary Greece, 2010–2014," in *Politics, Religion & Ideology*, Vol. 16, No. 2–3 (April 2015), pp. 226–227, https://doi.org/10.1080/21567689.2015.1077705.
23. Oulis, Makris, and Roussos, "The Orthodox Church of Greece" [note 9], p. 199.

24. Due to the evolving needs and the difficulties of the ongoing Greek independence war and in order to adapt the new conditions, three constitutions were adopted within the space of just 5 years.
25. Chrysoloras, "Why Orthodoxy?" p. 2.
26. Ibid., p. 1.
27. Elisabeth A. Diamantopoulou, "Religious Freedom in the Light of the Relationship Between the Orthodox Church and the Nation in Contemporary Greece," in *International Journal for the Study of the Christian Church*, Vol. 12, No. 2 (1 May 2012), p. 2, https://doi.org/10.1080/1474225X.2012.699425.
28. Münir Yıldırım, *Yunanistan ve Ortodoks Kilisesi* (Aziz Andaç Yayınları, 2005), p. 71.
29. Teuvo Laitila, "New Voices in Greek Orthodox Thought: Untying the Bond Between Nation and Religion," in *Journal of Contemporary Religion*, Vol. 30, No. 3 (September 2015), p. 529, https://doi.org/10.1080/13537903.2015.1081482.
30. Daniel P. Payne, "The Clash of Civilisations: The Church of Greece, the European Union and the Question of Human Rights," in *Religion, State and Society*, Vol. 31, No. 3 (2003), p. 265.
31. Makris and Bekridadis defend that this argument can be criticized especially because of its underlying claim "concerning an alleged continuous presence of Hellenism through long centuries of pre-nationalist, pre and early modern history." Gerasimos Makris and Dimitris Bekridakis, "The Greek Orthodox Church and the Economic Crisis Since 2009," in *International Journal for the Study of the Christian Church*, Vol. 13, No. 2 (May 2013), p. 111, https://doi.org/10.1080/1474225X.2013.793055.
32. Oulis, Makris, and Roussos, "The Orthodox Church of Greece" [note 9], p. 200.
33. Nikolaos Chrysoloras, "Religion and National Identity in the Greek and Greek-Cypriot Political Cultures" (London School of Economics and Political Science, 2010), p. 24, http://etheses.lse.ac.uk/3026/.
34. Oulis, Makris, and Roussos, "The Orthodox Church of Greece" [note 9], p. 193.
35. Molokotos-Liederman, "The Religious Factor in the Construction of Europe: Greece, Orthodoxy and the European Union (Work in Progress)," p. 4.
36. George Mavrogordatos, "Orthodoxy and Nationalism in the Greek Case," in *West European Politics*, Vol. 26, No. 1 (January 2003), p. 121, https://doi.org/10.1080/01402380412331300227.
37. Koumandaraki, "The Evolution of Greek National Identity," p. 49.

38. Nikos Alivizatos, "A New Role for the Greek Church?" in *Journal of Modern Greek Studies*, Vol. 17, No. 1 (January 1999), p. 34; Yannis Stavrakakis, "Religion and Populism: Reflections on the 'Politicised' Discourse of the Greek Church," Ph.D. dissertation (London School of Economics & Political Science, 2002), p. 8.
39. Oulis, Makris, and Roussos, "The Orthodox Church of Greece" [note 9], p. 195; Koumandaraki, "The Evolution of Greek National Identity," p. 48.
40. Kokosalakis, "The Political Significance of Popular Religion in Greece," pp. 44–45; Theodore A. Couloumbis, "The Greek Junta Phenomenon," in *Polity*, Vol. 6, No. 3 (1974), pp. 352–356, https://doi.org/10.2307/3233933.
41. Makris and Bekridakis, "The Greek Orthodox Church and the Economic Crisis Since 2009," p. 113; Oulis, Makris, and Roussos, "The Orthodox Church of Greece" [note 9]; and Stavrakakis, "Religion and Populism" [note 38], p. 8.
42. Effie Fokas, "A New Role for the Church? Reassessing the Place of Religion in the Greek Public Sphere," in *SSRN Electronic Journal* (2008), p. 12, https://doi.org/10.2139/ssrn.3256769.
43. George Th. Mavrogordatos, "Church-State Relations in the Greek Orthodox Case," *Church and State in Europe* (ECPR Workshop, Copenhagen, 2000), pp. 8–9.
44. VIIIth Revisionary Parliament of Greece, "The Constitution of Greece" (2008) Art. 3.
45. Ibid., Art. 13 & 14; "Greece," *End Blasphemy Laws*, https://end-blasphemy-laws.org/countries/europe/greece/ [last accessed 7 May 2019]; "International Religious Freedom Report for 2017" (United States Department of State, Bureau of Democracy, Human Rights and Labor, 2017), p. 1, https://www.state.gov/documents/organization/281156.pdf [last accessed 8 May 2019].
46. K. N. Kyriazopoulos, "The 'Prevailing Religion' in Greece: Its Meaning and Implications," in *Journal of Church and State*, Vol. 43, No. 3 (1 June 2001), p. 525, https://doi.org/10.1093/jcs/43.3.511; Fokas, "A New Role for the Church?" pp. 13–14; Constantine P. Danopoulos, "Religion, Civil Society, and Democracy in Orthodox Greece," in *Journal of Southern Europe and the Balkans*, Vol. 6, No. 1 (2004), p. 43, https://doi.org/10.1080/1461319042000187256; and Makris and Bekridakis, "The Greek Orthodox Church and the Economic Crisis Since 2009," p. 113.
47. PM Karamanlis gave a speech saying: "…. concepts of Hellenism and Orthodoxy are inseparable in consciousness of nation." Kokosalakis, "The Political Significance of Popular Religion in Greece," p. 45.

48. Kyriazopoulos, "The 'Prevailing Religion' in Greece," p. 532; Stavrakakis, "Religion and Populism" [note 38], p. 24; and Kokosalakis, "The Political Significance of Popular Religion in Greece," p. 45.
49. Karagiannis, "Secularism in Context" [note 6], p. 159.
50. Kokosalakis, "The Political Significance of Popular Religion in Greece," p. 45.
51. Karagiannis, "Secularism in Context" [note 6], p. 159; Lina Molokotos-Liederman, "Looking at Religion and Greek Identity from the Outside: The Identity Cards Conflict Through the Eyes of Greek Minorities," in *Religion, State and Society*, Vol. 35, No. 2 (June 2007), pp. 140–141, https://doi.org/10.1080/09637490701271145.
52. Koumandaraki, "The Evolution of Greek National Identity," pp. 48–50.
53. Lina Molokotos-Liederman, "Looking at Religion and Greek Identity from the Outside: The Identity Cards Conflict Through the Eyes of Greek Minorities," in *Religion, State and Society*, Vol. 35, No. 2 (June 2007), p. 141, https://doi.org/10.1080/09637490701271145; Evangelos Karagiannis, "Secularism in Context: The Relations Between the Greek State and the Church of Greece in Crisis," in *European Journal of Sociology*, Vol. 50, No. 1 (April 2009), p. 136, https://doi.org/10.1017/S0003975609000447.
54. Oulis, Makris, and Roussos, "The Orthodox Church of Greece" [note 9], *passim*; Victor Roudometof, "Eastern Orthodox Christianity and the Uses of the Past in Contemporary Greece," in *Religions*, Vol. 2, No. 2 (May 2011), p. 106, https://doi.org/10.3390/rel2020095.
55. Roudometof, "Eastern Orthodox Christianity and the Uses of the Past," p. 106.
56. Mavrogordatos, "Church-State Relations in the Greek Orthodox Case," pp. 10–14.
57. Oulis, Makris, and Roussos, "The Orthodox Church of Greece" [note 9], p. 201.
58. Chrysoloras, "Religion and National Identity in the Greek and Greek-Cypriot Political Cultures," p. 4.
59. Sotiris Mitralexis, "The Liberation of Church from State in Greece, and the Administrative Fragmentation of Ecclesial Jurisdictions," in Magdaleny Małeckiej-Kuzak (ed.), *Ex Oriente Lux: Relacje Wschodu i Zachodu Na Przestrzeni Wieków* (Cracow: Ignatianum Academy Press, 2007), p. 164.
60. Oulis, Makris, and Roussos, "The Orthodox Church of Greece" [note 9], p. 192.
61. Chrysoloras, "Religion and National Identity in the Greek and Greek-Cypriot Political Cultures," p. 5.
62. Ibid., 9.

63. Koumandaraki, "The Evolution of Greek National Identity," p. 48.
64. Stavrakakis, "Politics and Religion" [note 2], p. 166.
65. Makris and Bekridakis, "The Greek Orthodox Church and the Economic Crisis Since 2009," pp. 111–112.
66. Molokotos-Liederman, "The Religious Factor in the Construction of Europe: Greece, Orthodoxy and the European Union (Work in Progress)," p. 5.
67. Oulis, Makris, and Roussos, "The Orthodox Church of Greece" [note 9], p. 194.
68. Mitralexis, "The Liberation of Church from State in Greece, and the Administrative Fragmentation of Ecclesial Jurisdictions," p. 159.
69. Hercules Moskoff, "Church, State, and Political Culture in Greece Since 1974: Secularisation, Democratisation, Westernisation," PhD thesis (London School of Economics and Political Science, 2005), p. 70, http://etheses.lse.ac.uk/1769/.
70. Kokosalakis, "The Political Significance of Popular Religion in Greece," p. 38; Mavrogordatos, "Orthodoxy and Nationalism in the Greek Case," p. 121; and Stavrakakis, "Religion and Populism" [note 38], p. 10.
71. "Regulation of Church Estate," Pub. L. No. 1700/1988 (1988).
72. Fokas, "A New Role for the Church?" pp. 19–20; Makris and Bekridakis, "The Greek Orthodox Church and the Economic Crisis Since 2009," p. 113.
73. Paul Anastasi, "Greece Legalizes Abortion," *The New York Times*, 27 January 1984, at https://www.nytimes.com/1984/01/27/style/greece-legalizes-abortion.html [last accessed 2 May 2019].
74. Eugenia Georges, "Abortion Policy and Practice in Greece," in *Social Science & Medicine*, Vol. 42, No. 4 (February 1996), pp. 511, 516, https://doi.org/10.1016/0277-9536(95)00174-3; Kokosalakis, "The Political Significance of Popular Religion in Greece," p. 45.
75. Mark Fr. Hodges, "Greek Clergy: State-Supported Abortion Is 'Destroying' Our Nation," *LifeSiteNews*, 3 January 2018, https://www.lifesitenews.com/news/greek-clergy-state-supported-abortion-is-destroying-our-nation [last accessed 8 May 2019].
76. Stavrakakis, "Religion and Populism" [note 38], p. 32.
77. Ibid., pp. 30–34.
78. Ibid., p. 8.
79. The status in Thrace was agreed on the Lausanne Treaty with Turkey in 1923. The Muslims in Thrace are constitutionally recognized Muslim minority. The state appointed muftis in Thrace, has jurisdiction only in their area and Muslim cemeteries can only operate in Thrace. Molokotos-Liederman, "Looking at Religion and Greek Identity from the Outside," p. 143; Mavrogordatos, "Orthodoxy and Nationalism

in the Greek Case," pp. 121, 129; although there are ECHR decisions over the rights of Muslims to elect their muftis, Greek state violates their rights and appoints its preferred muftis. Charalambos K. Papastathis, "Greece: A Faithful Orthodox Christian State," in J. Martinez-Torron and W. C. Durham, Jr. (eds.), *Religion and the Secular State: Interim National Reports Issued for the Occasion of the XVIIIth International Congress of Comparative Law* (Provo, UT: Brigham Young University Press, 2010), p. 370.
80. Mavrogordatos, "Church-State Relations in the Greek Orthodox Case," p. 7; Mavrogordatos, "Orthodoxy and Nationalism in the Greek Case," p. 121; and Danopoulos, "Religion, Civil Society, and Democracy in Orthodox Greece," p. 46.
81. Danopoulos, "Religion, Civil Society, and Democracy in Orthodox Greece," p. 46; Sakellariou, "Anti-Islamic Public Discourse in Contemporary Greece," p. 516.
82. Danopoulos, "Religion, Civil Society, and Democracy in Orthodox Greece," p. 46; Roudometof, "Eastern Orthodox Christianity and the Uses of the Past," p. 101; Madeleine Speed, "The Battle to Build a Mosque in Athens," *Financial Times*, 1 February 2019, at https://www.ft.com/content/ae4fa654-2416-11e9-8ce6-5db4543da632 [last accessed 12 March 2019]; "Lack of Mosque in Athens Stokes Fears of Radicalism," *Kathimerini* (3 April 2016) at http://www.ekathimerini.com/207570/article/ekathimerini/news/lack-of-mosque-in-athens-stokes-fears-of-radicalism [last accessed 12 March 2019].
83. Stavrakakis, "Religion and Populism" [note 38], p. 8.
84. Ibid., p. 10; Mavrogordatos, "Orthodoxy and Nationalism in the Greek Case," p. 118.
85. Stavrakakis, "Religion and Populism" [note 38], pp. 29–30; Danopoulos, "Religion, Civil Society, and Democracy in Orthodox Greece," p. 49.
86. Mavrogordatos, "Orthodoxy and Nationalism in the Greek Case," p. 123.
87. Kathimerini, 30 August 2001, as cited in Stavrakakis, "Religion and Populism" [note 38], p. 11.
88. Anastassiadis, "An Intriguing True–False Paradox" [note 5], p. 53.
89. D. Oulis, G. Makris, and S. Roussos, "The Orthodox Church of Greece" [note 9], p. 198.
90. Diamantopoulou, "Religious Freedom in the Light of the Relationship Between the Orthodox Church and the Nation in Contemporary Greece," p. 1.
91. Mavrogordatos, "Church-State Relations in the Greek Orthodox Case," p. 1.

92. Diamantopoulou, "Religious Freedom in the Light of the Relationship Between the Orthodox Church and the Nation in Contemporary Greece," p. 5.
93. Ibid., pp. 1–2.
94. Alexandros Sakellariou, "Fear of Islam in Greece: Migration, Terrorism, and 'Ghosts' from the Past," in *Nationalities Papers*, Vol. 45, No. 4 (July 2017), p. 511, https://doi.org/10.1080/00905992.2017.1294561.
95. Mavrogordatos, "Church-State Relations in the Greek Orthodox Case," p. 12.
96. Sakellariou, "Fear of Islam in Greece," [note 94], p. 514.
97. Papastathis, "Religious Discourse and Radical Right Politics" [note 23], p. 238.
98. Ibid.
99. Payne, "The Clash of Civilisations," p. 261.
100. Ibid., p. 263.
101. Kyriazopoulos, "The 'Prevailing Religion' in Greece," p. 514.
102. Ibid., p. 515.
103. Ibid., p. 514.
104. VIIIth Revisionary Parliament of Greece, The Constitution of Greece; Molokotos-Liederman, "Looking at Religion and Greek Identity from the Outside," p. 140.
105. The environment was not completely peaceful. One Orthodox zealot slapped the Archbishop in front of the cathedral to protest Papal visit because they saw this visit as a submission of Greek Orthodoxy to Vatican. Anastassiadis, "An Intriguing True–False Paradox" [note 6], p. 56; Stavrakakis, "Religion and Populism" [note 38], p. 8; some clergy in the Synod also revolted against the visit and firstly permission by Archbishop. See Michael Howard, "Greek Priests Revolt as Church Backs Pope's Visit," *The Guardian*, 20 March 2001, at https://www.theguardian.com/world/2001/mar/20/catholicism.religion [last accessed 15 January 2019].
106. Stavrakakis, "Religion and Populism" [note 38], pp. 41–42; Victor Roudometof, "Greek Orthodoxy, Territoriality, and Globality: Religious Responses and Institutional Disputes," in *Sociology of Religion*, Vol. 69, No. 1 (Spring 2008), pp. 74, 77, https://doi.org/10.1093/socrel/69.1.67.
107. Anastassiadis, "An Intriguing True–False Paradox" [note 5], p. 42; Karagiannis, "Secularism in Context" [note 6], p. 159.
108. Roudometof, "Eastern Orthodox Christianity and the Uses of the Past," p. 100.

109. Helena Smith, "Sex and Fraud Woe for Greek Church," *The Guardian*, 19 February 2005, sec. World news, https://www.theguardian.com/world/2005/feb/19/religion.uk [last accessed 10 January 2019]; Harry de Quetteville, "Corruption Scandal Hits the Greek Church" (5 February 2005), at https://www.telegraph.co.uk/news/worldnews/europe/greece/1482856/Corruption-scandal-hits-the-Greek-Church.html [last accessed 5 February 2019]; Richard Galpin, "Greek Church Rocked by Scandals," BBC, 4 February 2005, at http://news.bbc.co.uk/2/hi/europe/4237135.stm [last accessed 22 April 2019]; and Doug Saunders, "Scandal Reaches Highest Echelon of Greek Orthodox Church," at https://www.theglobeandmail.com/news/world/scandal-reaches-highest-echelon-of-greek-orthodox-church/article977436/ [last accessed 2 May 2019].
110. Fokas, "A New Role for the Church?" p. 28.
111. "Church of Greece to Participate in Athens' FYROM Rally," Amna, http://www.amna.gr/en/article/226107/Church-of-Greece-to-participate-in-Athens-FYROM-rally [last accessed 22 March 2019]; Sinisa Jakov Marusic, "Ecumenical Patriarch Rebuffs Macedonian Church's Plea for Recognition," *Balkan Insight*, 18 October 2018, at https://balkaninsight.com/2018/10/18/macedonia-church-receives-cold-shower-from-constantinople-10-18-2018/ [last accessed 2 May 2019]; Sarantis Michalopoulos, "Local Orthodox Church Asks to Drop 'Macedonia' from Name as Talks with Greece Continue," Euractiv.Com, 31 May 2018, at https://www.euractiv.com/section/enlargement/news/local-orthodox-church-asks-to-drop-macedonia-from-name-as-talks-with-greece-continue/ [last accessed 2 May 2019]; Helena Smith, "Greek MPs Ratify Macedonia Name Change in Historic Vote," *The Guardian*, 25 January 2019, at https://www.theguardian.com/wrld/2019/jan/25/greek-mps-ratify-macedonia-name-change-historic-vote [last access 2 May 2019]
112. Alain Salles, "Orthodox Church Appears to Be Exempt from Austerity Measures," *The Guardian*, 4 October 2011, at https://www.theguardian.com/world/2011/oct/04/greece-orthodox-church-economic-crisis [last accessed 1 May 2019].
113. Makris and Bekridakis, "The Greek Orthodox Church and the Economic Crisis Since 2009," pp. 119–125.
114. The Metropolitan of Kalavryta and Aegialia Ambrose, "Metropolitan of Kalavryta and Aegialia: SLAUGHTER OF SOCIETY WAS HEAD!" *Metropolitan of Kalavryta and Aegialia* (blog), 9 December 2015, http://mkka.blogspot.com/2015/12/blog-post_9.html [last accessed 1 May 2019]; Peter Montgomery, "Greek Orthodox Bishop Says Spit on Inhuman Gay Scum: This Week's LGBT Global Recap," *Religion*

Dispatches, 17 December 2015, at http://religiondispatches.org/greek-orthodox-bishop-says-spit-on-inhuman-gay-scum-english-version-of-synod-report-cheers-conservative-catholics-australian-jesuit-urges-marriage-legislation-to-avoid-nasty-plebiscite-lgbt-glo/ [last accessed 1 May 2019].

115. Umur Yedikardeş (25 December 2015), "Kilisemiz eşcinsel evliliği kutsamaz," http://www.cumhuriyet.com.tr/haber/yasam/453706/_Kilisemiz_escinsel_evliligi_kutsamaz_.html [last accessed 25 April 2019].

116. "'Greece Stands on the Brink of Destruction'—Clergy of Diocese of Orestiada," OrthoChristian.Com, at http://orthochristian.com/109577.html [last accessed 27 April 2019]; "Current Education Minister Is New Nero, Bishops of Church of Greece Say," OrthoChristian.Com (3 October 2016), at http://orthochristian.com/97552.html [last accessed 28 April 2019].

117. GCT, "Greek Government Passes Law Allowing People from 15 to Change Their Legal Gender," *Greek City Times*, 10 October 2017, at https://greekcitytimes.com/2017/10/11/greek-government-passes-law-allowing-people-15-change-legal-gender/; Hodges, "Greek Clergy"; and Emmilio Polygedis, "The Reaction of Mount Athos to the 'Gender Identity'," ROMFEA, 5 October 2017, https://www.romfea.gr/agioritika-nea/17373-i-antidrasi-tou-agiou-orous-gia-tin-tautotita-tou-fulou [last accessed 5 May 2019].

118. "Greek Church Comes Out Against Cancellation of Morning Prayers in School," OrthoChristian.Com, at http://orthochristian.com/96859.html [last accessed 27 April 2019]; "Current Education Minister Is New Nero, Bishops of Church of Greece Say."

119. Paul Wilkinson, "Greek Orthodox Priests to Lose Civil Servant Status—and State Pay—Under New Deal," 23 November 2018, https://www.churchtimes.co.uk/articles/2018/23-november/news/world/greek-orthodox-priests-to-lose-civil-servant-status-under-new-deal [last accessed 14 April 2019]; Greek City Times, "Greek Priests to Remain on Civil Service Payroll," *Greek City Times*, 12 February 2019, at https://greekcitytimes.com/2019/02/13/greek-priests-to-remain-on-civil-service-payroll/ [last accessed 10 February 2019].

120. "Greece Revises Constitution to Fight Corrupt Politicians," France 24, 14 February 2019, at https://www.france24.com/en/20190214-greece-revises-constitution-fight-corrupt-politicians [last accessed 28 April 2019]; T. N. H. National Herald, "SYRIZA Church-State Separation Narrowly Backed by Parliament," *The National Herald*, 17 February 2019, at https://www.thenationalherald.com/230807/syriza-church-state-separation-narrowly-backed-by-parliament/ [last accessed 25 April 2019]; "Greek Parliament Adopts

Constitutional Revisions Proposed by Gov't," *Keep Talking Greece*, 14 February 2019, at https://www.keeptalkinggreece.com/2019/02/14/greece-church-state-constitution/ [last accessed 10 April 2019].

121. Sarah Francesca Green, "The Imia/Kardak Dispute: The Creation of Rocky Grey Zones in the Aegean Between Greece and Turkey," *Border Disputes: A Global Encyclopedia*, 2015, p. 3; For more on Greek-Turkish political relations, see: A. Günal and Sepli, A., "Türkiye'nin Yunanistan Dış Politikası," in *Türk Dış Politikası: Aktörler, Krizler, Tercihler, Çözümler* (Ankara: Barış Kitap, 2017).

122. Olimpia Dragouni, "The Macedonian Dispute in the Activity of the Metropolitan of Thessalonica Anthimos," *Poznańskie Studia Slawistyczne*, no. 10 (4 June 2016), p. 73, https://doi.org/10.14746/pss.2016.10.5.

CHAPTER 8

The Macedonian Orthodox Church in the New Millennium

Zachary T. Irwin

Abstract This chapter examines the political challenges, potential, and environment of the Macedonian Orthodox Church during the twenty-first century. It interprets the Church's place in shaping Macedonian identity, expressed by the idea of Church as a national "pillar," and support of its quest for acknowledged "autocephaly," proclaimed unilaterally in 1967. The chapter develops several themes. First, it examines the Macedonian Church's relations with the Serbian Orthodox Church, the abortive "Niš Agreement," and Serbian formation of a rival Orthodox entity under Bishop Jovan Vraniškovski. Second, the chapter comments on a "syndrome" of attitudes and values associated with the Macedonian Church: intolerance, homophobia, nationalism, and conservatism. The final section considers Archbishop Stefan's offer to the Ecumenical Patriarch, to rename the Church the "Archbishopric of Ohrid," possibly in connection with the "Prespa Accord," resolving the "name dispute" with Greece. A conclusion speculates whether an autocephalous

---

Z. T. Irwin (✉)
School of Humanities and Social Science, Behrend College
of Pennsylvania State University, Erie, PA, USA
e-mail: zti1@psu.edu

© The Author(s) 2019
S. P. Ramet (ed.), *Orthodox Churches and Politics in Southeastern Europe*, Palgrave Studies in Religion, Politics, and Policy,
https://doi.org/10.1007/978-3-030-24139-1_8

Macedonian Church might diminish espousal of those aforementioned values conflicting with Macedonia's EU membership.

The values of conservatism, nationalism, homophobia, and religious intolerance inspire and underpin Orthodox Church politics in the Balkans. Owing to the Orthodox Church's centrality in the national identity of several of the Balkan states, conservatism and nationalism lie at the core of the dominant political culture of Orthodox societies in the region. Moreover, levels of homophobia and intolerance figure as limits to each state's potential for integration in the larger European project, whether we think of Romania and Bulgaria, which were admitted to the European Union in 2007, or Serbia, Montenegro, and Macedonia, which are still hoping to join the EU. Where the Macedonian Orthodox Church is concerned, its claim to autocephaly and the Serbian Orthodox Church's denial of that claim and insistence that it retains jurisdiction over ecclesiastical affairs in Macedonia (renamed North Macedonia) represent what is probably the single most important challenge to the Macedonian Church. I shall return to the four values after discussing their context in the development of Macedonian identity.

This chapter is broadly divided into six sections. In the first, the struggle over the autocephaly of the Macedonian Orthodox Church and its troubled relations with its Serbian counterpart are discussed. In the second section, I look at the changed legal framework following the collapse of the Socialist Federated Republic of Yugoslavia and establishment of an independent Macedonian state. This is followed by a discussion of the case of Bishop Jovan Vraniškovski, who swore his allegiance to the Serbian Patriarchate. Then, in the fourth section, I take up the theme of religious inequality and religious intolerance, followed, in the section "Conflating Nationalism and Conservatism," by an analysis of the dynamic of nationalism and conservatism. Then, in the penultimate section, I discuss manifestations of homophobia in which the Church is complicit, followed by a conclusion.

AUTOCEPHALY IN THE CONTEXT OF MACEDONIAN IDENTITY

As Sabrina Ramet has noted, "[t]he term *autocephalous* comes from the ancient Greek and means that the body in question has its own head and is therefore independent or self-governing."[1] Thus, ecclesial autocephaly entails that the given Church is subject to no higher authority than God. Autocephaly entails not only juridical authority within the Church but also political symbolism and canonical consequences neither fully consistent nor obvious.[2] The status of an Orthodox community depends on the tradition and meaning of the concept as understood by the Church leadership, and for Macedonia, a population within Macedonia and its diaspora beyond (chiefly in the English-speaking world). General recognition of an autocephalous Macedonian Orthodox Church would affirm Macedonian nationality and confirm its canonical regularity. However, recognition of autocephaly requires consent by the community of autocephalous Churches, and in Macedonia's case, by a "Mother Church," implying close historical association. Were the Serbian Orthodox Church or the Ecumenical Patriarch to recognize the Macedonian Church's autocephaly, the result would affirm legitimacy unlike similar action by other Orthodox Churches. However, the Macedonian Orthodox Church's claim to autocephaly has no foundation other than its unilateral declaration in 1967, unless one appeals to the long-standing tradition that every nation is entitled to have its own autocephalous Church. But that raises complications in another dimension since the Bulgarian Orthodox Church and the Bulgarian state claim that Macedonians are merely the western branch of the Bulgarian nation, while there have been Serbian Orthodox clerics in the past who described Macedonians as "South Serbs."

The quest for Macedonian ecclesiastical autocephaly developed both after and coincidentally with the claims of a Macedonian language and nationality distinct from Bulgarian. The first mention of the Macedonian nation is associated with Georgi Pulevski (1817–1893) and Kiril Pejchinovich (1771–1865). Work on Pejchinovich affirms his "important role" in the "development" of a "Macedonian ethnic-cultural identity."[3] Significantly, the ethnographer Krste Petkov Misirkov (1874–1926) affirmed the existence of a Macedonian national identity separate from other Balkan nations and attempted to codify a standard Macedonian language based on the Central Macedonian dialects. It is difficult, however, to separate nineteenth-century linguistic, literary, and historiographic scholarship from broader regional rivalry, especially that in opposition to Greek, and later, Serbian influence.

Disputes about the distinctiveness of the Macedonian language reinforced claims for a separate Macedonian Church. While the Macedonian language enjoys a claim of difference from Bulgarian arguably greater than recent claims on behalf of "Serbian, Bosnian, or Croatian," Serbia's dominant relationship with Macedonia reinforced the importance of a distinctive Macedonian Orthodoxy. The Macedonian Church's claim to authenticity has been emphasized through the historic Archbishopric of Ohrid.[4] The latter had existed as an autonomous Orthodox Church under the tutelage of the Ecumenical Patriarch of Constantinople between 1019 and 1767. The Ottoman Sultan abolished the Archbishopric in 1767. During the nineteenth century, the idea of a distinct patriarch in an autocephalous Macedonian Church using the Macedonian language was revived by the claims of Teodosij (Theodosius) (Vasil) Gologanov (1846–1926); the latter was Bishop of the Exarchate of Skopje in 1885. The Metropolitan favored restoring the Ohrid Archbishopric as a separate Macedonian Church in which the Macedonian vernacular would be used in the religious service.[5] Greek opposition to this goal brought Gologanov to establish contacts with Rome, to explore the question of a Uniate confession. Teodosij's efforts to separate the Macedonian dioceses from the Bulgarian Orthodox Church resulted in 1892 in his dismissal from his post as bishop. Serbian Bishops were appointed to sees in Macedonia, an outcome actuated after the Second Balkan War and World War One.[6] During the interwar era, dioceses in "South Serbia" (as Serbs were apt to call Macedonia) and Montenegro were conjoined to the Serbian Orthodox Church.

Contacts between Macedonia's clergy and the Partisan resistance originated in clerical disillusionment with Bulgarian occupation and found a receptive response in Partisan appeals to "all nations and faiths."[7] The Partisan ideal of a Macedonia separate from Serbia implied separation of its Church from Serbian hegemony. Thus, the first assembly of Macedonian clergy in modern times was held near Ohrid in 1943 under the auspices of the Communist Party of Yugoslavia. The origins of the meeting are unclear. Stella Alexander considers it "probable" that the clergy took the initiative, since the Antifascist Council for the National Liberation of Macedonia (ASNOM) made no mention of a Macedonian Orthodox Church at its first meeting in 1944.[8] During the following year, an "Initiative Board for the Organization of the Macedonian Orthodox Church" was officially formed. In 1945, the First Clergy and People's Synod adopted a Resolution for the Restoration of the Ohrid Archbishopric as a Macedonian Orthodox Church. The Resolution was submitted to the Serbian Orthodox Patriarchate, since, after 1919, the

Serbian Church had been the sole Church in Vardar Macedonia (i.e., the portion of Macedonia which had come under Belgrade's rule).

The Serbian Church refused to recognize the Macedonian Church, possibly because of the protection of the Serb communist Aleksandar Ranković, who served as deputy prime minister from 1949 to 1963 and vice president from 1963 to 1966. Any polemics were confined to the respective hierarchies and the priests' associations. Clearly, promoting a Macedonian autocephalous Church was unacceptable in some circles. Gradual rapprochement between Belgrade and Athens after the Soviets expelled Yugoslavia from the Cominform in 1948 allowed the Serbian Church to resist more easily accommodation with Orthodox hierarchs in Skopje. As early as January 1952, Greek State Radio broadcast an account of Macedonia's quest for a Church separate from Serbia's to be a Soviet-inspired ploy intended to be "the first move" in a bid for Macedonia to secede from Yugoslavia.[9] In a similar spirit, Serbian and Macedonian clergy associations, despite their differences, pledged complete cooperation with communist efforts to reconstruct Yugoslavia.

However, the Macedonian Church required consecrated bishops to achieve canonical status, which in turn seemed to require the cooperation of the Serbian Orthodox Church. The postwar Serbian Church constitution recognized the use of languages other than Serbian in Church services in "exceptional circumstances," but dioceses in Macedonia were still listed as dioceses of the Serbian Orthodox Church.[10] A compromise was achieved, recognizing Serbian Church administration of the Orthodox Church in Macedonia, and providing for elevation of the Macedonian Serb, Dositej, as Metropolitan. Macedonian clergy and laity met in October 1958 to proclaim the reestablishment of the Archbishopric of Ohrid and, without Serbian Synodal approval, to elect Bishop Dositej as Metropolitan of the Macedonian Church. After initial refusal, the resolution for a separate "autonomous" Church was accepted by the Serbian Patriarchate only on 17 June 1959.

The 1966 ouster of Aleksandar Ranković may have removed the principal obstacle to the Macedonian Church's unilateral declaration of autocephaly. Thus, in 1967, on the 200th Anniversary of the abolition of the Ohrid Archbishopric by Ottoman Sultan Mustafa III, an assembly of the Church proclaimed autocephaly, along with two new dioceses: (1) Velika Makedonija and (2) America, Canada, and Australia.

Meanwhile, the new Macedonian Church enjoyed positive relations with the communist regime at all levels. The Church became a useful, if passive party to the historical "debates" about Macedonian identity with Greece and Bulgaria in the Yugoslav press during the 1970s. Much of the reason for the status of the Church centered on the nagging question, "who are the Macedonians?" Vjekoslav Perica, a Croatian historian and member of Socialist Yugoslavia's Committee for Relations with Religious Communities from 1985 to 1990, suggested an answer; "Macedonians are members of the Macedonian Orthodox Church."[11] No Macedonian government or Church official might publicly agree, among other reasons because Macedonian President Boris Trajkovski (1956–2004) was a Methodist, but Perica's viewpoint suggests why an autocephalous Church was vigorously defended, even given the presence of Muslims, Methodists, and members of other religious bodies.

There was little change for half a century after the proclamation of autocephaly, but in May 2018 Archbishop Stefan offered to drop the name "Macedonian" in applying for reconciliation with the Ecumenical Patriarch.[12] The Church would become the "Archdiocese of Ohrid." Prime Minister Zoran Zaev endorsed the request in an accompanying letter to the Ecumenical Patriarch. The change could have satisfied certain Church objectives. First, the "Archdiocese of Ohrid" would have harmonized the Church's identity with the Prespa Agreement reached between Athens and Skopje in June 2018, ending the "name dispute" by renaming the country *North Macedonia*. Second, invoking the "Archdiocese of Ohrid" would have recalled the Church's title during the height of its historic influence (1018–1763). Third, through recognition on the part of the Ecumenical Patriarch, the Church would effectively have denied the Serbian Orthodox Church's claims to superordination. Associations with "Ohrid" have a relation to Macedonian identity that could be compared with the historical and religious significance of "Cetinje" for Montenegro. On 25 January 2019, the Greek Parliament ratified the Prespa Accord recognizing "North Macedonia," as the resolution of the long-standing "name dispute." (At this writing, it is not certain that the Prespa Agreement will overcome continued resistance within both Greece and Macedonia.)

A New Reality in the Post-Yugoslav Era?

The demise of Socialist Yugoslavia presented both new opportunities for the Macedonian Orthodox Church and new threats. Introducing religious education in public schools occasioned a proposal by the Council for Religious Education to reform the curriculum.[13] In 2009, the VMRO-DPMNE (Internal Macedonian Revolutionary Organization-Democratic Party for Macedonian National Unity) government proposed that religious instruction be introduced as an elective in public schools. The curriculum would have offered both Orthodox and Islamic versions along with a secular alternative" ("Getting to Know Religions"). Parents objected that children were required to declare their religious identity, and the Constitutional Court declared the curriculum an unconstitutional violation of the separation of Church and state, that is, exceeding "the academic and neutral character of primary education."[14] Authorities replaced the curriculum with one allegedly more neutral, "The Ethics of Religions." However, parents found little substantive difference from the repudiated religious education class.[15]

The European Court of Human Rights examined the question of religious freedom in Macedonia. One case involved the distinct identity and property rights of the Bektashi Muslims from the larger Islamic Religious Community. Ruling in favor of the Bektashi in 2014, the European Court limited the application of Chapter 8 of the Law on the Legal Status of Churches, Religious Communities, and Religious Groups. The law recognized a single religious entity representing a particular tradition. The Court held that such constraints must be based on "public order, health or morals, or [serve] for the protection of the rights and freedoms of others." More generally, it maintained that a "democratic society presupposed religious pluralism" with the result that registration of religious entities would be transferred from the executive to the judiciary.[16] This decision would become relevant to relations between the Macedonian and the Serbian Churches.

After Macedonia's 1991 declaration of independence, tension between Belgrade and Skopje focused on the status of the Serbian minority and Macedonia's decision to accept a small contingent of American troops intended to block a plan for Greek-Serbian partition of Macedonia.[17] Relations worsened between the Macedonian and the Serbian Churches; without an avowedly anti-religious communist party, religious conflict became a matter of political interest. As early as 1993, Macedonian President Kiro Gligorov (1917–2012) deplored the Serbian Church's "pure spiritual aggression" in seeking to "impose its authority" on the Macedonian Church.[18] Meanwhile in 1994, the Macedonian Church reaffirmed its autocephaly through a new constitution as a "Holy, Catholic, and Apostolic Church, which protects the dogmas, canons, and unity of the divine services with the Eastern Orthodox Ecumenical Church."[19] In response, the Serbian Church called on Macedonians "to enter into the [Serbian] Church canons and canonical order, appointing Bishop Pahomie of the Eparchy of Vranje as "administrator of Macedonian eparchies." This demand had the greatest impact on the Serbian minority. Consisting of about 35,000 persons living in and around Kumanovo, the Serbian minority had boycotted Macedonia's 1991 independence referendum. Instead, many of them had organized Serbian parties and interest groups, including some associated with the Serbian Radical Party. The latter sought to create a "Serbian Autonomous Region of Kumanovo Valley and Skopska Crna Gora," an ambition that found little resonance in Belgrade.[20] The Helsinki Committee for Human Rights found no formal evidence that Skopje sought to provoke the Serbian minority, although the question of separate Church organization was, of course, an irritant for at least some Serbs.[21] In 1993, Macedonia's Minister of the Interior, Ljubomir Frčkovski, insisted that Serbs enjoyed equal status, but that the right of the Serbian Orthodox Church to "to form its own diasporic unit was another matter."[22] Not only did the Serbian Orthodox Patriarch appoint a Bishop for Macedonia, but the Serbian Church also sought to infiltrate Serbian priests across the border into Kumanovo, persons who would be expelled subsequently for the crime of fostering "religious hatred."[23] Serbian and Macedonian Metropolitans met, only to disagree vehemently.

THE VRANIŠKOVSKI THREAT: THE MACEDONIAN CHURCH ON THE DEFENSIVE

Instead of a challenge from the Serbian minority, the Macedonian Church confronted that of the Bishop of Veles, Jovan Vraniškovski, who announced his loyalty to the Serbian Church. Vraniškovski raised a fundamental threat—as loyalty to Serbian Orthodoxy could no longer be assumed to be an attitude exclusive to ethnic Serbs, but appealed apparently also to some Macedonian clergy. The episode constituted a direct challenge to the status of the Macedonian Church, and in the Orthodox tradition, the destabilizing threat of schism. Left unresolved, Vraniškovski's action would have posed a threat to the very existence of the Macedonian Church. Bishop Vraniškovski, born in 1966, had graduated in civil engineering from the University of Skopje and had earned theological degrees at the University of Belgrade's Faculty of Orthodox Theology. In 1995, he started his master's studies, ultimately completing a doctoral dissertation on "The Unity of the Church and the Contemporary Ecclesiological Problems."[24] In 1998, he was ordained as Bishop of Dremvitsa and was assigned to be a vicar to the Bishop of Prespa and Pelagonia. In March 2000, he was elected Bishop of the diocese of Veles.

However, the Macedonian Church was also changing. After a decade of state independence, some Macedonian Bishops sought to compose their differences with the Serbian Church. In 2002, three Macedonian Bishops (Metropolitan Petar of Australia, Metropolitan Timotej of Debar and Kicevo, and Metropolitan Naum of Strumica) negotiated and signed the Niš Agreement, a divisive document rejected by the Macedonian Church Synod. The agreement had sought to recognize broad but formal trappings of the autonomy of the Macedonian Church, but the agreement included the following controversial clause: "The Primate represents his Church before the Serbian Orthodox Church, and the establishing of the Eucharistic communion and canonical unity with the Serbian Orthodox Church is the witness for Church unity with the remaining local Orthodox Churches."[25] In addition, the document anticipated "brotherly agreement" for the "correct pastoral care" of members of the respective nationality in each state. The two Churches would provide for the appointment of priests "of the same nationality" under corresponding jurisdictions. Finally, the agreement provided for the creation of single Church under Serbian administration, whose Primate would officially bear the title of Archbishop of Ohrid and Metropolitan of Skopje.

This outcome stirred an unprecedented public conflict in which the three bishops were accused of "treason" by more conservative clerics. The Synodal Chair, Bishop Georgi Naumov, spoke about the loss of status were the agreement to be implemented, as one of "degradation … without the name 'Macedonian Orthodox Church', its head will automatically lose the status of Archbishop of Ohrid and Macedonia, and will have to ask for permission from the SPC [Serbian Orthodox] Patriarch for all of his activities."[26] The Macedonian Synod's rejection might have ended temporarily this phase of relations, but Bishop Vraniškovski decided to align his allegiance with an ecclesial entity anticipated but uncreated by the Niš Agreement. That is, Vraniškovski became the new

Serbian Orthodox-sponsored Archbishop of Ohrid and Metropolitan of Skopje. In 2005, the Serbian Patriarch and the Serbian Orthodox Synod confirmed the new Archbishop of Ohrid and Metropolitan of Skopje. In response, the Serbian Synod demanded the ouster of Bishop Jovan, an outcome, possibly accelerated by his public appeal to other clergy to follow him in unity with the Serbian Church.[27] In addition, the Macedonian Church altered its name to prevent any confusion with the Serbian-sponsored Church; it became the "Macedonian Orthodox Church-Ohrid Archbishopric (MOC-OA)."[28] The new entity in union with the Serbian Orthodox Church left little room for negotiation or compromise. In 2004, Serbian Patriarch Pavle described Macedonian Church autocephaly as having been responsive to the "needs of the Communists (sic)…to break up the unity of the Churches in the former Yugoslav regions in order to control it better and to destroy it systematically [and] to control the Macedonian diaspora that could not have been controlled by any other state apparatus."[29] That comment, relevant to established Macedonian communities in North America and Australia, gratuitously implied that somehow a Macedonian Church presence overseas had permitted control of émigré communities by Socialist Yugoslavia.

Meanwhile, three new bishops were elevated to the Synod, who presumably would not waiver on the matter of autocephaly. According to Zoran Bojarovski a journalist with ALFA TV Skopje, "these bishops belong to a new generation, which has a more progressive stance compared to the old members of the synod."[30] Apparently "progressive" meant less willing to compromise. Bishop Vraniškovski was stripped of his clerical rank by the Macedonian Synod and in early 2004, arrested for holding an unauthorized service outside a church.[31] Further prosecutions followed. Vraniškovski was charged with serious offenses, including "causing national, racial or religious hatred, discord and intolerance" under Article 319 of the Criminal Code and embezzlement of Church funds. Outside Macedonia, the case raised questions of human rights. The World Council of Churches, Helsinki Watch, and Amnesty International took up the Bishop's cause. The Commission of the Churches in International Affairs of the World Council of Churches (CCIA-WCC) summarized his case as one based on "unfounded charges" in which the defendant was denied the "basic right to defense."[32]

Although the WCC report had been included in the case "at the request" of Serbian Patriarch Irinej (Patriarch since 2010), the result implied a violation of the "essential right to freedom of religion or belief, as guaranteed in the Universal Declaration of Human Rights." Amnesty International had adopted Vraniškovski as a "prisoner of conscience" in 2004.[33]

The issue became relevant to European Union accession. As early as 2005, the EU's "analytical opinion" considered the case a violation of freedom of conscience, citing Article 8 in the Law on Religious Communities to the effect that any national community was entitled to only one Orthodox Church, thus, creating "particular difficulties for the 'Ohrid Archbishopric'."[34] The finding criticized Vraniškovski's sentencing for incitement of national, racial and religious hatred, advising, "[I]t is essential to intensify dialogue between the MOC and the SOC in good faith and based on respect for religious tolerance. In addition, all legal avenues must be pursued to resolve this matter in a manner that reflects the established principle of religious tolerance."[35] Finally, in November 2017 the European Court of Human Rights rendered its opinion. Acknowledging the "utmost importance [of the] autocephaly and unity of the Macedonian Orthodox Church, the decision was unequivocal:

> This cannot justify, in a democratic society, the use of measures which, as in the present case, went so far as to prevent the applicant comprehensively and unconditionally from even commencing any activity ....[T]he role of the authorities in a situation of conflict between or within religious groups is not to remove the cause of tension by eliminating pluralism, but to ensure that the competing groups tolerate each other.[36]

The Court found a violation of Article 11 of the Convention, interpreted in light of Article 9.[37] Clearly, the human rights community perceived a denial of religious freedom.

For Skopje, the political value of an autocephalous Church exceeded the possible diplomatic gain of its abandonment. Moreover, the election of conservative Nikola Gruevski (b.1970) in 2006 as Prime Minister, may have invigorated elements in the Macedonian Church who considered Vraniškovski especially dangerous and desired his further imprisonment. Belgrade had no obvious way to break the impasse between the two Churches despite the diplomatic cost of the situation which had no silver lining for Serbia. Macedonian Church statements professing a desire for "dialogue" with the Serbian Church were ignored.

Ultimately, however, Vraniškovski would be released before finishing his prison sentence, an outcome which, nonetheless, did not signify inter-Church reconciliation. Secular officials were involved in the dispute from the start, and among the first announced, discussion involved a meeting between President Boris Trajkovski and the Serbian Chairmen of the BK [Braća Karić] Group and the Belgrade Commercial Bank. The former sought Vraniškovski's release while the latter "welcomed efforts for an *equal dialogue* between the two Churches."[38] One reason for Serbian interest in resolving the dispute emerged from Skopje's then-uncertain attitude concerning the issue of recognition of Kosovo. Soon after his election, Gruevski raised the issue of Serbian recognition of the MOC-OA with the speaker of the Serbian Parliament, but to no avail.[39] Gruevski persisted, but talks suffered from excessive publicity and inconsistent positions. The Serbian President in office at the time of Vraniškovski's release, Tomislav Nikolić (b.1952), allegedly offered to recognize Macedonian Church autocephaly in exchange for a complete pardon of Vraniškovski.[40] Such an outcome, assuming it could have been delivered, could have left the Ohrid Archbishopric intact. How could so emphatic a conviction as that meted out to Vraniškovski be easily pardoned? In fact, the Vraniškovski question was resolved differently. Secret talks started in 2009 between the two Churches, although they soon foundered over the proposal for a guaranteed amnesty in exchange for a written promise by the Serbian Church to recognize autocephaly.[41] Neither side may have satisfied the other's objectives. Ultimately Vraniškovski received "clemency," i.e., neither an amnesty nor a pardon, nor was there a public promise to recognize the Church's autocephaly. Vraniškovski was released on 2 February, after missions to Skopje and Belgrade by Russian Bishop Illarion, head of the International Relations department of the Russian Orthodox Church. The Macedonian Holy Synod recommended clemency for Vraniškovski after Bishop Illarion met with leaders of Church and State in December. Any constraints on Vraniškovski's future activity were not revealed. A committee charged with the goal of resuming relations also emerged, however, doubtful its mandate.

A postscript to the conflict with Serbia took place in November 2017. The Macedonian Church advised the Bulgarian Orthodox Church Synod of its readiness to recognize the Bulgarian Patriarchate as its Mother

Church, to be followed by the latter's recognition of its autocephalic status. Qualifications for a "mother Church" involve the political character of autocephaly, yet one without obvious precedent. Some of the ambiguity has emerged from the Bulgarian Church's willingness to hold talks with its Macedonian counterpart, despite the Greek Orthodox Church's "concern" over the development.[42] Sofia and Skopje signed a Friendship, Neighborhood, and Cooperation Agreement, but clerical relations did not advance.

Religious Inequality and Religious Intolerance

Article 19 of the 2001 Ohrid Framework Accord (OFA) specifies that religious communities are "separate from the state and equal before the law...[and] are free to establish schools and other social and charitable institutions, by way of a procedure regulated by law."[43] I have mentioned religious education. Controversy has centered on the question of an earlier draft of the Ohrid Framework Accord that identified the Macedonian Orthodox Church, the Islamic Religious Community (IVZ),[44] and "other religious communities." Zhidas Daskalovski has observed that any provision mentioning specific religions enjoying rights and prerogatives "on an equal basis" would symbolically rank the members of religious communities mentioned in the document higher than the citizens of different religious beliefs.[45] Instead, disagreement about Church and state has been more challenging than multi-confessional equality.

Separation of Church and state, in the Ohrid Framework Agreement, was not definitively accepted by the Church. Rather, the Church enjoyed the rhetorical support of the then-ruling VMRO-DPMNE, and conversely, Social Democratic governments, more respectful of the separation question, appeared politically vulnerable. In 2009, VMRO-DPMNE spokespersons vehemently criticized the Constitutional Court for prohibiting religious instruction in Macedonian primary schools. Beyond the Court itself, there was criticism of former President Branko Crvenkovski (b.1962) for having allegedly "orchestrated" a decision based on "party and politically motivated rulings." In turn, Crvenkovski rejected VMRO-DPMNE's position as an "unprecedented attack on the integrity" of the Court. VMRO spokesmen equated "attacks" on the Church with attacks on the Macedonian nation and its statehood, demanding that Crvenkovski's government "abandon the ignorant relation [to the Church] and more actively to support the MOC."[46] The meaning of "support" was unclear. The Church sought specific objectives, e.g., further denationalization of Church property, inclusion of the Orthodox Theological Faculty and high schools in the country's educational system, as well as inclusion of religious communities in the preparations for a new law on religious communities.[47] This "wish list" was not a practical agenda for any political party, but engaging the Macedonian Church in conflict could be politically unwise since public trust in the Church far exceeded trust in political institutions.

Some 68.7% of the ethnic Macedonians and 6.5% of the ethnic Albanians expressed "trust" in the MPC-OA, whereas 81% of the ethnic Albanians and 19.7% of the ethnic Macedonians trusted the IVZ.[48] Neither major Slavic party could express disinterest in the autocephaly issue or alienate Church spokesmen. In 2007, on the 40th Anniversary of its proclamation of autocephaly, then-Prime Minister Gruevski effusively praised the Church as a "pillar" of the nation the restoration of which had "mended a great historic injustice of 1767."[49] On the same occasion, Social Democratic leader and Macedonian President, Branko Crvenkovski, used the identical word "pillar" to describe the Church as a "guardian of Macedonian identity [and its] spiritual and cultural treasure." He also mentioned the "role in nourishing the [Macedonian] diaspora."[50] By contrast Serbia's Democratic Party (later the New Democratic Party) leader and President Boris Tadić, dismissed a role for Belgrade in mediating the inter-ecclesiastical conflict because "the state does not interfere in Church affairs."[51]

Although survey data from Macedonia and Eastern Europe are not conducive to precise comparison, they identify the key role of religious belief in public life. In Macedonia, 83.5% of Slavic Macedonians consider themselves members of a Church; of these 81.9% believe in God and 45.8% are "strongly attached" to their religious community and only 12.6% "faintly attached."[52] These figures are similar to figures for other Balkan nationalities and distinctive from figures from elsewhere in Eastern Europe. Broadly speaking belief in God corresponds with belief in the importance of religion for national identity. For example, 59% of Hungarians believe in God and 43% consider religious belief "very important" for national identity. In Serbia, 87% are believers and 78% consider religious affiliation to be "very important" in being a member of their community.[53] The data for Macedonia express high levels of trust in their religious communities—68.7% for Macedonians and 81% for Albanians.

Research conducted by Ružica Cacanoska between 1996 and 2012 on religious affiliation in Macedonian society found increasing rates of "positive religious affiliation." The trend could be associated with a decline in the "cross-cutting cleavages" that lessen social polarization. Cacanoska also confirmed a "disintegration" of the community, which is "burdened with disputes, [and] conflicts, particularly in the period after independence."[54] The study revealed a strong and continuous association of ethnic and religious identification. Another survey contrasted the attitudes of Slavic and Albanian Macedonians in response to the question whether religion was "essential" for the existence of the nation. A majority of Slavic Macedonians (67%) "definitely agreed" or "agreed," but only 13% of Albanians did so.[55] Differences may arise from the existence of the state of Albania and its distinctive language.

The distinction in attitudes concerning the Macedonian Church between Macedonia's Social Democrats (SDSM[56]) and VMRO-DPMNE appears relatively subtle since both have praised the Macedonian Church's role in the nation. But there is nonetheless a difference in attitudes of the SDSM and VMRO-DPMNE concerning the Church. Alexandar Spasenovski, a VMRO-DPMNE official, explained the distinction obliquely, arguing that the Social Democrats advocated "more strongly" for the separation of Church and state than did the VMRO-DPMNE. "[T]his means that [the Social Democrats] do not interfere in religious institutions,…[while] at the same time making it impossible for religious communities to interfere in the work of [other] institutions.(sic)."[57] However, a broader spectrum of issues has involved the VMRO-DPMNE government of Nikola Gruevski including some issues of interest to the Church, if not those affecting it directly. More exactly, attitudes about toleration and gender equality have become more prominent as have unfavorable demographic trends involving Slavic Macedonians.[58] One critical study points to the tendency to "dissolve secularism" through such actions as "the carnival in the Vevcan village near Struga, the building of a church in the Skopje Fortress, and the erection of giant crosses in the Skopje Municipality of Aerodrom."[59] In 2009, the Gruevski government passed legislation intended to increase birthrates in areas of low fertility, i.e., Slavic areas. The Court annulled the subsidies as discriminatory against areas with high birth rates.[60]

The Macedonian Church continues to express particular concern about the demographic situation, if less emphatically than Serbian Patriarch Irinej's comment that "Serbian women [were] obliged to give birth."[61] The Macedonian Church supported passage of a more restrictive abortion law in 2013. Revising a 1972 law, the Gruevski government's "Law on the Termination of Pregnancy" required a formal request for the procedure, as well as mandatory counseling, and a waiting period. A report submitted to the UN Human Rights Commission considered these and other provisions discriminatory and effectively, to stigmatize women seeking an abortion.[62] The Church took part in an extensive public campaign equating abortion with murder.[63]

Church affiliation strengthens with the decline of civic values. That decline may be demonstrated by the failure of the 2017 elections to improve civic trust. One indication that avoids direct identification with any MOC issue involves recent elections. Nikola Gruevski's VMRO-DPMNE government was defeated by Zoran Zaev's SDSM.

Conflating Nationalism and Conservatism

Nationalism is a politically assertive attitude toward collective identity, and as frequently, a political response that assumes that the value of identity itself is in jeopardy. *Conservativism*, distinctively, elevates traditional social practices and values over "rational" attempts devoted to social improvement or innovation and is typically critical of what qualifies as "post-modern." Observations about these concepts require a contextual qualification within a specific setting. The conflation of nationalism and conservatism has been a feature of Macedonian politics since the state's independence. Briefly, what is meant by the relation of the two is useful in understanding why policy toward the Macedonian Orthodox Church hardly changes regardless of which party or coalition holds power.

As Sabrina Ramet has explained, the historical experience of Orthodox Churches and their emphasis on the early experience of Christianity has made them "less disposed to liberalization and habituated them to thinking in terms of threat and survival."[64] The result presumes an "idyllic" past, a decadent present, and a future of imperative "repurification, revival, and regeneration." As communism once attributed its perceptions of social pathology to "[Western] capitalist survivals," so Orthodoxy is inclined to blame Western influences on similar behaviors, with additional distrust of internal dissent and ecumenism. The result is a resonance between Orthodoxy and conservatism evident in political parties on the right. However, attitudes about the past and corresponding attitudes about national revival have particular meaning in Macedonia, i.e., restoring the Archbishopric abolished in 1767. Likewise, comparing party attitudes with other predominantly Orthodox countries requires caution. For example, both the "conservative" Macedonian VMRO-DPMNE and the less conservative SDSM claim to have sought membership in the European Union, but the former is more skeptical of universal "European" civic values in conflict with perceptions of Macedonian tradition. The distinction is less clear where the Macedonian Orthodox Church is concerned. In view of Macedonia's aspirations for EU membership, openly expressed distrust in Western liberalism may be less prominent than in other Orthodox Churches. However, clerical use of the social media site "Facebook" has been condemned as undesirable.[65]

Since the 2001 Ohrid Accords, Albanian parties have looked to constitutional innovation and ethnic quotas as a means of preserving and asserting national identity. Slavic parties have, perhaps unconsciously, promoted similar policy versions of common values shared by all political systems. Harold Lasswell identified such values as power, enlightenment, security, and well-being.[66] Each value offers corresponding policy choices shared broadly by both Macedonian Slavic parties, e.g., anti-corruption reform (power), language and culture (enlightenment), étatism (well-being), and the name dispute (security). Notwithstanding differences between party leaderships, similarities in governance link and affect the character of "conservatism" and "nationalism." As mentioned, this linkage embraces the attitudes of the two parties concerning the centrality of the Church as a "pillar" of the nation. Similarly, I have mentioned the high level of public trust in the Church compared with political institutions.[67] The level of public trust implies that neither the VMRO-DPMNE nor the SDSM could afford to alienate Church spokesmen by neglecting the autocephaly issue.[68] Practical policy differences between the parties appear more strident than substantive. Despite Church opposition, neither party has sought to revise the notion of separation of Church and state in the Ohrid Accords despite the greater rhetorical support for the Church expressed by VMRO-DPMNE spokesmen. Despite the parties' policy similarity, high levels of support for the Church ensure its politics will remain contentious.

Homophobia and Intolerance: Seeking Support on the Cheap

Homophobia is manifested, inter alia, in government statements and policies that denigrate or disadvantage persons who are not of heterosexual orientation. Intolerance may also affect ethnic minorities negatively. Unlike discrimination, intolerance is more likely a social phenomenon than a deliberate policy, although intolerance is promoted by distinct policies. Governments express intolerance and homophobia through passive sanction or by policies that make legitimate such attitudes in society. Typically, homophobia has been manifested, for example, in insufficient police response to a 2013 Macedonian gay pride parade and the Macedonian Church's vehement condemnation of non-heterosexual relationships. British Human Rights advocate, Peter Tatchell "considered that such violence has been encouraged by the silence and inaction of the Macedonian government and police."[69] Archbishop Stefan considers that gay marriage "is not only a violation of the holy will of God but ... an introduction and a prerequisite for the dissolution of the family as the basic cell of every civilization and society."[70] Such assertions are a commonplace trope among homophobes outside Macedonia. Comparing non-heterosexual unions to the practice of bestiality, Bishop Petar of the Pelagonija-Prespa Diocese remarked, "We should not ruin the morality of the whole state just to please a handful of people."[71] According to representatives of some non-governmental organizations (NGOs), there is a "holy matrimony" between the Church, Muslim leaders, and the government on LGBT issues in the sense that all three actors strongly oppose the rights of LGBT persons.[72] Slavcho Dimitrov, an authority on the history of LGBT policy in Macedonia, considers the Church's position especially important because of its claim to "ultimate moral authority."[73]

Arguably the Church finds sanction for intolerance and homophobia in the actions of elected officials. Nikola Gruevski's government (2006–2016), for example, adopted homophobic policies, seeking electoral support in actions indirectly affecting Church concerns. Policies and statements involving ethnic toleration, gender inequality, and religious symbolism have promoted values appeasing Church supporters, yet involve little material cost to the government.[74] Non-discriminatory policies have been identified with secular values; conversely, homophobia has been correlated with certain expressions of religiosity. One critical study points to the tendency to "dissolve secularism" through such actions as the aforementioned sponsorship of the carnival in the Vevčani village near Struga, building of the church in the Skopje Fortress, and erection of giant crosses.[75]

The problem of homophobia represents a particular subset of policies the origins of which probably should be traced to "populist" homophobic attitudes.[76] Some 61% of Macedonian adults said they would not vote for a political party that championed the rights of LGBTI people. The VMRO-DPMNE promotes the homophobic image of a "real man" as representative of its supporters.[77] Both VMRO-DPMNE and the Macedonian Orthodox Church have elevated homophobia to an institutional value. There was also substantive controversy concerning the 2010 Law on non-discrimination whose final version excluded an explicit section on sexual orientation as a basis for determining discrimination.

Intolerant attitudes are varied and include the Macedonian Church's opposition to recognition of an Albanian Orthodox Church in Macedonia. Branislav Sinadinovski, an adviser to the President of DUI [Democratic Union for Integration], claims that some 70–75,000 Christian Orthodox Albanians live in Macedonia and that merely holding services in the Albanian language "does not solve the problem of Orthodox Albanians. Registering an Albanian Orthodox Church in Macedonia could be a way out. We expect support from the MOC as the establishment of an Albanian Orthodox Church in Macedonia can only be to the benefit of the MOC."[78] Bishop Timotej, Metropolitan of the Diocese of Debar and Kichevo, dismissed the request as a "typical political manipulation" [that is] a chauvinistic and nationalist project [that has] "nothing to do with religion." Dissenting religious minorities such as Bektashi Muslims and the "True Orthodox Christians" have been denied the right to register under the 2007 Law on Religious on Registration, despite the aforementioned decision of the European Court of Human Rights.[79]

Despite the inclusion of Albanian parties in governing coalitions, policies favoring Slavic Macedonians have been adopted, I have mentioned the 2009 effort of the Gruevski government to increase birth rates in areas with a higher Slavic population as well as the restrictive law on abortion adopted under the Gruevski government in 2013. In June 2018, the Social Democratic Minister of Health Venko Filipce announced that a revised law would "put women's wishes first" by requiring only consultation with a gynecologist on abortion during the first 12 weeks of pregnancy.[80]

Other instances of intolerance involve perceived anti-Islamic discrimination. Such episodes increased under the Gruevski government. The Islamic Religious Community (IZV) refused to take part in the World Religions Conference held in Podgorica (Montenegro) in October 2014 under the theme "Islam, Religions and Pluralism in Europe." The IZV leader Sulejman Rexhepi demanded guarantees for the construction or restoration of several mosques and the return of Albanian-claimed assets in the Old Bazaar in Skopje. At the Conference, a professor at the South Eastern European University in Tetovo, Ali Pajaziti, referred to a "Macedonian Culture War" initiated by VMRO-DPMNE upon coming to power in 2006. "A key point of this strategy was the 'defense of the Macedonian ethnos', the national iconography, the MOC...the racist law on fertility (in which only Macedonian zones would have benefits), the re-reading and re-writing of Macedonian history, morality, and [the defense of] politics."[81] It is difficult to know if the Albanian public shared these opinions or identified the Macedonian Orthodox Church with the Gruevski government.

Conflict between public attitudes and Macedonian aspirations to enter the European Union further complicates the issue. The latter presumes that successful candidacy entails robust legislation supporting non-discrimination. Ivo Vajgl, Member of the European Parliament, author of the report on the Republic of Macedonia, and Member of the Parliament's LGBTI Intergroup, remarked that "Macedonia has the dubious honor of having one of the worst records on LGBTI rights of all Balkan countries."[82] The report expressed concern about Macedonia's Commission for Protection against Discrimination. The Chairman had complained about the Commission's inadequate budget, the "widely spread" toleration of hate speech, violence, and intolerance in Macedonian media and state agencies, and the lack of "human resources" for legal investigation.[83] The European Parliament's investigation has been more emphatic in its condemnation and "reiterate[d] its call for the Anti-Discrimination Law to be aligned with the *acquis* as regards discrimination on grounds of sexual orientation."[84]

It is likely that the Macedonian Orthodox Church would not oppose EU membership and demands from Brussels as the probability of membership increases. The Church's apparent decision not to oppose EU membership may have resulted from the high level of public support for accession, that is, between 77% in 2014 and 80% in 2016. Similarly, the high levels of existing support for the Church in Macedonia indicate that criticizing liberal values would yield only a slight increment in popular approval of Church policies.[85]

Intolerance is related to the dominant place of ethnicity in identity. The journalist Radmila Zarevska has described this phenomenon in the context of religious authority.

> Let us not forget that every conflict in our state is immediately put into an ethnic-religious context, even when it has nothing to do with any kind of intolerance…. [T]he religious communities must work on the ground …. Only in this way can the believers become acquainted with the possible consequences of riots on religious grounds and avert major conflicts.[86]

Ironically, Zarevska's observation is compatible with Church claims on behalf of its overarching role in Macedonian society. The Holy Synod has elevated the Church as the "spiritual mother of all Orthodox Christian believers and all others, regardless of their national and ethnic background. Taking a protective role as a parent, it is advocating [that it is ready] to defend [the] national, ethnic and religious dignity of every community."[87] Such a role for Orthodoxy that transcends ethnicity enables the Church to defend a privileged position for the Macedonian language and culture, typically in the census and public instruction.

Concluding Thoughts

Intolerance, homophobia, nationalism, and conservatism are interrelated and mutually reinforcing. Macedonian social attitudes toward homosexuality, clerical insecurity concerning Western values, and the identification of nationalism with conservatism collectively shaped a reinforcing complex of values and attitudes hostile to change. To be a nationalist, at least in the Balkans, is to be a conservative and, more often than not, also a homophobe. I have suggested that the Church's strength is derived from its place in defining national identity. Neither the alternation of parties in power nor the Ohrid Accord, has threatened to change those values defended by the Church. Moreover, outspoken views of diaspora Macedonian Orthodox clerics reinforced the situation in Macedonia. Nevertheless, I believe that the Prespa Accord may contribute to altering the Church's political environment. Assuming the Accord's implementation, Skopje would confront the choice between membership in a wider European Union and defending values incompatible with EU membership. Indeed, the coincidence of the Accord with Archbishop Stefan's willingness to seek reconciliation with the Ecumenical Patriarch in omitting reference to "Macedonian" in the Church's title suggests Church involvement in the Accord's negotiation.

Further considerations suggest a distancing of the Church from traditional stances of intolerance and homophobia. First, the prospect of Macedonia's admission to the EU sharpens the conflict between traditional Church attitudes and overwhelming public endorsement of European institutions. Second, the defeat of VMRO-DPMNE in the December 2016 parliamentary elections and the conviction on charges of involvement in an illegal purchase of a luxury Mercedes of its former leader, Nikola Gruevski, removes a governing alternative that had sought legitimacy, among other ways, in an intolerant Church policy. Finally, should the renamed "Archbishopric of Ohrid" attain autocephalous status, the influence of other Orthodox primates on Macedonia in resisting change in the Church's status would be diminished. However, a less "traditional" Orthodoxy would still not have surmounted the legacy of "Caesaropapism," as it is generally understood, that is, a potentially disruptive relationship between Church and state. The idea of a Church–state "symphony" did not transfer well from fourth-century Byzantium to the multiple Balkan sovereignties. The Macedonian Church confronts an enduring challenge beyond its political environment described generally in H. Richard Niebuhr's classic work, *Christ and Culture*, that interprets various outcomes of the collision of secularism and Christian values.[88] Among those outcomes is one in which Christian Churches are "institutionalized" in a "temporal embodiment" that deliberately overlooks the "radical evil present in all human work." Arguably this assertion could be relevant to criticism of other Orthodox Churches by qualified comparison with a Church's political context.

The four themes highlighted in the introduction to this volume are clearly part of a single syndrome. There may be such a thing as a "liberal nationalist," depending on how "nationalist" is defined, but there is no such thing as a liberal homophobe or an anti-nationalist conservative. In association, these four elements work against change, keeping, in this case Macedonia, moored to a foggily remembered past, imagining the Macedonian community as surrounded by currents which are not to be tolerated.

Notes

1. Pedro Ramet, "Autocephaly and National Identity in Church–State Relations in Eastern Christianity: An Introduction," in Pedro Ramet (ed.), *Eastern Christianity and Politics in the Twentieth Century* (Durham, NC: Duke University Press, 1988), p. 5.
2. For further discussion of Orthodox Church traditions, see Aristeides Papadakis, "The Historical Tradition of Church–State Relations Under Orthodoxy," in Pedro Ramet (ed.), *Eastern Christianity and Politics in the Twentieth Century*, pp. 37–58.
3. Michael Seraphinoff, *The 19th Century Macedonian Awakening: A Study of the Works of Kiril Pejchinovich* (Lanham, MD: University Press of America, 1996), p. 132.
4. Ružica Cacanoska, "Religious Polarization of Macedonian Modern Society," in Branislav Radeljić and Martina Topić (eds.), *Religion in the Post-Yugoslav Context* (Lanham, MD: Lexington Books, 2015), p. 121.
5. "Teodosij: Renewal of the Archbishopric of Ohrid 1891!" *Makedonika: The Macedonian Blog*, n.d., at https://makedonika.wordpress.com/2008/03/06/teodosij-renewal-of-the-archbishopric-of-ohrid-1891/ [accessed 13 March 2018].
6. Doné Ilievski, *The Macedonian Orthodox Church: The Road to Independence*, translated by James M. Leech (Skopje: Macedonian Review Editions, 1973), pp. 60–61.
7. Stella Alexander, *Church and State in Yugoslavia Since 1945* (Cambridge: Cambridge University Press, 1979), pp. 48–49, 182–184.
8. Ibid., p. 183.
9. *USSR's Hand Seen in Macedonian* Church, Radio Athens, 15 January 1952, *Foreign Broadcast Information Service* (FBIS), 16 January 1952 (FBIS-1952-16).
10. Alexander, *Church and State in Yugoslavia Since 1945*, p. 187.
11. Vjekoslav Perica, *Balkan Idols, Religion and Nationalism in Yugoslav States* (Oxford: Oxford University Press, 2002), p. 174.
12. "Macedonian Church Gets Entangled in Name Dispute," *Balkan Insight*, 31 May 2018, at https://balkaninsight.com/2018/05/31/macedonia-name-dispute-spill-into-church-territory-05-31-2018/ [accessed 20 April 2019]. See also "FYROM Church Requests to Rejoin Ecumenical Patriarch After Dropping 'Macedonia'," *Greek City Times* (Sydney), 31 May 2018, at https://greekcitytimes.com/2018/05/31/fyrom-church-requests-to-rejoin-ecumenical-patriarchate-after-dropping-macedonia/ [accessed 26 April 2019].
13. Todor Cepreganov/Maja Angelovska-Panova/Dragan Zajkovski, "The Macedonian Orthodox Church," in Lucian N. Leustean (ed.), *Eastern*

Christianity and Politics in the Twenty-First Century (London: Routledge, 2014), pp. 429–430.

14. See "Macedonia 2016: International Religious Freedom Report," at https://www.state.gov/documents/organization/269084.pdf [accessed 27 April 2019].
15. "Secular Voices in the Balkans Oppose Religious Education in Public Schools," *Global Voices*, 8 August 2017, in *Nexis-Uni* [accessed 20 October 2017].
16. Albana Metaj-Stojanova, "Religious Freedoms in Republic of Macedonia," *SEEU Review*, Vol. 2, No. 1 (2015), pp. 163–164, at https://www.degruyter.com/downloadpdf/j/seeur.2015.11.issue-1/seeur-2015-0019/seeur-2015-0019.pdf [last accessed 20 April 2019].
17. Sabrina Petra Ramet, "The Macedonian Enigma," in Sabrina Petra Ramet and Ljubiša S. Adamovich (eds.), *Beyond Yugoslavia, Politics: Economics and Culture in a Shattered Community* (Boulder, CO: Westview Press, 1995), p. 219.
18. *Večernji list* (Zagreb), 9 August 1993, trans. in *FBIS* (FBIS-EEU-93-156) [accessed 22 August 2017].
19. Chapter 1 of the Constitution of the Macedonian Orthodox Church [1994], *LiCoDu* [*Freedom of Conscience and Human Rights*] (Bologna: University of Bologna), at http://licodu.cois.it/?p=7939&lang=en [last accessed 20 April 2019].
20. John Philips, *Macedonia: Warlords and Rebels in the Balkans* (London: I. B. Taurus, 2004), p. 52.
21. Helsinki Committee for Human Rights in the Republic of Macedonia, *Report on Minority Rights in the Republic of Macedonia* (Skopje), September 1999, at http://www.cilevics.eu/minelres/reports/macedonia/macedonia_NGO.htm [last accessed 20 April 2019].
22. MILS News (Skopje), 27 August 1993, in *FBIS* (FBIS-EEU-93-166) [accessed 23 September 2017].
23. MIC (Skopje), 14 June 1994, in *FBIS* (FBIS-EEU-94-115) [accessed 23 September 2017].
24. "Biography of the Archbishop of Skopje and Metropolitan of Skopje Kyr Kyr, John IV," at http://poa-info.org/archbishop [accessed 30 May 2018].
25. "Niš sopimus," 17 May 2002, at http://www.ortodoksi.net/index.php/Ni%C5%A1-sopimus [accessed 27 April 2019].
26. *MIA News Agency* (Skopje), 5 June 2002, in *BBC Monitoring International Report*, in *Access World News* [accessed 4 October 2017].
27. Zoran Bojarovski, "Macedonia: Bishop Accused of Treason After Accepting the Authority of the Serbian Orthodox Church," in *Religioscope*, 3 July 2002, at https://english.religion.info/2002/07/03/

macedonia-bishop-accused-of-treason-after-accepting-the-authority-of-the-serbian-orthodox-church/ [last accessed 20 April 2019].
28. *MIA News Agency*, 9 October 2009, *Access World News* [accessed 10 October 2017].
29. *MIA News Agency*, 5 January 2004, in *BBC Monitoring European*, 5 January 2004, in *ProQuest* [accessed 1 October 2017].
30. "New Bishops Strengthen Macedonian Church's Hand," Institute for War and Peace Reporting, at https://iwpr.net/global-voices/new-bishops-strengthen-macedonian-churchs-hand [accessed 1 October 2017].
31. *MIA News Agency* (Skopje), 11 January 2004, in *BBC Monitoring Internal Reports* in *Access World News* [accessed 4 October 2017].
32. Minute Adopted by the WCC Central Committee on the Unlawful Detention of Archbishop Jovan of Ochrid and Metropolitan of Skopje of the Serbian Orthodox Church (sic), *Kolympari* (Crete), 28 August–5 September 2012; and *The Churches in International Affairs 2010–2013*, Commission of the Churches on International Affairs (Geneva, 2014), p. 364.
33. Amnesty International, "Macedonia: Prisoner of Conscience: Zoran Vraniškovski(m), Religious Leader," EUR 65/08/2004, at https://www.amnesty.org/en/search/?q=vraniskovski&sort=date [last accessed 20 April 2019].
34. Analytical report for the Opinion on the application from the former Yugoslav Republic of Macedonia for EU membership (COM[2005] 562 final COM[2005] 557 final), 9 November 2005, p. 25, at https://ec.europa.eu/neighbourhood-enlargement/sites/near/files/archives/pdf/key_documents/2005/package/sec_1425_final_analytical_report_mk_en.pdf [accessed 20 April 2019].
35. Ibid.
36. European Court of Human Rights(Strasbourg) Orthodox Ohrid Archdiocese (Greek-Orthodox Ohrid Archdiocese of the Peć Patriarchy) v. the former Yugoslav Republic of Macedonia—First Section Judgment, pp. 37–38, at https://www.strasbourgconsortium.org/common/document.view.php?docId=7459 [last accessed 20 April 2019].
37. European Court of Human Rights (Strasbourg), "Greek Orthodox Ohrid Archdiocese v. FYROM: Grand Chamber Referral Request," 5 April 2018, at https://hrwf.eu/macedonia-orthodox-ohrid-archdiocese-greek-orthodox-ohrid-archdiocese-of-the-pec-patriarchy-v-the-former-yugoslav-republic-of-macedonia-grand-chamber-referral-request/ [accessed 27 April 2018].
38. *Dnevnik* (Skopje), 30 January 2004, in *Access World News* [accessed 10 October 2017].

39. *MIA News Agency* (Skopje), 20 July 2007, in *Access World News* [accessed 10 October 2017].
40. *Nova Makedonija* (Skopje), 29 October 2012, in *Access World News* [accessed 13 October 2017].
41. *Vest* (Skopje), 4 August 2009, in *Access World News* [accessed 13 October 2017].
42. "Church of Greece Concerned by Bulgarian Orthodox Decision on Macedonia Church," *Sofia Globe*, 18 December 2018, at https://sofiaglobe.com/2017/12/18/church-of-greece-concerned-by-bulgarian-orthodox-church-decision-on-macedonia-church/ [last accessed 20 April 2019].
43. *Constitution of the Republic of Macedonia* (as amended up to 2011), at http://www.wipo.int/edocs/lexdocs/laws/en/mk/mk014en.pdf [last accessed 20 April 2019].
44. Islamska Vjerska Zajednica.
45. Zhidas Daskalovski, "Language and Identity: The Ohrid Framework Agreement and Liberal Notions of Citizenship and Nationality in Macedonia," *Journal on Ethnopolitics and Minority Issues in Europe* (Budapest), Vol. 1, No. 1 (2002), pp. 18, 24–25, at http://www.ecmi.de/fileadmin/downloads/publications/JEMIE/2002/nr1/Focus1-2002Daskalovski.pdf [last accessed 20 April 2019].
46. "Macedonia's Ruling Party' Attacks Constitutional Court'," *Balkan Insight*, 22 April 2009, at https://balkaninsight.com/2009/04/22/macedonia-s-ruling-party-attacks-constitutional-court/ [accessed 20 April 2019].
47. *MIA News Agency* (Skopje), 1 March 2005 in *Access World News* [accessed 10 October 2017].
48. *Nova Makedonija* (Skopje), 7 March 2012, in *BBC Monitoring Europe in Access World News* [accessed 22 March 2018].
49. *MIA News Agency*, 7 July 2007, in *BBC Monitoring Europe* in *Proquest* [accessed 23 October 2017].
50. *MIA News Agency*, 7 July 2007, in *Access World News* [accessed 24 October 2017].
51. *Dnevnik* (Skopje) 9 June 2005, in *Access World News* [accessed 24 October 2017].
52. "Survey on Religion and Religious Hate Speech in the Republic of Macedonia," 'A' Rating Agency (Skopje), October 2014, at http://bezomrazno.mk/wp-content/uploads/2013/10/Survey-on-religion-and-religious-hate-speech-in-the-republic-of-Macedonia.pdf [last accessed 20 April 2019].
53. "Religious Belief and National Belonging in Central and Eastern Europe," 10 May 2017 (Washington, DC), at http://www.pewforum.

org/2017/05/10/religious-belief-and-national-belonging-in-central-and-eastern-europe/ [last accessed 20 April 2019].
54. Ružica Cacanoska, "Religious Polarization of Macedonian Modern Society," in Branislav Radeljić and Martina Topić (eds.), *Religion in the Post-Yugoslav Context* (Lanham, MD: Lexington Books, 2015), p. 135.
55. Jonuz Abdullai and Xhemali Çupi, "Policy Making and Secularism in Macedonia," in *Revista de Stiinte Politice* (Craiova), No. 50 (2016), at https://search-proquest-com.ezaccess.libraries.psu.edu/docview/1807503966/7F05B2A7DCA547C0PQ/1?accountid=13158 [accessed 23 October 2017].
56. Социјалдемократски сојуз на Македонија–СДСМ (Social Democratic Union of Macedonia SDSM).
57. Alexandar Spasenovski,"Politićkite partii i granicite sekularizmot vo republika *Makedonija,*" *Policy Briefs,* Berlin/ Konrad Adenauer Stiftung, December 2014, at http://www.kas.de/wf/doc/kas_40070-1522-2-30.pdf?141225140859 [accessed 23 October 2017].
58. Zachary T. Irwin, "The Importance of Tolerance: Intolerance and Its Consequences in the Balkans," in Sabrina P. Ramet, Christine M. Hassenstab, and Ola Listhaug (eds.), *Building Democracy in the Yugoslav Successor States: Accomplishments, Setbacks, and Challenges Since 1990* (Cambridge: Cambridge University Press, 2017), pp. 66–67.
59. Sinisa Jakov Marusic, "Giant Macedonian Cross, 'Not Anti-Muslim Symbol'," *Balkan Transitional Justice,* 26 June 2014, at https://balkaninsight.com/2014/06/26/macedonia-s-giant-cross-not-a-provocation-initiator-says/ [accessed 23 October 2017].
60. Sinisa Jakov Marusic, "Macedonians Shrink as Ethnic Albanians Expand," *Balkan Insight,* 14 February 2011, at https://balkaninsight.com/2011/02/14/white-plague-decimates-macedonians/ [accessed 27 April 2019].
61. *MIA News Agency* (Skopje) in 30 June 2015, *Access World News* [accessed 23 October 2017]; and Maja Zivanovic, "Serbian Patriarch 'Motherhood Is Obligatory' Declaration Condemned," *Balkan Insight,* 25 October 2017, at https://balkaninsight.com/2017/10/25/serbian-patriarch-s-statement-on-maternity-sparked-anger-on-social-networks-10-25-2017/ [accessed 21 April 2019].
62. Concluding observations on the Third Periodical Report of the Republic of Macedonia; for the complete report, see the previous note.
63. See note 60. See also Ana Miškovska Kajevska, "The 2013 Law on Termination of Pregnancy: A Clear Case of the Suspension of Democracy in Macedonia," Paper presented at the World Congress of Political Science (IPSA) (Poznan), July 2016, at http://hera.org.mk/wp-content/uploads/2016/09/Ana-M-Kajevska-Abortus-Ukinuvanje-na-demokratijata_ENG.pdf [last accessed 21 April 2019].

64. Sabrina P. Ramet, "The Way Were—And Should Be Again? European Orthodox Churches and the 'Idyllic Past'," in Timothy Byrnes and Peter Katzenstein (eds.), *Religion in an Expanding Europe* (Cambridge: Cambridge University Press, 2006), pp. 149–150.
65. Sinisa Jakov Marusic, "Macedonian Church's Facebook Ban Annoys Clerics," *Balkan Insight*, 28 October 2013, at https://balkaninsight.com/2013/10/28/macedonian-church-facebook-ban-disturbs-clerics/ [accessed 21 April 2019].
66. Harold D. Lasswell and Abraham Kaplan, *Power and Society, a Framework for Political Inquiry* (New Haven, CT: Yale University Press, 1950), pp. 55–56.
67. *Nova Makedonija* (Skopje), 7 March 2012 [note 48].
68. *MIA News Agency*, 7 July 2007 [notes 54, 55].
69. Dan Littauer, "LGBTI Center in Macedonia Torched in Latest Wave of Anti-Gay Violence," *LGBTQ Nation*, 6 July 2013, at https://www.lgbtqnation.com/2013/07/lgbti-center-in-macedonia-torched-in-latest-wave-of-anti-gay-violence/ [accessed 21 March 2019].
70. "Macedonian Local Elections Whip Up Anti-Gay Hate," *Gay Star News*, 5 February 2013, at https://www.gaystarnews.com/article/macedonia-local-elections-whip-anti-gay-hate050213/#gs.6y2m9u [accessed 21 April 2019].
71. Sinisa Jakov Marusic, "Activists to Sue Macedonian Church Over Anti-Gay Remarks," *Balkan Insight*, 14 January 2011, at https://balkaninsight.com/2011/01/14/human-rights-activists-to-sue-macedonian-orthodox-church/ [accessed 21 April 2019].
72. COWI (Danish Institute of Human Rights), "Study on Homophobia, Transphobia and Discrimination on Grounds of Sexual Orientation and Gender Identity: Sociological Report: In the Former Yugoslav Republic of Macedonia," n.d., p. 3, at https://www.coe.int/t/Commissioner/Source/LGBT/FYROMSociological_E.pdf [last accessed 24 April 2019].
73. Slavcho Dimtrov, "The Triumphant Distribution of the Heteronormative Sensible: The Case of Sexual Minorities in Transitional Macedonia, 1991–2012," in Christine M. Hassenstab and Sabrina P. Ramet (eds.), *Gender (In)equality and Gender Politics in Southeastern Europe: A Question of Justice* (Basingstoke and New York: Palgrave Macmillan, 2015), p. 231.
74. Irwin, "The Importance of Tolerance" [note 58], pp. 66–67.
75. Jonuz Abdullai and Xhemali Cupi, "Policy Making and Secularism in Macedonia," in *Revista de Ştinte Politice* (RSP) (Craiova), No. 50 (2016), pp. 166–179, at http://cis01.central.ucv.ro/revistadestiintepolitice/files/numarul50_2016/15.pdf [accessed 4 June 2018].

76. ILGA Europe (Brussels), *Annual Review of the Human Rights Situation of Lesbian, Gay, Bisexual, and Intersex People in Europe 2017*, May 2017, p. 12, at https://www.ilga-europe.org/sites/default/files/Attachments/annual_review_2017_online.pdf [last accessed 25 April 2019].
77. Misha Popovikj, "Homophobia in the Contemporary Public Discourse in Macedonia: Constructing Homosexuality as National Other" (Skopje, 2010), pp. 14–15, at https://www.academia.edu/13448645/Homophobia_in_the_Contemporary_Public_Discourse_in_Macedonia_Constructing_homosexuality_as_national_Other [accessed 15 December 2017]. See also, "Videos of VMRO-DPMNE/Real Men," 2016–2017, at https://www.bing.com/videos/search?q=vmro-dpmne%2freal+man&qpvt=+VMRO-dpmne%2freal+man+&FORM=VDRE [accessed 16 December 2017].
78. *Makfax News Agency* (Skopje), 1 December 2014, in *Nexis-Uni* [accessed 12 January 2018].
79. US Department of State, Bureau of Democracy, Human Rights and Labor, *International Religious Freedom Report for 2017—Macedonia 2017: International Religious Freedom Report*, pp. 6–8, at https://www.state.gov/j/drl/rls/irf/religiousfreedom/index.htm#wrapper [last accessed 25 April 2019].
80. Sinisa Jakub Marusic, "Macedonia to Ease Restrictions on Abortion," *Balkan Insight*, 8 June 2018, at https://balkaninsight.com/2018/06/08/macedonia-to-ease-abortion-restrictions-06-07-2018/ [accessed 21 April 2019].
81. Ali Pajaziti, "Interreligious Dialogue in the Macedonian Context; from Natural Diversity to Secular Theocracy," in Ednan Aslan, Ranja Ebrahim, and Marcia Hermansen (eds.), *Islam, Religions and Pluralism in Europe*, Wiener Beiträge zur Islamforschung (Vienna: Springer VS, 2016), p. 199.
82. "For LGBTI Rights in 2014–2019?" Intergroup on LGBT Rights [European Parliament], at https://lgbti-ep.eu/ [accessed 27 April 2019].
83. Dusko Minovski, *Commission for Protection Against Discrimination: Experiences of the First Equality Body in Macedonia in Its First Three Years of Operating*, at https://www.scribd.com/document/245730073/Dusko-MINOVSKI-COMMISSION-FOR-PROTECTION-AGAINST-DISCRIMINATION-EXPERIENCES-OF-THE-FIRST-EQUALITY-BODY-IN-MACEDONIA-IN-ITS-THREE-YEARS-OF-OPERATING [last accessed 27 April 2019].
84. European Parliament, "Report on the on the 2016 Commission Report on the Former Yugoslav Republic of Macedonia (2016/2310(INI)," Committee on Foreign Affairs, Rapporteur: Ivo Vajgl, 6 March 2017 (A8-0055/2017), at http://www.europarl.europa.eu/doceo/document/A-8-2017-0055_EN.pdf?redirect [last accessed 26 April 2019].

85. According to a WIN/Gallup International Poll, 88% of people in Macedonia, 83 in Kosovo and 77% in Romania consider themselves religious. See Marcus Tanner, "Religion Remains Powerful in Balkans, Survey Shows," *Balkan Insight*, 15 January 2018, at https://balkaninsight.com/2018/01/15/religion-remains-powerful-in-balkans-survey-shows-01-15-2018/?utm_source=Balkan%20Insight%20Newsletters&utm_campaign=17584edcca-BI_DAILY&utm_medium=email&utm_term=0_4027db42dc-17584edcca-319704473 [accessed 21 April 2019].
86. *Nova Makedonija* (Skopje), 7 March 2012, trans. in *BBC Monitoring* (9 March 2012), *Access World News* [last accessed 26 April 2019].
87. *MIA News Agency* (Skopje) in English, 23 February 2017, in *Nexus-Uni*, 10 January 2018.
88. H. Richard Niebuhr, *Christ and Culture* (New York: Harper & Row, 1951), pp. 147–148.

CHAPTER 9

Navigating the Challenge of Liberalism: The Resurrection of the Orthodox Church in Post-Communist Albania

Isa Blumi

Abstract Surviving the Balkans' twentieth century was no simple task for Albanian Christians. Facing a regime of capitalism that absorbed the socialist Balkans in the 1990s, the efforts of Albanian Orthodox Christians to adapt seem inadequate. This chapter explores how one may read the struggles of the post-communist Albanian Autocephalous Orthodox Church that confronted the "universal" liberal enterprise in the context of the concurrent tensions within Albanian circles seeking the reaffirmation of ethno-nationalist concerns. In questioning how the rebuilding of the Church reflected an aggressive missionary approach led by Greek-born Archbishop Anastasios Yannoulatos, it will become clear how necessary it is to read this ongoing process of rebuilding on several institutional and ideological/spiritual planes.

I. Blumi (✉)
Stockholm University, Stockholm, Sweden
e-mail: isa.blumi@su.se

© The Author(s) 2019
S. P. Ramet (ed.), *Orthodox Churches and Politics in Southeastern Europe*, Palgrave Studies in Religion, Politics, and Policy,
https://doi.org/10.1007/978-3-030-24139-1_9

Subject to persistent violence—physical, psychological, and material—those inhabiting the southern fringes of the Albanian-speaking world have a particularly difficult twentieth-century story to tell. Targeted by competing ethno-national states hoping to steer individual loyalties toward Athens, Constantinople, Belgrade, Sofia or Tirana's orbit, the affiliations of Albanian Orthodox Christians (AOC) have taken numerous convoluted paths. In the last century, many insisted that concessions given to other "national peoples" by the Ecumenical Patriarch in Constantinople/Istanbul—recognizing autonomously administered churches like the Bulgarian Orthodox Church—also applied to them. The problem was that pan-Hellenist advocates, many deeply invested in the expansionist Greek state realizing the "Megali Idea," refused to surrender the claim that Albanian Christians were culturally Greek. The resulting struggle to utilize local Albanian to disseminate the Church's teachings shaped much of the subsequent history of the region. The conflict has served as the enduring question that informs recent attempts at reconstituting the Orthodox Church leadership destroyed by decades of state persecution under the communist regime of Enver Hoxha (1944–1991).

In the following, we explore how in this distinctive post-communist era, Albanian Christian struggles to reconstitute a community otherwise eviscerated from the cultural terrain reflects an enduring tension about the subsequent role of the Church's foreign-born leadership. Complicating the process is the rise of Euro-American liberalism in the Balkans, both economically and culturally. The underlying task of reconstituting a community of believers in face of globalization has complicated a transitional story repeated often in the literature on the Balkans today.[1] While parallels are evident, the Albanian case proves unique.[2]

BEFORE THE RESURRECTION (NGJALLJA)

For much of the period from the 1880s until World War One, Albanian members of the Orthodox Church sacrificed life and limb to practice their faith in a manner that reflected their distinctive cultural heritage. Crucial to this struggle was countering the ideological and theological denial of the existence of an Albanian Christian community explicitly made by Greek, Bulgarian, and Serbian nationalists. A component of this hostility to Albanian national rights was the collaboration between Constantinople-based authorities and their locally based allies such as the Metropolitan of Kastoria, Karavangjelis. This collusion to enforce Hellenist cultural hegemony included using Ottoman authorities to violently persecute Albanian-speaking priests using their mother tongue during mass. Papa Kristo Negovani, for instance, was murdered on 12 February 1905, just two days after performing a sermon in his native Tosk Albanian in front of the outraged Metropolitan Karavangjelis. This act of defiance and the formal institutional response served as the platform for a generation of would-be nationalists to invest in collaborative activism across the world.[3]

Following Negovani's lead, Petro Nini Luarasi defied Church authorities by translating many critical Christian texts into local Tosk Albanian.[4] While today celebrated, these efforts, repeated throughout the larger Mediterranean world where Albanians lived, provoked considerable debate at the time. Well into the interwar period, Albanian-speakers in the diaspora struggled to conjoin their spiritual needs with the necessity to adjust to a new liberal political order that broke apart multi-ethnic empires. The investment toward securing some ethnic national home in the Balkans meant greater collaboration among various Albanian diasporas against the pan-Hellenist creed of the Church. In part because the Church's cultural politics became indistinguishable from Greek nationalism, the nature of this deadly struggle for a multifaith Albanian homeland would prove the primary reason that AOC members have remained alienated by Constantinople's rigid cultural politics, no matter how "universalist" Constantinople may claim to be.

By the end of the Ottoman Empire, Albanians realized they too would have to secure autonomy from the various religious institutions like the Diyanet in Kemalist Turkey and the Orthodox Church, now co-opted to serve as extensions of an ethno-national state building project in "Greater Greece" and Serbia. From as far away as Boston, Cairo, or Bucharest, AOCs laid the foundations for the establishment of an Autocephalous Albanian Orthodox Church (AAOC) in the 1920s.[5] Cairo-based activist Milo Duçi (1870–1933) spent most of his life seeking to mobilize AOC in Egypt to secure separation from the increasingly Greek nationalist clergy ministering there. Among his activities was serving as president of an organization called Vellazerise Shqipëtarëve, or Albanian Brotherhood, which promoted the cultural preservation of Albanians in Egypt. He also edited various publications, including *Besa*, in collaboration with Thoma Abrami, and *Shqipëria*, written specifically for AOC members living in Cairo. By 1922, Duçi had also arranged for the creation of the publishing company Shoqëria botonjëse shqiptare/ Société albanaise d'éditions to help distribute translated religious texts produced by priests such as Luarasi. In apparent coordination with activists from Boston and throughout the Balkans, Duçi's publications of crucial religious texts translated into regional Tosk Albanian corresponded with the distribution of aid the diaspora collected to build schools in the homeland. The efforts to help teach Christianity in the native language of the Western Balkans' inhabitants would carry on beyond the truncated and besieged Albania's formal independence.[6]

By this time, the AOC elite that emerged around the charismatic activism of men like Boston-based Theofan (Fan) Noli declared during the Berat Congress of 1922 an Autocephalous Church. With considerable pressure applied from the sizable diaspora in the Americas and Egypt, by 1937 the Ecumenical Patriarchate of Constantinople could no longer resist and recognized its autocephaly.[7] The hard-earned distinction, however, would face devastation under Enver Hoxha's regime.

This latter period of persecution and the resulting destruction of the institutional and intellectual superstructure of Albanian religious practices prove invaluable to understanding the current status of Albanian Orthodox Christians living under the authority of their hesitantly reconstructed Church, led by Greek-born Archbishop Anastasios Yannoulatos (b. 1929) appointed by the Ecumenical Patriarchate in 1991. Crucially, the context of "the reconstruction from ruins of the fully disintegrated Autocephalous Church of Albania," was enduring fears of Greek irredentism. As much as xenophobic "afterimages" afflicted Albanians in an era rapidly shifting from communist rule to Euro-American hegemony, Greek, Montenegrin, Macedonian, and Serbian nationalism proved equally resilient. Indeed, the enduring pressure from Greek nationalists since World War Two accounts for much of the visceral nationalism in communist-era Albania and its aftermath.[8]

Facing a NATO state along its southern border that persistently claimed that the Orthodox Christians living in Albania were ethnically Greek, much of the investment in destroying associations with Hellenism required a heavy dosage of Albanian particularism.[9] In this respect, the subsequent post-communist "afterimage" of strident nationalism among Church members reflected suspicions that Greek nationalism was behind the aggressive push by Church authorities, led by Greek Priest Sebastianos throughout 1991–1992, to tie a resurrection of the Church with "Greek" rights. For this, the appointed Greek-born leadership has since been under suspicion, a legacy of fear that obviously shapes much of the current state of disconnection between the Church and many Albanian Orthodox in Albania today.

Preaching to the Wrong Choir

The particularly devastating consequences of state-imposed atheism in communist-era Albania proved to be the disappearance of indigenous clergy, especially vital for the AOC in the context of a post-communist period of regeneration. The lack of indigenous clergy, at a time when the old regime was collapsing and religious organizations were flooding the country, meant the entirety of the rebuilding process would be in the hands of foreign (Greek-born, no less) personalities. The simple fact so few Albanians alive were "qualified" to lead the rebuilding process gave Church authorities the justification to push for what many believed was a renewed campaign by Greek nationalists to annex southern Albania.

Contributing to the struggle over hearts, souls, and minds was the "victorious West." As a project to subordinate/integrate the region to service the new regional hegemon based in Brussels/Washington, "integrating" the Balkans into the West's sphere has had a deep impact on how several hundred thousand Albanians have made spiritual choices. In the face of severe austerity and the emigration of millions to the West, many Orthodox Albanians proved more resolutely nationalist and refused to blindly offer their fealty to an Orthodox Church leadership that initially could not hide its pan-Hellenist colors. The aggressive, and ineptly public, campaign by Church officials throughout 1991–1992 had the effect of alienating the very Albanian Christians targeted by the program of "resurrection" promoted by the Church. Worse, many sources interviewed for this chapter connect efforts to exploit Albania's post-communist chaos by the "Greek" nationalist leadership to the larger imposition of neoliberal economic (dis)order.[10]

What Albanians associate with globalism has been both deindustrialization (with the concomitant unemployment and massive demographic shifts as Albanians emigrate) and new expectations of cultural liberalization (and thus denationalization). To those desperately seeking to protect what was left of the Albanian nation, the waves of fellow citizens fleeing to Italy or Greece (often to continue onwards to larger Western Europe) opened the door for irredentists to renew the "Megali Idea" agenda long associated with the conservative factions in civic and spiritual Greek life.[11] For many, the agendas of irredentist Greeks and the liberals pushing the discourse of tolerance and open markets were intertwined. Often, those signaling a need to adapt to "Western" values of tolerance, especially in respect to embracing "minorities" in society—cultural, economic, and ethnic—seemed closely associated with efforts to subdue the Albanian nation. To many, even among the first generation growing up since the fall of the Hoxha regime, nationalism and religious tradition were equally evil remnants of the past. In sum, fears of neighbors exploiting the chaos associated with globalism ignited a reactionary wave of the three often mutually reinforcing "syndromes"—nationalism, conservatism, and intolerance—as itemized by Ramet in the introduction to this volume.

For members of the Albanian Orthodox Church interviewed over the last year, the new, almost entirely uncontested liberal order imposed on their homelands at the material level has its spiritual equivalent. To many, their wish to regain their faith while retaining their ethnic distinctiveness and strengthening their nation clashes with the Church administration that since the early 1990s has adopted "contradictory agendas." This tension is largely unreported in sanctioned Church material but legible indirectly when reading between the lines of official statements. Such readings are made possible further by the eager help of numerous AOC interviewees who point out the divergence of needs respective to the post-communist project of rebuilding the newer Autocephalous Albanian Orthodox Church.

At the heart of the enduring mistrust of the Church leadership is the fact that much of the past 30 years has been clouded by the lingering impression pan-Hellenist agendas are still being served. The reported "lack of indigenous clergy" and the subsequent, "opportunistic" appointment of a Greek-born Archbishop, despite the explicit demands that the AAOC be led by native-born clergy, has clearly upset those hoping for a Church that explicitly serves the nationalist instincts of its people. In this respect, it is interesting to monitor how official Church media respond to these accusations. Rather than dutifully engaging in a search for suitable clergy, for instance, the choice by the primary representatives of the Church has been an attempt to smear dissenters as mere "communists."[12]

In the face of this debate tactic, some self-declared faithful feel alienated by a "foreign" leadership unable to communicate to them as Albanians. For many, the Catholics are the working model of a nationalist church. Under the leadership of Archbishop Rrok Mirdita, long serving the powerful Albanian Catholic diaspora in the Bronx, New York, the Catholic Church's reconstruction since the early 1990s reflects the right combination of openly nationalist and religiously responsible leadership.[13] Indeed, according to those supporting an Elbasan-based opposition to the current AAOC leadership, failure from the start to make it clear that the Church, as it was being rebuilt, would follow the Catholic lead, has meant a significantly divided constituency.

The opposition has had two principal concerns, largely silenced in the official media of the Church. The first is the underlying principle established in 1929 that only an Albanian national can serve as Archbishop of the AAOC. Obviously, the appointment of Greek-born Archbishop Anastasios did not fit this criterion. Faced with much the same criticism directed at Sunni Muslim institutions rebuilt with Saudi and Turkish money, the AAOC leadership has been consistently accused of being under the influence of "foreign" powers. It has not been reassuring to see how adamant "the Church" has remained with its choice. The struggle over the initial arrival of foreign-born clergy would last until 1998 but many claim the Church has done little to assuage the concerns that they are serving foreign agendas after this agreement with the government.[14]

Perhaps the greatest ongoing tension is with the aggressive campaign to retrieve Church properties. Led largely from abroad via organizations close to Greece, Serbia, and Russia, the efforts to reclaim properties confiscated in the Hoxha-era meant those either living or working in these facilities faced eviction and unemployment. More damning still was the way foreign Church officials characterized the resistance from local communities affected by these legal battles over property. Periodic clashes with local government and civic courts over properties the Church (again, supported by foreign entities) loudly claims as its own is generally accompanied with crude references to an Albanian hostility to European traditions, reflecting their cultural backwardness. What Church declarations fail to acknowledge is that the efforts to enforce local court rulings that seek to limit the AAOC's claims on municipal properties, in for instance to southern town of Përmet throughout 2014, are applauded by Albanians of all religious backgrounds.

These clear conflicts of interest that pitted civil society against the "Greek" authorities had become international scandals.[15] They also reignited an undercurrent of opposition to the Archbishop in particular, a discomfort to which the Church regularly responds by characterizing those raising concerns as infected with "sick fantasies" that hark back to old tropes about the Albanian Church circulating in some circles.[16]

Subsequent efforts through sympathetic newspaper editorials to defuse the scandal focused on the accomplishments of this Archbishop—from building the largest cathedrals in the Balkans to receiving humanitarian awards in the US. These narratives, however, failed to impress. Worse, the tone of the communication was considered condescending and neocolonial. It is pointed out, for instance, that the Russian and Serbian Orthodox Church webpages regularly reported on "Albanian thuggery" when the locals resisted the huge land grabs by "the Church." Coupled by the equally ostentatious construction projects of massive cathedrals visited by thousands of foreign pilgrims as well as Serbian, Russian, and Greek dignitaries, the subsequent lecturing from official Church media about the need to embrace the global agenda adopted by Archbishop Anastasios proved especially corrosive.[17]

Worse still is the concern that the leadership has failed to stand up to the moral collapse of Albanian society as it faces the tidal wave of liberalism. Far from creating a strengthened moral and theological barrier, the AAOC leadership is accused of being far too "liberal" in its embrace of interfaith dialogue and the "western discourse" of tolerance. The explicitly ecumenical and "inclusive" narrative promoted by Archbishop Anastasios thus directly contradicts the sensibilities of Albanians feeling their nation is "under siege." Sources tied to the Elbasan-based opposition to the current AAOC leadership complain that their struggle against the hegemony of liberal discourses and the associated liberal hostility to exclusive ethno-national, homophobic, hegemonic religious paradigms is directly undermined by Archbishop Anastasios' widely distributed lectures on ecumenical tolerance. To many, the messages distilled in his numerous published interviews and lectures all seem to at best indirectly respond to demands from Albanians for the AAOC to reflect first the concerns of Albanians, not those in the rest of the world.[18] With a large group of missionaries from the US aiding in projecting this universal message from a pulpit Albanians feel is exclusively meant to address their needs, there remains a strong divide that periodically manifests itself in open defiance of the hierarchy on the part of the ordinary clergy and civilian population.[19]

In short, a strong contradiction exists between official Church doctrine that openly tries to accommodate a "liberal" sensibility and the frustrated expectations of self-identified Albanian laymen fearing foreign influence. The tension over losing the youth to immorality is especially crucial to fully appreciate the multiple pressures peoples affected by these transitions are experiencing. One reflection of this has been an apparent residual mistrust of formal organized religion among Albania's population; the results of various (albeit disputed) polls and censuses seem to suggest Albanians have not recovered from the old regime's allergy to religion.[20] Albanians have consistently made it clear to pollsters, academics, and state census takers that they believe in God while being hostile to the institutions representing their faith. In fact, the numbers for the Orthodox Church in particular have proven consistently dismal. A 1999 study conducted by sociologists at the University of Tirana found that only 3.1% of those asked went to a place of worship once a week, even if 90% believed in God.[21] These numbers would be reflected again in a 2011 census that specifically exposed Orthodox Christians as being detached from their faith.

Laypersons wishing to see a more pro-active, national Church that would resist the evils of a liberal culture infecting their children seem the most disappointed today. While their voices are largely shut out from the official documentation produced by the Church, the manner in which their combined fears as a dying Albanian Christian community facing predatory foreigners and their corrupted local politician allies stealing their property, in tandem with the flight to Greece of tens of thousands (and their "conversion for papers"), many AOC have expressed quite visceral forms of the syndromes as outlined in the introduction to this volume.[22]

The most evident manifestation of this is the blaring islamophobia that operates within the larger context of xenophobia directed at Saudis and Turks and extended to Greek, Slav, Vlach, and Macedonian minorities. There is also a cultural/lifestyle dynamic in the growing displays of intolerance among the frustrated members of the AOC. As throughout the Balkans since the rise of liberalism in the 1990s, there is an element of homophobic regressive back-tracking in this segment of Albanian society.[23]

That said, research on the ground both in the Balkans and among North America's sizable Orthodox Christian diaspora suggests a far more present concern. There is an apparent realization that the AAOC may in fact represent what has long been a stated fear preached by the former regime: religious institutions and their clergy are nothing better than "agents of foreign states" seeking to destroy the unity of the Albanian people. Albania's sectarian diversity, long deemed a weakness by neighbors and imperialist powers alike, seems to have come to surface since the mid-1990s and more and more beleaguered, reactionary members of the AOC community want an aggressively nationalistic and sectarian clergy.

While many Orthodox Albanians had hoped for an explicitly nationalist Church to arise from the debris left behind as the former regime collapsed, the actual policies of the Greek and American-born leaders appointed by Constantinople point to a different trajectory.[24] Interlocutors constantly stress the contradictory public statements made by clergy, especially those of Archbishop Anastasios. They lament that the process of resurrecting the Church—building massive, expensive cathedrals that rarely fill—appears to have promoted a decisively "universalist" agenda and therefore antidote to the explicit needs of a threatened nation.

The simple explanation for why the Church is not responding to Albanian interests is that the Hellenistic Ecumenical Patriarch in Istanbul appointed an explicitly non-ethnic oriented clergy. More suspicious still is the fact that the members of the team supporting Archbishop Anastasios' reign in Albania all come from a "missionary" background. Indeed, many, including Archbishop Anastasios himself, previously served in Africa or seminaries in North America, addressing a decidedly "foreign" audience with missionary passion for a universal faith.[25] That a seasoned Greek-born missionary in Africa would be, after considerable hostility from the government of Sali Berisha, given the responsibility of resurrecting the AAOC proved immediately suspect. The consistent preaching of a universalist message, even with a suggested Greek-centric underpinning, has only exasperated Albanian nativist fears.[26]

The problem for Albanians when observing "foreigners" preaching tolerance toward some of the same minority Greek and Macedonian communities actively championed by irredentist projects in neighboring states is self-evident. To many, the project since the Archbishop formally assumed his present office in 1992 after a long political battle with then Prime Minister Sali Berisha has been to deemphasize the particularities of a Church serving a nationalist cause. In its place, the Church is promoting a universal spiritual message, repeated often as the Archbishop travels the world proclaiming his role in bringing peoples together.[27] It is the general concern that surrendering to this "new" doctrine of tolerance and universalism, unhesitatingly associated with the parallel expansion of the "West," suggests that the hard fought-for autonomy of Albanian spiritual institutions prior to World War Two has now been lost.

The suspicion that the Church no longer invests in the required fortifying role of consolidating the nation seems warranted when one considers the public statements and the heavy investment in emphasizing the "diversity" of practising Christians in Albania by the official Church. The equally celebrated global presence of the Archbishop's personality extends to being the honorary President of the Conference of Religions for Peace (the largest interfaith organization in the world) and thus exhibits a self-declared goal to be "present in various ecumenical activities and contributing to efforts for peaceful cooperation and solidarity in our region and beyond."[28] To Albanian nationalists of all varieties—practising Christians or not—these gestures are incongruent to a nationalist position necessary in face of regional challenges.

The Church organizations busily building new infrastructure in Albania seem remarkably tone-deaf to the demands of Albanians for a Church reassuring them of their national heritage. Rather than seeing homegrown leaders taking the mantel of protecting the nation from globalism, liberalism, Greek irredentists, and other threats, it is American-born missionaries who are the most active advocates of the Church in Albania today. Like Archbishop Anastasios himself, when holding mass and speaking to the larger community via various media, the feeling is that these men have adopted the kind of patronizing attitudes about which Albanians often complain when dealing with Protestant Evangelical and Turkish- or Saudi-trained imams. Especially problematic is the constant reiteration of the discourse of "tolerance" and "inter-faith dialogue" associated with the liberal institutes funded by International Organizations and western-based NGOs that have flooded Albania since 1991. As with those other foreign organizations, the "aggressive imposition" [*imponim aggressive*] of foreign ideals by the official Church leadership frustrates Albanians for the utter lack of any nationalist underpinnings in the liturgies of their religious institutions. Tied to an equally unrepresented political class ruling Albania since the early 1990s, the frustrations with an ineffective AAOC have translated into open street protests that point to many culprits today.[29]

According to those close to the Albanian-born clergy and the leaders, or "guardians" (*mbrojtës*) of what remains of the AOC community that is opposing the current AAOC leadership, the transition led by an Archbishop with no nationalist credentials has ruined a critical branch of Albanians' ecumenical national heritage. In response, AOC leaders publicly lament the waves of younger Albanians who, seen at one time as potential adherents, now aggressively resist overtures to return to the Church on precisely these partisan, nationalist concerns. Preferring to embrace secular nationalism, or simply fleeing the homeland in search work, those responsible for what Albanian nationalist Church officials suggest is an "anti-religious" generation have become unequivocally associated with "the West." In this respect, the immorality promoted by Westernization is the result of a generation of Albanians who eagerly seek to shed their "traditions" that include associating with an ethno-national community. The demand among many Albanians for a Church clergy that devotes its teachings to reaffirm the distinctive Albanian cultural heritage is thus in direct contradiction to a message of universal love for others, regardless of language and national association. In other words, Albanian Christians have been pitted against new forms of social engineering via either a market-driven commercial apparatus or a selective use of universal (and not exclusively Albanian) Christianity that itself proves to be struggling in face of lingering nostalgia for the old communist party.

The story of rebuilding a once threatened tradition seems to have taken less precedence as clergy and community leaders are pressured to reposition their faith and institutional capacities to suit the larger demand of the European Union to embrace diversity, not reinforce national distinctions. The result has not been reassuring as Albanians report alienation from the Church leadership that deemphasizes their unique historic place in Christianity. While constantly hoping to convey the opposite, many point to the census of 2011 as evidence that this formula of deemphasizing the Albanian presence in the liturgy of the (formally) Autocephalous Church has turned people away. No longer the standard bearer of 10–15% of Albanians presumably willing to accept their affiliation with a Church preaching tolerance for non-Albanians and non-Christians, a new ideological struggle has infested the haphazardly reconstituted Church infrastructure in the early 1990s. Again, the seeming contradiction of roles expected from the layman, both seeking to regain some spiritual guidance as Albanian Christians and fending off the onslaught of Greek irredentism many believe the current Archbishop facilitates, leads many to conclude that there is no recourse but to leave the community.

How this Church's leadership mediated these challenges facing the local populations becomes relevant once policies of survival are more closely observed through the challenges brought by a new era of openness. A new sensitivity toward ethnicity, history, and authority over the interpretation of their relevance to the lives of the faithful reflects the syndromes Ramet highlights in her valuable introduction.

Krishti u Ngjall (Christ Is Risen)

One may read the transformation of the post-communist AAOC through the works of its primary agents of "rebirth" as they haltingly emerge around the personality of Archbishop Anastasios. New publications of spiritual guidelines for Albanian Christians confronted by the liberal world order fall short, according to sources, in part because the specificities of the Albanian struggle are rarely addressed. They are tired of being told they are but part of a larger phenomenon, a Third World problem. Indeed, Archbishop Anastasios refers to the challenges facing Albanians as akin to, if not even worse than, what he witnessed over decades of missionary work in Kenya, Tanzania, and Uganda:

> The experience of these last years in Albania has revealed to me the kind of surprises God reserves for us in our effort to live the global vision of the spreading of the Gospel. During the first phase of my missionary search and diakonia, the words "to the ends of the earth" were rather colored by geographical meanings - the depths of Africa or Asia. I had never thought that "the ends of the earth" could be so near geographically. That it could be in Albania, where for decades the breath of Hades reigned, where they had crucified and buried Christ again, and where an obstinate communist regime socially and spiritually brought the country to the ends of the earth. ... In Africa or Asia, at least people never stopped addressing God, in their own way, as a supreme reality.
>
> The large majority of the [Albanian] people, including the new generation, are still imbued with the theories of Marxist atheism, which for almost fifty years dominated the country. This is an element that makes them rather close with the other former socialist countries. Through the recent democratic and financial changes, a speedy secularization is creating problems and situations similar to those that are faced by the Orthodox Churches living in western cultural areas. At the same time, the financial situation is so low that it is creating phenomena known mainly in the Third World.[30]

Such statements by the Church are being interpreted as the product of a lingering Eurocentric chauvinism that is simply inserting one missionary's current project—Albania—into a normative frame that conservative Albanians resent (despite being xenophobic and borderline racist themselves). The comparison with "the Third World" confirms the larger criticism of Archbishop Anastasios that he and his foreign allies regard Albanians as mere objects. The focus on Albania's alien place in the community of Christians has left the country's faithful exposed to what many identify as a patronizing disregard of all things that make Albanians distinctive. In the end, their Archbishop is indeed rebuilding a Church, but one that explicitly classifies Albania and its people as culturally alien, and thus targets for neocolonial missionary work. The result of this criticism is that most of those opposing the leadership of the Church cannot entirely embrace what has been accomplished to date, no matter how often they are celebrated by friendly media.[31]

From the heavy investment in rebuilding the infrastructure of the Church (1608 Churches and missionaries were in ruin by 1991), to adopting an aggressive missionary approach vis-à-vis the larger Albanian population, both in the Balkans and in the diaspora, many think of their opposition over the last 20 years as an indigenous retort to globalist agendas that include the attempt to reinstate foreign spiritual authority over Albanians. While it was a clearly stated demand from the Berisha government and likely the majority of Albanians that the leader of the resurrected AAOC be Albanian, the insistence from the Patriarchate that it would be a Greek national continues to vex even the most loyal among Albanian laypersons. That struggle lasted from August 1992, when the Archbishop was initially "enthroned" in Tirana, to late 1998. Periodic subsequent attempts to dislodge Archbishop Anastasios were all justified on the grounds he was a Greek and thus his underlying mission was suspect.

Official Church narratives about this period speak of unity in the Church despite the acknowledged fact that Albanians were not "of one mind." This concession seems justified in that a year and a half later some members of the Albanian clergy quietly supported Sali Berisha's rash call for a referendum to redraft the Albanian Constitution so that the law would insist the Archbishop must be native born. While the 6 November 1994 referendum did not pass, once again in 1996 the Albanian government and a wide range of civilians and local clergy resisted the arrival of Greek-born Bishops the Patriarch insisted would serve in Albania.[32]

In a process lasting until July 1998, the Ecumenical Patriarchate, via arbitration from Albanian members of the AAOC, agreed with the Albanian state to form a Synod consisting of two Church leaders of Greek origin and two of Albanian heritage. The ongoing question was why such a long process was necessary when the available Albanian leaders eventually were, as a compromise granted by the Patriarchate, allowed leadership roles? Joan Pelushi became Metropolitan of Korça and Kozma Qirjo became Bishop of Apollonia. To many, these battles constituted a principled intransigence on the part of a government trying to protect the Albanian Church and an equally resilient insistence by the Grecocentric leadership in Istanbul. Unfortunately, the tensions have not been resolved, regardless of the public exclamations otherwise.

The subsequent decade resulted in some significant gains for the Church. The reconstruction of hundreds of structures and the development of a seminary at Saint Vlash have produced results that even the most vocal opponents must concede. The clergy seem to have consolidated and were able to rewrite a Constitution for the AAOC in November 2006. The resulting expansion of the Church, with the elevation of three archimandrites to a metropolitan—Gjirokaster—and two Bishops, Nicholas Hyka of Apollonia and Anthony Merdani of Kruja, reflects the internal development of Albanian clergy. All three were trained at the "Resurrection of Christ" Theological Academy in the previously mentioned St. Vlash institution, located in Durrës. By November 2008, relations with the Albanian state improved to the point that the two institutions signed an agreement that became state law after ratification by the Albanian parliament.

As such, the consolidation and settlement have resulted in several "elevations" to Bishop since 2009, leading to a current composition of the Holy Synod of the AAOC consisting of 8 members, the first in the history of the Church. Able to establish parishes in most towns, the public ordination since 1992 of 165 clergymen, all Albanian nationals, was possible because of investment in their training locally. While the general consensus among otherwise hostile interlocutors is that the infrastructure of the Church in regard to education and rebuilt churches has been commendable, the enduring questions about the larger quality of life and the deterioration of morals remain a problem in need of far more direct attention.[33] In this respect, Albanian clergy are much more eager partners to engage with local civilians, report critics of the AAOC in general. They are, however, regularly "interrupted" by American or other "foreign" visitors whose "missionary" zeal entirely reflects an understanding of local conditions in terms of inter-ethnic strife. What many conclude, therefore, is that the primary problem is a heavy investment in a message of "tolerance" and "brotherhood" that extends beyond the Albanian context.

Again, the Archbishop is a global personality, with years of experience preaching to large audiences a message largely deemed insensitive to specific, parochial Albanian needs. By traveling the world and preaching unity with "others," the needs of local Christians-as-Albanians are frustrated. Drawing on this palpable critique of the whirlwind activities of Albania's globalist Archbishop, many believe an undercurrent of resentment still exists within even the inner circles of the AAOC, evidenced in recent interventions by the Archbishop in the form of statements on Ukraine. In a case where local nationalist Ukrainians seek separation from the Russian Church, Archbishop Anastasios has taken a public position to declare it anathema to seek to divide the jurisdiction of the Ecumenical Patriarchate.[34]

Some account for these extensive, recent statements not only as demonstrations of loyalty to the recognized structures centered around the Ecumenical Patriarchate, but also as reflecting an attempt to address enduring internal dissension. By voicing fears and laying out a legal argument to deny Ukrainian Orthodox Christians the right to separate, it may be a public attempt to pre-empt a direct challenge to the Church leadership within Albania. Indeed, interlocutors loyal to the faction of opposition based in Elbasan hint that a challenge to Archbishop Anastasios´ jurisdiction will include a similar act of separatism.

Another cloud hovering over the leadership today is the perception that it has failed to protect the community from hemorrhaging members, either by way of conversion to more effective evangelical groups or as a result of cultural alienation. These criticisms draw from the results of various polls and a national census, the last being in 2011, which all indicate that the numbers of the AOC are dropping. In response, the AAOC official media have regularly published declarations penned by the Archbishop, with supplementary public letters, to protest the faulty methods of the last few censuses that consistently report only 6.75% Albanians see themselves as Orthodox Christians. The arguments against these results are revealing. They took the form of formal declarations with extensive explanations on the official website and print/radio media, as well as large segments of books published over the last several years.

RESPONDING TO THE CENSUS

The 1990s proved especially difficult for Church authorities as they had to fight constant legal battles initiated by nationalists in Tirana, a realignment that left its inner core at odds with the obvious needs to "update" a message to a youthful society with little to no moral foundations that tolerate Church dictates. This was apparent with the census of 2011 which reported that only 6.75% of the population see themselves as belonging to the Orthodox community. The shock of these numbers required an immediate response from the Church already suspect for failing to rebuild the community among the most nationalist factions of the indigenous clergy and laypersons.[35]

The response from the Church was revealingly desperate. The message it wished to convey in challenging the numbers was not only to suggest that Albanians were far more loyal to the Orthodox Church than indicated by the statistics, but oddly it emphasized that a good number of those not counted were in fact non-Albanian minorities. The message has long been conveyed by the leadership that it wanted to integrate other national groups, a small minority by any count. In the Church's communiques, however, the language was problematic for Albanians seeking a nationalist leadership; instead of challenging the results along straight-forward lines of argument, the Church statements tried to puff up the numbers of Greeks (whom, it is claimed, state authorities never count). More still, there is a lingering insinuation in the text of the official Church statements that "certain groups" want to undermine the authority of the Church and, more importantly, deemphasize the presence of these uncounted Greeks:

> … it is surprising and to be wondered at why certain groups attempted to show with various manipulations that the Orthodox population has been reduced by two-thirds…All the evidence supports the fact that the vast majority of those who were registered as "did not answer 13.79%" and "undefined believers 5.49%" are Orthodox Christians. This would include: a) Those who willingly chose not to answer the questions regarding faith and religious affiliation, i.e., most of the Greek minority, as well as members of the Vlach, Montenegrin and other ethnic minorities; [and] b) those who avoided a direct declaration of their religion because of psychological pressure created by some extremist groups and threats in connection with the optional declaration of religion and ethnic identity.

The Advisory Committee considers that the results of the census should be viewed with the utmost caution and calls on the authorities not to rely exclusively on the data on nationality collected during the census in determining its policy on the protection of national minorities. It is a well-known [fact] that in the country national minorities are affiliated with a concrete religion. Based on the above facts: We denounce the unscientific method followed for this sensitive religious issue. We protest the lack of professionalism, ignoring international standards. *We do not recognize* the final results regarding religious affiliation of the population given by INSTAT. Plans and actions of this type undermine the religious coexistence and harmony for which we strive.

The search for the truth is foundational for a civilized society, especially in a case as sensitive as the religious identity of the citizens. Only the truth can help Albania on its journey towards a united Europe and, in general, for progress in the twenty-first century.[36]

Conclusion

As discussed throughout, what constituted a new opportunity proved a complex experience for Albanian Christians of the Orthodox faith. Faced with persistent questions from erstwhile rival "ethnic" churches laying claims on the faith of so many of Albania's inhabitants, the story of the AAOC at the end of the twentieth century forewarns a dangerous shift toward marginality for one particular constituency and larger structural confusions for others. With the spread of liberal secularism, the institutions seeking reentry into the lives of Albanians have been laboring to field a compelling message to youthful audiences who were, until the 1990s, free of any formal education on what it meant to be Christian. The sole recourse for authorities outside Albania, whose privilege extended to the fact no living Albanian could take on the role of leading a resurrection of the Orthodox Church (unlike the case with the Catholic community), has proven to be an opportunity to reassert non-Albanian authority over a once short-lived pestilent nationalist challenge to traditional authority based in Constantinople.

It is not difficult to see how open conflicts between nationalist projects elsewhere in the Orthodox world necessarily were submerged with the appointment of a Greek-born Archbishop with a long history of missionary work in Africa.[37] The Albanian case is thus a story of navigation, one that requires wondering aloud how the Orthodox community could survive in the face of the plethora of challenges the end of the communist era introduced.

There is a seemingly unbreachable chasm created by what others in the context of Muslim societies call liberal secularism with the arrival of Euro-American economic and political power. I suggest here that what is analyzed in Muslim societies by Talal Asad, Saba Mahmoud, and others warrants similar investigation in the Balkans among Orthodox Christians.[38] Unlike, however, the narrowed Muslim-majority confines in which scholars studying liberal secularism are forced to operate, it may be argued that the Balkans offers us a unique context to analyze the postmodern world. Indeed, as noted with this case of Albanians navigating the post-communist arena created by the resurrection of the Orthodox Church, how many invest in retaining what Sabrina Ramet correctly identifies as afterimages of the twentieth century, principally ethno-national identity or nationalism, does reflect unique tensions contrastive to those found in, for instance, the Middle East. In as much as we are inspired by those Asadian affiliates exploring how accurate "secular" sensibilities clash or complement "traditional" or "revivalist" ones in an entirely different socio-political setting like Egypt today, the cases in Albania and perhaps elsewhere in Southeast Europe reflect different sensibilities and concerns.[39] For one, the project of identifying ontological others as much as creating/reaffirming what it means to be Albanian, Greek, or Serb seems indelibly challenged with the arrival of liberal sensibilities constantly restated in Archbishop Anastasios' lectures on universal values.

In this regard, the project here is perhaps entirely reserved to opening up suggestively new channels of inquiry, with some preliminary observations of what the unique Albanian context offers us as we position the transitions from post-communism within a study of the role of institutions of faith as critical as the various national Churches. According to interlocutors, it is a secularism that seems to, in affective spirit, take form in the iterations of the nation's Orthodox Church. This secularism constitutes a pervasive Western liberalism that is behind a fundamental disconnect between very powerful, now opposing sensibilities festering inside an Albania facing new waves of economic austerity. Paradoxically, as much as the official statements from the Church media reassure a global audience that their project not only addresses the fears of sectarian intolerance and associated violence (never a problem in Albanian society), but also is winning over the hearts and minds of previously "atheistic" devoutly secular people (rarely identified as Albanians), consultations with sources on the ground suggest a far less successful tenure in post-communist Albania. The teachings of the Orthodox Church as articulated currently (and, to be fair, those of most religious institutions in Albania today) are incapable of confronting a wave of activism promoting "lifestyle" choices deemed antithetical to traditional moral values. Indeed, the open embrace of "others" and the preaching of tolerance have been viewed as an ambiguous but nevertheless "contradictory" position on increasingly charged debates surrounding globalization and the cultural "innovations" and "infringements" associated with it. As much as the Archbishop wishes to indulge these liberal values, it is still coming from a moralizing entrenched patriarchal institution with equally dubious Albanian nationalist credentials.

The difficult task of keeping internal criticism from undermining the authority of already precarious roles suggests clergy should embrace a more nuanced appreciation for what is happening within the larger community. Their sensitivity requires being not entirely faithful to the ideological cracks within Orthodox traditions and more willing to hint at concessions through "modern" designed webpages. It is when the researcher consults these sources that perhaps reading against the grain of discourse is necessary to appreciate the actual depth of the tensions within the Church.

In other words, all efforts to instill confidence while also navigating new "innovative" waters may require our not seeking clear-cut answers as to how the Albanian Orthodox Church is faring locally. Investigating more deeply how its message conflicts with more resilient affiliations that do indeed prove to have an "afterlife" in Albania has compelled entrenched leaders to accept that different interests within this institution are possible when presented as ecumenical and universalist, but never also as Albanian.

The previous accounting of this process of adaptation and perhaps fundamental reorientation reflects the larger forces of change afflicting the Balkans and its inhabitants of all faiths. Far more than a sectarian issue, however, the experience of AOC can serve as an interesting entry-point to appreciate better the larger structural, existential, and ideological underpinnings of traumatic changes in the region for the entirety of the twentieth century and now well into the present day. By examining specifically at how the values of the Albanian Orthodox Church have evolved to fit external political, socioeconomic, and cultural forces far greater than its own, it is possible to introduce a new set of analytical tools to appreciate change in a region perhaps most directly impacted by events over the last century, events whose "afterimages" resonate in ways familiar to those who have studied the Balkans for some time.

Notes

1. Victor Roudometof, "Greek Orthodoxy, Territoriality, and Globality: Religious Responses and Institutional Disputes," in *Sociology of Religion*, Vol. 69, No. 1 (2008), pp. 67–91.
2. Vasilios Makrides, "Why Are Orthodox Churches Particularly Prone to Nationalization and Even to Nationalism," in *St. Vladimir's Theological Quarterly*, Vol. 57, No. 3–4 (2013), pp. 325–352.
3. Isa Blumi, *Reinstating the Ottomans: Alternative Balkan Modernities, 1800–1912* (Basingstoke: Palgrave Macmillan, 2011), pp. 165–168.
4. Many examples of Luarasi's translations, using a now archaic, early Latin-based alphabet, are digitally available on a website loyal to the current Archbishop, http://albanianorthodox.com/kisha-shqiptare/deshmi-historike/ [accessed 20 April 2019].
5. In Albanian: *Kisha Ortodokse Autoqefale e Shqipërisë*.
6. Blumi, *Reinstating the Ottomans*, pp. 118, 205.
7. For a narrative of the history of Orthodoxy in Albania, as presented by loyalists to the current Church leadership, see http://historia-e-kishes-english.blogspot.com/ [accessed 1 April 2019]. For an official rendition of events leading to the formal recognition of the AAOC, see http://orthodoxalbania.net/index.php/en-us/lajme-3/blog/4291-autocephaly-granted-to-the-orthodox-church-of-albania-80-years-ago [accessed 10 April 2019]. Details of the extensive hostility Albanians faced from expansionist neighboring states Yugoslavia and Greece throughout the interwar period can be found in Robert C. Austin, *Founding a Balkan State: Albania's Experiment with Democracy, 1920–1925* (Toronto: University of Toronto Press, 2012), pp. 78–122 and in reports from the League of Nations. Called on by the struggling government set up by Fan Noli to conduct an investigation to refute the claims made by Greece that the Orthodox Christians in Southern Albanian were ethnically Greek, the subsequent report secured, for the time being, Albania's southern frontiers from Athens' irredentism. See League of Nations, C. 93. M. 48. 1922. VII, "Albania. Report of the Commission of Enquiry," dated Tirana, 18 January 1922: "…the minority wishing to be under Greek domination is extremely small…The influence of the clergy, and especially of the Greek Metropolitans, who, … are working openly for the detachment of Southern Albania and for its union with Greece."
8. Rodanthi Tzanelli, "'Not My Flag!' Citizenship and Nationhood in the Margins of Europe (Greece, October 2000/2003)," in *Ethnic and Racial Studies*, Vol. 29, No. 1 (2006), pp. 27–49.

9. Gus Xhudo, "Tension Among Neighbors: Greek-Albanian Relations and Their Impact on Regional Security and Stability," in *Studies in Conflict & Terrorism*, Vol. 18, No. 2 (1995), pp. 111–143.
10. Lina Molokotos-Liederman, "Identity Crisis: Greece, Orthodoxy, and the European Union," in *Journal of Contemporary Religion*, Vol. 18, No. 3 (2003), pp. 291–315.
11. Konstantinos Papastathis, "Religious Discourse and Radical Right Politics in Contemporary Greece, 2010–2014," in *Politics, Religion & Ideology*, Vol. 16, No. 2–3 (2015), pp. 218–247.
12. The official newsletter of the Church—*Ngjallja* (Resurrection)—has been especially keen on using this tactic when addressing this hostility to the appointment of Archbishop Anastasios. Throughout its periodic responses, they assert such questions are mobilized by old Communists who want to stop the return of Christianity to Albania. That much of the articulated resistance continues to be from those professing great faith to AAOC heritage seems to disqualify this line of argument from the Church. To resort to calling all dissent the product of old Communists fails to reflect the myriad of concerns, leaving many to conclude the Church is incapable of engaging its internal doubters. "Akt që u bë baza e rimëkëmbjes së vrullshme të kishës sonë," *Ngjallja* (August 1999), pp. 1–2.
13. Antonia Young, "Religion and Society in Present-Day Albania," in *Journal of Contemporary Religion*, Vol. 14, No. 1 (1999), pp. 5–16.
14. In fact, it would take another ten years for the government and the Church to reach an agreement on the allocation of confiscated property; an addendum to the country's constitution recognized the Church's extra-legal status and the right of return of previously confiscated Churches, Monasteries, and other Church properties. Law no. 10057 Article 22/2 dated on 22/01/2009, the "Agreement between the Government of the Republic of Albania and the Albanian Orthodox Church." For a copy of the agreement provided by the Church official website, see http://orthodoxalbania.net/index.php/en-us/kisha-jone-3/marveshja-me-qeverine [accessed 22 April 2019].
15. With headlines from a notorious Greek nationalist newsletter that read: Maria Korologou, "Albania Seizes Orthodox Church," *Greek Reporter* (20 August 2013), at https://eu.greekreporter.com/2013/08/20/albania-seizes-orthodox-church/ [last accessed 24 April 2019] and the website of the Serbian Orthodox Church characterizing of court-ordered return of community property occupied by the Church as "Albanian Thuggery" the conflict between powers of state and a "foreign" religious entity quickly takes on the frame of a nation's struggle with a foreign cohort of irredentists. "Another Orthodox Church Profaned in Albania," 18 July 2017, http://www.spc.rs/eng/another_orthodox_church_profaned_albania

[accessed 12 March 2019]. The official statement from the AAOC itself referred to the local civil authorities as having no jurisdiction over sovereign Church property (confiscated according to the Church during the Hoxha-era). See statement of protest https://orthodoxalbania.org/alb/index.php/en-us/besimi-orthodhoks-3/multimedia/gazeta-ngjallja/2-uncategorised/823-official-declaration [accessed 21 April 2019]. For a report on the incident under discussion see "Orthodox Church Denounces the Violence of Local Officials to Priests," *Independent Balkan News Agency*, 16 August 2013.

16. "Response of the Orthodox Clergy of the Archdiocese of Tirana to Some Recent False Statements" (22 December 2012), http://orthodoxalbania.net/index.php/en-us/lajme-3/blog/947-response-of-the-orthodox-clergy-of-the-archdiocese-of-tirana-to-some-recent-false-statements [accessed 31 March 2019].

17. The enduring struggle of the poor, inhabiting the kinds of megalopolis surrounded by slums Anastasios likely ministered in while in Africa prior to his election as Archbishop in 1991, remains a constant in his message to the larger world. Throughout his writings, he frames this in terms of a "human enterprise" that is directed toward, by way of the preaching of scripture, "the entire world." Promoting a particular understanding of "human rights" that considers a complicated relationship between culture and the gospel, while continuing to emphasize the need to maintain a "dialogue with Islam," while celebrated in the global media, are failing to reassure Albanians the Archbishop's work is primarily aimed to secure their homeland from new globalist and old rival nationalist projects. Anastasios Yannoulatos, "The Global Vision of Proclaiming the Gospel," in *Greek Orthodox Theological Review*, Vol. 42, No. 3–4 (1997), pp. 401–417.

18. A telling section of a recent book may help support why many AOC feel the Archbishop is ignoring their demands and addressing them to a global audience through a language not accessible to them: "The global vision is the correct Orthodox framework for everything that we do or transmit on the local, parochial level. There exists no correct understanding of the living Orthodox tradition when this perspective of universality is missing. This is not a vision we observe as spectators, but an area of existence, of thought, of acting, within which we live….A person bearing the Spirit (pneumatophoron) thinks, feels and acts with a universal perspective. His reflection, his prayer, his interests and efforts acquire a worldwide horizon. …a genuine Orthodox spiritual life is realized and completed within the wider global frame…" Archbishop Anastasios, *Facing the World: Orthodox Christian Essays on Global Concerns* (Grand-Saconnex: World Council of Churches, 2003), pp. 170–172.

19. The World Council of Churches based in the US has been especially active in Albania, with the Hoppe family becoming known throughout the world for their efforts. For a brief accounting see Eleni Kasselouri-Hatzivassiliadi, "Mission, Gender, and Theological Education: An Orthodox Perspective," in *International Review of Mission*, Vol. 104, No. 1 (2015), pp. 37–45, esp. 43–44; Lynette Katherine and Anastasios (Archbishop of Tirana and all Albania), *Resurrection: The Orthodox Autocephalous Church of Albania, 1991–2003* (Tirana: Ngjallja Publishers, 2004).
20. Ina K. Zhupa, "New Social Phenomena in the Optics of Values in Post-communist Albania," in *European Journal of Social Science Education and Research*, Vol. 2, No. 1 (2015), pp. 106–111.
21. The numbers were quite damning of the entire religious order of Albania. Only 9% claimed to visit once a week a place of worship, while 33% claimed to go only very rarely. Gjergj Sinani, "Fenomeni fetar në Shqipëri," in *Shqipëria në tranzicion dhe vlerat* (Tiranë: Departamenti i Filozofi-sociologisë, Universiteti i Tiranës, 1999), pp. 67–108.
22. On the conflicted expectations of Orthodox Christian women to uphold Albanian heritage while trying to sustain a family as cheap labor in Greece, the options for long-term stability actually mean contradicting the first role by formally declaring oneself ethnically Greek in order to secure EU citizenship. Dimitra Charalampopoulou, "Gender and Migration in Greece: The Position and Status of Albanian Women Migrants in Patras," in *Finisterra*, Vol. 39, No. 77 (2004), pp. 77–104; Panos Hatziprokopiou, "Albanian Immigrants in Thessaloniki, Greece: Processes of Economic and Social Incorporation," in *Journal of Ethnic and Migration Studies*, Vol. 29, No. 6 (2003), pp. 1033–1057.
23. Urjana Curi, "Legal Provisions, Discrimination and Uncertainty on LGBT Community in Albania," in *Academicus International Scientific Journal*, Vol. 9, No. 17 (2018), pp. 111–121; Erka Çaro, Ajay Bailey, and Leo Van Wissen. "'I am the God of the House': How Albanian Rural Men Shift Their Performance of Masculinities in the City," in *Journal of Balkan and Near Eastern Studies*, Vol. 20, No. 1 (2018), pp. 49–65.
24. There are regular contributors to mainstream Albanian websites and newspapers trying to persuade readers to trust the foreign-born leadership and celebrate their accomplishments. And yet, as these interventions follow scandals that hurt this message, it is clear the attempts to assuage Albanian fears fall on deaf ears. Compare Miron Çako, "Moment për të reflektuar dhe kërkuar falje Kishës Ortodokse," *TEMA*, 30 Shtator 2014; Miron Çako, "Janullatos, njeriu që ka punuar dhe ka bërë më shumë për shqiptarët nga viti 1991 deri më sot!" *TEMA*, 8 April 2015.

25. Anton C. Vrame, "Transforming a Nation Through Mission: A Case Study on the Church in Albania," in *Journal of Ecumenical Studies*, Vol. 45, No. 2 (2010), pp. 245–248.
26. Tonon Gjuruaj, "A Stale Ecumenical Model? How Religion Might Become a Political Message in Albania," in *East European Quarterly*, Vol. XXXIV, No. 1 (March 2000), pp. 21–49.
27. This official message the Archbishop wishes to convey has appeared often in publications such as Archbishop Anastasios and John Chryssavgis, *In Albania: Cross and Resurrection* (Yonkers, NY: St. Vladimir's Seminary Press, 2017).
28. Luke A. Veronis, "Anastasios Yannoulatos: Modern-Day Apostle," in *International Bulletin of Missionary Research*, Vol. 19, No. 3 (1995), pp. 122–128.
29. For an accounting of the wave of unrest in Albanian-inhabited territories since late 2018, see Isa Blumi, "Albanian Slide: The Roots to NATO's Pending Lost Balkan Enterprise," in *Insight Turkey*, Vol. 21, No. 2 (2019), pp. 149–170.
30. Archbishop Anastasios, *Facing the World: Orthodox Christian Essays on Global Concerns* (Grand-Saconnex: World Council of Churches, 2003), pp. 119–124.
31. Jim Forest, *The Resurrection of the Church in Albania: Voices of Orthodox Christians* (World Council of Churches, 2002).
32. Peter Bartl, "Albanien," in Erwin Gatz (ed.), *Kirche und Katholizismus seit 1945*, 4 vols—vol. 2: Ostmittel, Ost-und Südosteuropa (Paderborn, 1999), pp. 29–40, 35–37.
33. For an official report on the successes of the Church's activities, see http://orthodoxalbania.net/index.php/en-us/kisha-jone-3/veshtrim-i-pergjithshem [accessed 12 April 2019].
34. Quoted from published letter by the Orthodox Autocephalous Church of Albania to Patriarch, "On the Ukrainian Ecclesiastical Question. 2nd Reply. Speaking the Truth in Love," dated 29 March 2019. Translated from Greek. http://orthodoxalbania.net/index.php/en-us/lajme-3/blog [consulted on 18 April 2019].
35. Gëzim Visoka and Elvin Gjevori, "Census Politics and Ethnicity in the Western Balkans," *East European Politics*, Vol. 29, No. 4 (2013), pp. 479–498.
36. Quoted from published letter by the Orthodox Autocephalous Church of Albania to Patriarch, "The Results of the 2011 Census Regarding the Orthodox Christians in Albania Are Totally Incorrect and Unacceptable," at http://orthodoxalbania.net/index.php/en-us/lajme-3/822-officialdeclaration [accessed 12 November 2018], emphasis in the original.

37. The disputes over authority and the particular demands of specific nationalist interests versus perceived Greek chauvinism, if not overt irredentism, is study in depth by Victor Roudometof, "Greek Orthodoxy, Territoriality, and Globality: Religious Responses and Institutional Disputes," in *Sociology of Religion*, Vol. 69, No. 1 (2008), pp. 67–91.
38. Ovamir Anjum, "Islam as a Discursive Tradition: Talal Asad and His Interlocutors," in *Comparative Studies of South Asia, Africa and the Middle East*, Vol. 27, No. 3 (2007), pp. 656–672.
39. See special issue debate, Meditation on Fadil, Nadia and Mayanthi Fernando, "Rediscovering the 'Everyday' Muslim: Notes on an Anthropological Divide," in *Hau: Journal of Ethnographic Theory*, Vol. 5, No. 2 (2015), pp. 59–88.

CHAPTER 10

The Orthodox Church of the Czech Lands and Slovakia: Survival of a Minority Faith in a Secular Society

Frank Cibulka

Abstract This chapter will focus on the fortunes of the autocephalous Orthodox Church of the Czech Lands and Slovakia in the aftermath of the collapse of the Czechoslovak communist regime in 1989 and the creation of new nation-states in Prague and Bratislava in 1993. The topic generates a special set of questions stemming from the fact that, not only does the Orthodox Church in the successor states of former Czechoslovakia represent a minority faith existing on the periphery of the post-communist societies, but it does so in the case of the Czech Republic, in one of the most secularized and atheistic countries in the world. Among the topics examined will be the strength of its membership and of its present societal role, its relationship with key governmental institutions, its leadership strife, social conservatism and religious tolerance, the impact of church restitutions, and its position on the evolving schism between the Ecumenical Patriarchate of Constantinople and the leadership of the Russian Orthodox Church over the issue of

F. Cibulka (✉)
Zayed University, Abu Dhabi, United Arab Emirates

© The Author(s) 2019
S. P. Ramet (ed.), *Orthodox Churches and Politics in Southeastern Europe*, Palgrave Studies in Religion, Politics, and Policy, https://doi.org/10.1007/978-3-030-24139-1_10

granting of autocephaly to the Orthodox Church of Ukraine. Finally, the question of foreign influence or control over this minority Church will also have to be addressed.

This chapter begins by thoroughly addressing the ambiguous historical context of the Orthodox Church in the territory of former Czechoslovakia in terms of the question whether it can be considered a natural religious creation within the national life, rooted in the eastward orientation of Christianity dating back to the Saints Cyril and Methodius, or a religious transplant from the powerful Slavic neighbors. The ambivalent early spatial orientation of the Church within the multinational First Czechoslovak Republic, its near-destruction during the Nazi occupation in World War Two, along with the nature of its accommodation with the Czechoslovak communist regime will also be explored. The analysis of the Church's historical journey in the seemingly alien heart of Europe is absolutely inevitable for achieving full understanding of its contemporary situation.

The Historical Context of the Czechoslovak Orthodox Church

The heart of Europe does not constitute a fertile environment for Orthodox Christianity and this is true also where the Czech Republic is concerned and, to a somewhat lesser extent, in the case of Slovakia. The 2011 population census indicated that the autocephalous Orthodox Church in the Czech Lands and Slovakia (*Pravoslavná církev v českych zemích a na Slovensku*) numbered just under 70,000 believers: only 20,533 in the Czech Republic and 49,133 in Slovakia.[1] In addition, the status of the Orthodox Church in former Czechoslovakia has been undermined by episodes of power struggle, allegations of misbehavior on the part of the top Church leadership, and very real instability of the top leadership.

The religious history of the Czech Republic or of its traditional territory of Bohemia presents a dramatic story of alternating fortune for Roman Catholicism and Protestantism, stemming from the stunning legacy of the Czech reformist priest and theologian Jan Hus (c.1369–1415) and from the Bohemian Reformation movement, an early fifteenth-century attempt to reform the Christian Church. The myths of the nineteenth-century Czech National Revival almost all center around the nation's dramatic fifteenth-century history—the burning of Jan Hus at the stake as a heretic, the stunning success of Hussite military machinery in resisting the Crusades, and the legacy of one of the religious factions which emerged out of the Hussite religious movement—the Unity of the Czech Brethren (Jednota Bratrská), best known because of its last bishop pre-exile, the theologian and educator Jan Amos Komenský (1592–1670). The one exception through which the Czech nation turns its eyes to the East was the role played in the ninth century by the Byzantine Christian missionaries, Saints Cyril and Methodius, Greek brothers from Thessaloniki, sent in the 862 by the Byzantine Emperor Michael III to help evangelize the population and reduce the Frankish influence in Greater Moravia. In fact, the Slav polytheist religion had for some decades been in retreat given the rapid spread of Christianity. But the Byzantine missionaries not only translated the Bible from Greek into Old Church Slavonic but invented a Glagolitic alphabet for it. The expulsion of their disciples from Greater Moravia by its ruler prince Svatopluk after the death of Saint Methodius in 885 signaled a turning toward a western version of Christianity.

But that was an exception. As Derek Sayer wrote in the *Coasts of Bohemia*: "Since the times of Cyril and Methodius, Czechs had been variously Catholic and Protestant, but never Orthodox; their language has been written in Roman and Gothic scripts, but never Cyrillic."[2] The defining event in the life of the nation was the defeat by the army of the Habsburg Emperor Ferdinand II at the Battle of White Mountain in 1620. This tragic event in Czech national history resulted not only in the loss of the sovereign statehood and in widespread repression, but also, in the context of the Habsburg Counter-Reformation, in the forced re-Catholization which endured for the next three centuries. During the nineteenth-century National Revival, this period was referred to as the Age of Darkness (*Temno*), for example, in the works of the nation's pre-eminent writer Alois Jirásek. The period of intense myth-making during the Czech National Revival and the early years of independence included an emphasis on the Slavic nature of the Czechs and Slovaks, the promotion of Pan-Slavism, and fellowship with Russia. These themes often figured in the works of prominent Czech artists, such as in Alfons Mucha's series of monumental historical paintings, the *Slovanská epopej* (*The Slav Epic*), painted from 1912 to 1926. As Sayer writes about this masterpiece, "The overall effect of Slovanská epopej is to (re)locate Czech history squarely in the pan-Slav context, while placing the Hussite drama at the heart of both. That Mucha freely mingles pagan, Orthodox, Catholic and Protestant references in a paean to Slavism is interesting. On one level his indiscriminate plundering testifies to the ascension of the national and the ethnic into the realm of the sacred."[3]

The creation of the independent Czechoslovak Republic in 1918 coincided with the crisis and the rapid decline of the Roman Catholic Church in the country. In 1910, 96% of the Czech population were Roman Catholic. This figure declined to 82% in 1921, but, by 2011, had sunk to only 10.4% or 1.3 million Catholics out of a population of 10.6 million in the Czech Republic. Many factors were responsible for this trend, including subsequent religious repression by the communist regime and secularization and atheization of the second half of the twentieth century. In the immediate post-World War One years, the return of religious freedom and an attendant reaction against the Catholic Church which was seen as pro-Habsburg and anti-national played their part. A revival in 1918 of the Jednota katolického duchovenstva (Association of Catholic Clergy), originally founded in the Czech lands in 1895 in the context of *Catholic modernism*, resulted in demands for a reform of the Catholic Church, including democratization of the Church, creation of a Czech national patriarchate, an economically more equal treatment of the clergy and the elimination of their mandatory celibacy.[4] The Vatican's refusal of the demands of the reformist clergy resulted in an exodus from the Catholic Church and the eventual creation in 1920 of the new national Church, the Czechoslovak Hussite Church (Československa církev husitská), which had the evident support of much of the governmental elite. This Church initially prospered, reaching a half a million members in 1921 and almost a million (946,800) in 1950. It created an excellent opportunity for the growth of religious Orthodoxy since the new national Church had undergone a divisive search for theology and institutional orientation and for a while seriously considered adopting Eastern Orthodox identity. This search and internal power struggle were only definitively resolved in 1924 with the victory of the first patriarch of the Czechoslovak Hussite Church, Karel Farský, who opposed unity with Orthodoxy.[5]

During the initial years of Czechoslovak independence, the number of Orthodox believers grew and came largely from four sources. One was the small number of Orthodox believers who had existed in the

Czech lands during the Habsburg era. In 1910, this figure was placed at 832 in the Czech Lands, 210 in Moravia and 21 in Silesia. The second group were the defectors from the Roman Catholic Church who chose to join the Orthodox Church rather than the Czechoslovak Hussite Church. The third and by far the largest group came from the autonomous region of Carpathian Ruthenia, where some 30,000 admitted being Orthodox in 1912,[6] in spite of repression from the politically dominant Ruthenian Greek Catholic (Uniate) Church. The fourth group came from the influx of political refugees coming out of Russia during the early 1920s, following the end of the Civil War. According to the Czechoslovak government, there were some 30,000 Russian refugees living in the country in 1926,[7] and the vast majority were Orthodox believers. In 1930, the total number of Orthodox believers in all of Czechoslovakia was 145,583, with some 24,573 in Bohemia and Moravia-Silesia,[8] and the rest in Carpathian Ruthenia and in Slovakia.

During the early years of the Czechoslovak Republic, the Orthodox Church found a significant source of support in the country's first Prime Minister during 1918–1919, Karel Kramař (1860–1937), a Russophile and an advocate of neo-Slavism, who had a Russian wife and converted to Orthodoxy because of his marriage.

During World War Two, the Orthodox Church suffered catastrophic repression following the assassination of the Acting Reich Protector Reinhard Heydrich in May 1942 by a group of Czechoslovak parachutists dispatched from London. The parachutists were allowed to hide in the crypt of the Orthodox Church of Saints Cyril and Methodius in Prague, where they were eventually discovered by the Gestapo and killed in a firefight. In a brutal reprisal, the Germans arrested and tortured the Metropolitan Bishop of the Church, Gorazd, and in September 1942 all the Czech Orthodox properties in the Protectorate of Bohemia and Moravia were confiscated by the Germans. With the churches closed, the Orthodox priests were removed to Germany to perform forced labor.[9] Bishop Gorazd (Matěj Pavlík, 1879–1942), who had headed the Church since 1921 was executed on 4 September 1942. It is somewhat ironic that today the perception of the Czech general public of the Orthodox Church is probably most closely associated with this tragic episode in the country's history.

Following the liberation from the German occupation in 1945, Stalin annexed Carpathian Ruthenia and Czechoslovakia was left with only about 20,000 Orthodox believers, with about 9000 consisting of former Uniates in eastern Slovakia and the remainder being Russian émigrés and converts to Orthodoxy. There were about twenty Orthodox priests left and subsequently, in 1946, the Church broke away from the patriarch of Constantinople and the Serbian metropolitan and placed itself under the jurisdiction of the patriarch of the Russian Orthodox Church instead.[10] During the years of communist rule, the Orthodox Church in Slovakia participated in the repression of the Uniates, but was itself treated with relative benevolence, escaping the severe persecution of the Roman Catholic Church.[11] As Pavel Marek has written, "...the Orthodox Church in Czechoslovakia, in the period after Second World War, enjoyed support from the state; this trend deepened after February 1948, reaching a stage of full control over the Church, of its directing and control by the party and state organs, and the Orthodox fulfilled tasks and orders assigned to them by the communist party, aiming at the building of the socialist system."[12] The Moscow Patriarchate granted autocephaly to the Czechoslovak Orthodox Church in 1951, but this was recognized by the Ecumenical Patriarchate of Constantinople only in 1998. The period of the 1950s was a time of the greatest numerical strength of the Orthodox believers in socialist Czechoslovakia. While the 1950 census reported some 57,000 believers, the realistic estimates a year later revealed the presence of 350,000–370,000 Orthodox believers in the country.[13] This was due to two factors: The mass forced conversions from the Greek Catholic Church in Slovakia and the return of some 40,000 Volhynian Czechs after World War Two, the vast majority of whom were Orthodox in their religious identity. These were descendants of the Czech migrants to the Volhynia region of Western Ukraine during the second half of the nineteenth century. However, the numbers of Orthodox dropped during the second half of the twentieth century down to 90,000 in 1981 and 53,000 in 1991 at the end of the communist regime.[14] Much of the drop in membership can be explained by the relegalization, during the 1968 Prague Spring, of the Greek-rite Catholic Church and subsequent return of many of the Orthodox believers to their original spiritual home. The alien nature of the Orthodox Church was underscored by the fact that its leadership was until 2000 in the hands of Russian-born metropolitan bishops. It has existed on the fringes of the Czech and Slovak societies, and its reputation among the population has not been helped by the evidence of secret police links on the part of some of its leaders.

The Czech and Slovak Orthodox Church and the State and Society Since 1989

In the period since the fall of communism, the Orthodox Church has been able to retain and even increase its membership more effectively than other Churches in the country. This is in part due to the dynamic ethnic base of the Church and to the continuing strength of the dominant Russian Orthodox Church to the East. The official figure of 70,000 believers is misleading as it does not include visitors and migrant workers from Ukraine and other Orthodox-majority countries, such as Russia and Bulgaria, and church attendance is therefore larger. The Orthodox Church claims to have around 100,000 Czech and Slovak adherents and an additional 180,000 foreigners residing or working in both states, who are adherents of the Eastern Orthodox faith.[15] Another set of figures effectively demonstrates the "foreign" nature of the Orthodox Church. It has been reported that, in 2017, there were 120,000 Ukrainians living permanently in the Czech Republic and another 50,000 residing there on short-term visas. Both the Russian Orthodox Church of the Moscow Patriarchate, with 6000 believers and headquarters in Karlovy Vary (Karlsbad), and the former Ukrainian Orthodox Autocephalous Church (later absorbed into the new Orthodox Church of the Ukraine) also operated in the Czech Republic at one time. At the same time, the "vast majority" of Orthodox believers in the Czech lands were also Ukrainians.[16] In 2001, the Orthodox Church reported to the Ecumenical Council of Churches that it had 82 parishes in the Czech Republic, served by 76 priests.[17] It has been alleged that, during the election of the new primate of the Church, the Ukrainian clergy were able to provide the two-thirds majority support of the delegates needed for election at the eparchial convention and have at times been subjected to pressure and blackmail to support candidates favored by Moscow Patriarchate.[18]

A few prominent Czech individuals have recently been identified as being Orthodox Christians. The best known is Jaromir Jágr, who is considered one of the greatest professional ice hockey players in history. Jágr, who converted from Catholicism, was baptized by Metropolitan Kryštof in 2001 and his Orthodox faith was further strengthened when he played for Avangard Omsk in Russia during 2008–2011. He later stated that, "At least I am improving my Russian in church. It is attended by such an unusual group of people who believe in something and whose energy is so strong that one feels well there."[19] He also recalled his experience while working in Omsk. "It was endearing how Russians accepted my faith. I was somehow closer to them and they to me as well. It helped me to better adjust to the country, its people. We understood each other better."[20]

After the dissolution of Czechoslovakia on 1 January 1993, two separate and equal Churches have emerged, but they have maintained canonical unity through a shared Holy Synod and through a common primate of the Church. The Orthodox Church in the Czech Lands and Slovakia is divided into four eparchies: In the Czech Republic, these are the Archdiocese of Prague and the Czech Lands, and the Diocese of Brno and Olomouc, while in Slovakia we find the Archdiocese of Prešov and Slovakia and the Diocese of Michalovce and Košice. The Church's primate, with the title of Metropolitan of the Czech Lands and Slovakia, is elected from among the two archbishops, and currently the post has been held since January 2014 by 41-year-old Archbishop Rastislav (Ondřej Gent) of the Prešov and Slovakia Archdiocese.[21] The Metropolitan, according to the Church constitution, "carries out together with the Holy Synod (composed of all the active bishops) the spiritual administration of the Church."[22] There are some 82 Orthodox parishes in both states and the training of priests takes place at the semi-independent Orthodox Theological Faculty of the University of Prešov, with a branch for distance study in Olomouc. The unity of the Czech and Slovak Orthodoxy is no doubt motivated by the constraint of needing to retain autocephalous status. According to the distinguished Church historian Pavel Marek, "The two Churches formerly functioned in a more connected way during Metropolitan Kryštof's term as primate. Today they are in fact two Churches, each in reality acting independently and having only a common name."[23] This should not be surprising given the great differences in religiosity of the two states. The Czech Republic has earned a reputation as the most atheistic state in Europe, while Slovakia's population remains much more religious, due to the strength of the Roman Catholic Church. While 63% of the Slovak population are Roman Catholics and 69% claim that they believe in God, only 29% of Czechs say that they believe in God and 72% are religiously unaffiliated. The Roman Catholic Church still represents by far the strongest religious faith in both republics. The overall figures of attendance at religious services are far lower than the Church membership in both countries, with only 31% of Slovaks and 11% of

Czechs attending monthly.[24] The Orthodox Church certainly has a stronger position in Slovakia than in the Czech Republic, but ranks as only the fifth largest among Slovakia's Churches, with just under 1% of the population, after the Catholic Church, the two Protestant denominations—the Evangelical Church of the Augsburg Confession in Slovakia and the Reformed Christian Church—and the Slovak Greek Catholic Church. The Slovak Orthodox can be found mostly in eastern Slovakia and areas with Ruthenian populations. Even in Prešov County, the site of the Slovak Archdiocese, Orthodox believers counted for only 4% of the population in 2002 and the highest concentration of Orthodox believers can be found in remote mountain villages of eastern Slovakia, where the proportion of the Orthodox population can range from 20 to 30%.[25] In the Czech Republic, the Orthodox believers constitute the fourth most numerous group with 0.2% of the country's population; after the Roman Catholic Church, the Evangelical Church of Czech Brethren, and the Czechoslovak Hussite Church. The area of greatest concentration of Orthodox believers in the Czech Republic is in the spa town of Karlovy Vary (Karlsbad), where there has long been a strong Russian community. It is also the site of the oldest and largest Orthodox church in the country—the Saints Peter and Paul Cathedral, next to which are located the offices of the rector of the Russian Orthodox Church representation in Karlovy Vary, the influential Archpriest Nikolay Lischenyuk.

It is ironic that, at the time of religious decline in the Czech Republic, the country does not have a constitutional separation of Church and state. The current model, common to both Czechoslovak successor states, is centered on the financing of religious organizations by the state. This function is delegated to the Department of Churches of the respective Ministries of Culture and includes also other key control functions, especially the task of registering Churches and religious organization. The Department of Churches (*Odbor církví* in the Czech Republic and *Cirkevný odbor* in Slovakia) continues in a significantly more benign way at least some of the functions of the communist-era Secretariat for Church Affairs (*Secretariát pro věci církevní*), which was part of the Czechoslovak Ministry of Education and Culture. The importance of the state management of religious affairs has grown substantially with the approval of religious restitutions, as the amount of money distributed to various Czech organizations increased. The Czech department has since 2006 been headed by its director Jana Bendová.

The top bishops of the local Orthodox Church do participate to some degree in the public life of the Czech Republic and Slovakia and appear alongside the countries' political and religious leaders during formal occasions of state. Metropolitan Kryštof kept a particularly high profile in that respect. Many of the public, non-religious occasions in which they take part are nevertheless often connected to the world of Orthodoxy. For example, Archbishop Michal of Prague and the Czech lands in January 2019 hosted a New Year reception in one of Prague's hotels for the ambassadors and other representatives of select countries, all of which had a majority of Orthodox believers: Serbia, Belarus, Moldova, Greece, Ukraine, Russia, Bulgaria, Romania, and Cyprus.[26] But he also attended in December of the previous year a reception on the occasion of Austria's national holiday, and here he met the former Czech President Václav Klaus.[27]

THE POWER STRUGGLE WITHIN THE CHURCH AND RELIGIOUS RESTITUTIONS

Two very likely interrelated aspects of the recent history of the Church need to be addressed: The religious restitutions and the crisis which gripped the Church after the April 2013 resignation of Metropolitan Kryštof (Radim Pulec), who had served as Archbishop of Prague and the Czech Lands since 2006 and as Metropolitan of the Czech Lands and Slovakia since 2010.[28] The subsequent scandal and power struggle divided the Church into various factions and reached an international dimension.

Metropolitan Kryštof has been a complex, contradictory, and controversial figure. He is a person of great charisma and erudition, an active scholar with doctoral degrees in theology and philosophy and with fluent knowledge of several foreign languages. He has brought unprecedented dynamism into his leadership role and to some degree re-oriented the Church from an almost exclusive Eastward orientation back to the Czech and Slovak societies. His ambition was not limited to the survival of the Church, as he genuinely believed that he could make missionary inroads in the mainstream domestic societies. In an interview, dating to 2011 and remarkable for its directness and ambition, he claimed that, "the number of the Orthodox in the Czech Republic is increasing every day" and that "many Czechs come to be baptized Orthodox; the Orthodox

Church is a refuge for all." He went on to say that "all Orthodox churches are full, even on holidays the people fill the church, even overflowing outside. Meanwhile the Catholic churches are empty."[29] He took aim at the country's dominant Catholic Church and explained its decline by the decline of the rural population and by historical factors:

> Catholicism was implanted by force, with almost the same methods as traditionally practised by the Nazis and the communists. If you were disobedient, they would take your property and send you into exile, and they may have even put an end to you…Of the 150,000 rural families there are only 30,000 left. It seems clear that the Czechs do not like Catholicism. So, Czechoslovakia became independent country, with about one million people leaving the Catholic Church and the establishment of the Orthodox Church of Czechoslovakia. More and more people today in the Czech Republic and Slovakia prefer the Orthodox Church. We now need to boost their morale, especially among the young people and teach them the truth that they did not know.[30]

At the same time, there has always been an apparent dark side to Metropolitan Kryštof. He has been reliably identified as an agent of the former State Security (StB), even though he was eventually cleared by a 1997 court decision. His economic activities have also come under scrutiny and suspicion due to his role in the IKONOSTAS company which was involved in the management of the Church property.

His tenure as primate came to an abrupt end in 2013, in the same year that the restitutions of religious property in the Czech Republic came into effect. They provided for almost US$4 billion in return of property confiscated by the communist regime in 1948 and US$3 billion in financial restitution to be spread over a period of thirty years. The bulk of these funds was provided for the Roman Catholic Church while the Orthodox Church was granted 1.16 billion Czech crowns (about US$60 million), not counting limited property restitution. It has been speculated subsequently that this has fueled a power struggle within the Orthodox Church. Metropolitan Kryštof, as the primate of the Church, controlled the Church's property, but he resigned as a result of allegations of sexual impropriety in April 2013. He retreated to a small monastery in Těšov, in western Czech Republic. He concentrated, with some success, on clearing his name and has retained significant support among the faithful.

The entire dramatic episode in the life of the country's Orthodox Church was the result of a complex combination of factors including human frailty of character, financial motives, struggle for power, and finally an involvement by foreign actors. Its beginning predates the restitution legislation. Apparently, Metropolitan Kryštof lost the support of the Russian Orthodox Church when in 2011 he complained in a letter to the Ecumenical Patriarchate that he had come under pressure from Moscow to take part in the celebration of the 60th anniversary of autocephaly, which was granted to the Czechoslovak Church by the Moscow Patriarchate (but not by the Ecumenical Patriarchate at that time) in 1951. Kryštof was subsequently criticized for being disloyal to the Russian "Mother Church" and this episode apparently marked the beginning of the process of his removal from his posts.[31] Allegedly motivated by the prospect of control over the restitution funds, the primate's rivals, allegedly with the support of the Moscow Patriarchate, took advantage of his known but hitherto ignored personal weaknesses and engineered his ouster on charges of violation of his priestly vows. In April 2013, television station TV NOVA came out with allegations that Kryštof had had sexual relations with several women and a number of illegitimate children. While denying the allegations, Kryštof resigned both his posts on 12 April for the good of his Church.[32] The administration of the Church, as *Locum Tenens*, was placed in the hands of Archbishop Simeon of the Olomouc-Brno diocese, and he struggled without success to remove the administrator of the Church property, the controversial priest Martin Marek Krupica, who now became the temporary administrator of the Prague Diocese. The situation developed into a full-blown struggle between the two senior clergymen for the control of the Church. Archbishop Simeon, weakened, completed his tenure as an interim administrator of the Church following the election in January 2014 of the new primate, Metropolitan Rastislav, who in turn attempted to remove the 87-year-old Archbishop from his post in the Olomouc-Brno diocese. At the same time, while the election of Rastislav was embraced by the Moscow Patriarchate, it was not recognized, on procedural grounds, by the Ecumenical Patriarchate in Istanbul till 2016. It has been alleged in some circles that Metropolitan Hilarion of Volokolamsk, the chairman of the Department of External Church Relations of the Russian Orthodox Church, during his visits to Prague had managed to engineer the election of Rastislav.[33]

The conflict gained intensity as the first payment of 38 million Czech crowns was about to be delivered to the Orthodox Church and the struggle over the control of the funds continued. There were accusations of "connection with *podvorje*," a representative organization of the Russian Orthodox Church, which defends Russian interests. In April, the Ecumenical Patriarch Bartholomew was sufficiently concerned about the matter that he sent a letter to the then Czech Minister of Culture Daniel Herman.[34] The issue drove the Church factions further apart and led to allegations, for example, by Marek Martin Krupica, of an involvement of "dark forces," such as of the former StB secret policy personnel or even Russian intelligence services.[35] The situation reached the point where the Czech press reported that, in late 2014, the Ministry of Culture suspended the restitution payments to the Orthodox Church. The 40 million Czech crowns which were to be transferred to the Church the following January were potentially headed into temporary court or notarial custody for safekeeping.[36] Minister Herman declared, "I did what was necessary to prevent misuse of the funds,"[37] and Krupica subsequently reacted on 24 October by filing a police complaint against the Minister, drawing in turn a condemnation of his own action from Archbishop Simeon.[38] But the matter is shrouded in confusion because, according to a recent statement by the Ministry Department of Church Affairs director, Pavla Bendová, the money was ultimately paid on time. She wrote, "I am unaware that Minister Herman would have suspended the payment to the Orthodox Church. All Churches, including the Orthodox, were paid their financial compensations at the same time, exactly according to the existing law."[39] Krupica was eventually removed from his key positions, moved to priestly duties in Litoměřice and died in a traffic accident in November 2018. Subsequently, the Orthodox Church experienced another major crisis, caused by the struggle for the control of the Diocese of Prague and the Czech Lands.

Roman Hrdý (born 1973) was elected Archbishop of Prague, in January 2014, as the successor to Metropolitan Kryštof; in this new post, he took the name Archbishop Jáchym. However, due to procedural issues, his election was not accepted by much of the country's Orthodox community or by the Ministry of Culture. It was also rejected by the Ecumenical Patriarchate, but not by the Russian Orthodox Church. A new election took place in November and Archbishop Jáchym was defeated for his post by Michal Dandár (born 1947), who was enthroned in March 2015 as Archbishop Michal of Prague and of the Czech lands. Archbishop Jáchym kept his rank and was removed to a titular post as Archbishop of Beroun. His successor, Archbishop Michal, who had spent time working for the Russian Orthodox Church in Germany, was identified as a former agent of the Czechoslovak StB; he has been regarded as being strongly Russian-oriented.

It is not easy to interpret the power struggle within this minority Orthodox Church. The Orthodox Church in Czechoslovakia's successor states has been secretive and its inner developments have been non-transparent even for experienced observers of Church history. It is certainly difficult to believe that Metropolitan Kryštof has been accused completely unjustly of the many episodes of violation of his priestly vows. At the same time, it is hard to believe that the accusations against him were not exaggerated and that they were not politically or financially motivated. The episode was very costly for the Orthodox Church because it damaged its reputation in both countries, and because it resulted in the removal from the scene of an erudite and charismatic leader who appeared to possess a vision of a greater societal role for the Church within the Czech and Slovak societies and who wished for the Church to break out of its historical, regional, and ethnic constraints. In the wake of his ouster, disturbing trends continued to be manifested in the Orthodox Church of the two countries. For example, there were reports that the original Czech and Slovak priests were being replaced by new ones coming from among migrants from the Ukraine, Russia, and Moldova, who have been more compliant with the new pro-Russian orientation of the Church.[40] It does seem, however, unlikely that the rich Russian Orthodox Church would attempt to strengthen its influence or even control over the Orthodox Church of the Czech lands and Slovakia in order to get access to the restitution funds. On the contrary, it has provided generous funding for the projects of the Czech Church, such as the renovation of the archbishop's residence. In Prague, Archbishop Jáchym has argued that "The Russians certainly do not seek to get our money and never interfered in our internal Church matters. It even sounds comical that the Russian Church, rich in comparison with us, should be dealing with the finances of our local Czech Church which barely secures its own operations."[41] It appears likely that, rather than for financial gain, the Moscow Patriarchate seeks greater control over the Czech and Slovak Orthodoxy in order to strengthen its position in the global Orthodox Church in relation to the Ecumenical Patriarchate in

Constantinople, as well as in order to ease the political penetration of the Russian state. In fact, the Orthodox Church has already been labeled "the Kremlin's Trojan Horse in the Czech Republic."[42]

Eventually, the leadership situation began to settle down, with the resolution coming in January 2016, during the visit of Metropolitan Rastislav to Istanbul, during which he met a delegation led by Metropolitan John of Pergamon at the Orthodox Patriarchate in Phanar. A communique stated that Rastislav "apologized for his statement against the Ecumenical Patriarchate and Greek People, thus decisively influencing the solving of the problems that the Orthodox Church of the Czech Lands and Slovakia has been facing." He was subsequently recognized in his post by the Ecumenical Patriarch Bartholomew. Furthermore, formal relations between Rastislav and Archbishop Simeon, the former *Locum Tenens*, had been restored, with Simeon remaining as the Archbishop of the troubled Olomouc-Brno diocese.[43] In a further indication of his international acceptance, Rastislav was received by Pope Francis in Rome in May 2018, as part of the Vatican's ecumenical agenda.[44]

THE CHURCH AND SOCIETY: THE EXPECTED CONSERVATISM

It remains to examine the attitude of the Church toward key social issues such as gender equality and homosexuality. The positions taken up by the hierarchs of the Orthodox Church of the Czech lands and Slovakia are consistent with the established views of world Orthodoxy, although articulated in a somewhat softer fashion than by the Russian Church figures. One important factor is that the Orthodox Church in the Czech Republic and Slovakia functions in the environment of a democratic polity and vibrant civil society, while being largely dependent on the government for its funding. This may serve as a moderating influence. In fact, the Church Constitution, adopted in 1999, states that, "This Constitution respects the constitution in the territory of the Czech Republic as well as all legal norms of the Czech Republic, and in the territory of Slovak Republic the constitution and all legal norms of the Slovak Republic, the Declaration of Human Rights and Freedoms, and other state, international and religious norms related to the activity of the Orthodox Church."[45]

The Ecumenical Patriarch Bartholomew expressed the official position of the Church on the issues of homosexuality and same-sex marriage during a homily in Tallinn, Estonia, in September 2013: "To our

Lord Jesus Christ, who blessed families through the Mystery of Marriage at Cana of Galilee and changed water into wine, that is, into joy and feasting, and to his Body, the Orthodox Church, the partnering of the same sex is unknown and condemned, and they condemn the contemporary invention of 'mutual cohabitation', which is the result of sin and not the law of joy."[46] The Orthodox Church of the Czech lands on 9 February 2005 issued a lengthy proclamation on the subject under the title "God Loves the Sinner, but Hates Sin. A statement of Bishops of the Orthodox Church of the Czech Lands Regarding the Issue of Homosexual Unions and About Some During Current Times Wide-Spread Sins." The statement was signed by the then-Prague Archbishop Kryštof and Bishop Simeon of the Olomouc-Brno diocese and contained a clear message: "Homosexual relationships are from the point of view of the Bible and also from the point of view of the teaching of the Church a sin which separates a man from God."[47] But remarkably, the statement continued to say, "But it would be a big mistake to select from many sins, to which people today surrender and which are very widespread, only one (for example the practice of homosexual unions), not to speak about many others, which are today considered acceptable, not only in today's society but sometimes even in the Church," listing "widespread selfishness and individualism, forgetting God, as well as in the widespread practice of extramarital relations, marital infidelity, divorces, and frequent abortions which have neither medical nor social justification," and also the "intemperate indulging in alcohol and addictive substances...In the forefront also emerges the sin of the consumerist lifestyle, resulting in its consequences in the destruction of Divine creation."[48] In a sense, the issue of homosexuality seemed almost marginalized in the wide-ranging indictment of the Czech society.

Another example of the conservatism of the Church came in early 2015, when the Holy Synod of the Orthodox Church of the Czech lands and Slovakia expressed its support for the Referendum for Protection of the Family (*Referendum o ochraně rodiny*) in Slovakia, which was set declared by President Andrej Kiska for 7 February of that year. The referendum was initiated by the conservative *Alliance for the Family* (*Aliancia za rodinu*). The Holy Synod requested that the citizens participate in the referendum and "thus show in a legitimate democratic way their Christian view in the form of triple 'yes'," because, "for Orthodox Christians, marriage has always been a union of one man and one woman who promise each other mutual respect and love before God and the

Church community."[49] The three propositions called for confirmation that only the union of one man and one woman can be considered a marriage, that same-sex couples or groups should not be allowed to adopt children, and that schools could not require participation of children in sex education or education about euthanasia, without their or their parents' agreement with the content of the curriculum.[50] Slovakia's LGBTI community opposed the referendum and requested its boycott. Ultimately, the referendum failed in its purpose and was declared invalid because of low voter participation of only 21.4%. However, the actual vote showed support ranging between 90 and 95% for the three referendum questions,[51] clearly displaying the enduring conservatism of Slovak society.

The final example deals with the opposition of the Orthodox Church of the Czech lands to the legislative ratification of the so-called Istanbul Agreement, which is to say, the Council of Europe's 2011 Convention on Preventing and Combating Violence Against Women and Domestic Violence. While the convention was signed by the Czech government, it has not yet been ratified. In June 2018, the Czech Orthodox Church joined as a signatory of a letter, prepared by some of the main religious institutions in the country and led by the Roman Catholic Church, calling on the Czech legislators to reject the convention. The letter tried to demonstrate that the convention is unnecessary for the states of the European Union and stated that "Gender harmony, meaning equality in dignity and acceptance within the framework biological or socio-cultural difference, is the correct goal, but the repression or hostile contest of power, is not the correct way to it."[52]

THE MINORITY CHURCH BETWEEN THE SECOND AND THIRD ROME

It is precisely because of the status of the Orthodox Church of the Czech lands and Slovakia as a minority Church suspended between the great Orthodox Sea in the East, consisting of Russia, Ukraine, and Belarus, and the ancient Orthodox lands of the Balkans, with Greece, Serbia, Romania, and Bulgaria prominent among them, that it presents such a valuable case study. To be more precise, the Czech and Slovak Church has long been located in the geographical and historical void between the Ecumenical Patriarchate of Constantinople, as the fading ghost of Christianity's Second Rome, and the increasingly more powerful Third

Rome of the Moscow Patriarchate of the Russian Orthodox Church. One can identify several key aspects of its minority status:

First, the Czech and Slovak Orthodox Church lacks the ability to address the Czech and Slovak societies regarding key issues and values, as its reach is limited to its baptized believers. It has no political clout and it has no political parties and interest groups within the political system that could articulate and promote its position on key issues. The dominant Roman Catholic Church can, for example, still successfully play such role in more religious Slovakia, but not in the highly secular and atheistic Czech Republic.

Secondly, the Czech and Slovak Orthodox Church is with its small membership limited in its ability to generate financial support from the ranks of the faithful, and is even more than other religious groups, heavily dependent on the Czech and Slovak governments for its funding. The supervision by the Ministry of Culture is a stark reality for the Church and serves as an inevitable constraint in the absence of the separation of Church and state. Thirdly, it has been able to preserve and even increase its core of believers through migration rather than through conversion or missionary activity among the Czechs and Slovaks.

Thus, it has become, to a significant degree, a "foreign church" with the majority of those attending religious services in the country being Ukrainians and Russians or citizens of various Balkan countries. The situation is further aggravated with the influx of foreign priests into the country. This can also be seen in the intensification of contacts between the Czech and Slovak Church hierarchs and the religious and political leaders in the Ukraine and Russia. Fourthly, as a minority Church, it is more vulnerable to being buffeted by power struggles within the world of Orthodoxy, and especially by the intensified competition and newly arisen conflict between the Ecumenical Patriarch Bartholomew of Constantinople and the powerful Patriarchate of the Russian Orthodox Church in Moscow. It has become obvious that the Czech and Slovak Orthodox hierarchs are increasingly drawn into the orbit of the "Mother Church" in Russia, while remaining unwilling to sever their ties to the Ecumenical Patriarchate in Constantinople.

The Eastern Orthodox Church may currently be undergoing one of its most serious crises since the Great Schism of 1054; the current crisis began in the aftermath of the grant of autocephaly to the Orthodox Church of the Ukraine by the Ecumenical Patriarch Bartholomew. This act has had strong implications for the political and military conflict between Russia and the Ukraine and can even be placed in the context of regenerating East-West tensions. Given the political and international context and consequences of this action, it is not surprising that it has provoked a fierce reaction, not only from Patriarch Kirill of Moscow, the Primate of the Russian Orthodox Church, but also from the Putin regime in the Russian Federation. Following Patriarch Bartholomew's confirmation in October 2018 that he would grant autocephaly to the Orthodox Church of the Ukraine, the Russian Orthodox Church severed its full communion with the Ecumenical Patriarchate in Constantinople.

Like a majority of Europe's Orthodox Churches, all the Czech and Slovak Orthodox bishops, including even the retired primate of the Church, Metropolitan Kryštof, have supported the position of the Moscow Patriarchate, but without severing their ties to the Ecumenical Patriarchate in Constantinople. Metropolitan Rastislav stated that, "the split was provoked by human egoism, which can be overcome only through penitence and return to the embrace of the Church," expressing the view that autocephaly can be achieved only through consensus.[53] In a meeting with Patriarch Kirill in Moscow on 31 January 2019, Rastislav stated: "There was a meeting of the Holy Synod of the Orthodox Church of the Czech Lands and Slovakia two days ago, and the members of the Holy Synod place on my shoulders the duty to appeal to the Primates of all Local Orthodox Churches to hold a pan-Orthodox meeting on the Ukrainian issue."[54] He also expressed his view that the restoration of relations between the Patriarchates of Moscow and Constantinople is impossible without dialogue.[55] Subsequently, in February, Archbishop Michal of Prague and of the Czech lands issued a directive labeling the autocephalous Orthodox Church of the Ukraine as non-canonical and prohibiting his own clergy and believers to participate in common religious services with it.[56] It can therefore be concluded that, caught in the conflict between the Constantinople and Moscow patriarchates, the Czech and Slovak Orthodox Church has supported the position of the Moscow Patriarchate but has so far displayed a degree of independence.

Conclusion

The Orthodox Church of the Czech Lands and Slovakia remains a minor religious component in one of the most atheistic countries in the world, but it is also a part of a vast religious community of perhaps as many as 300 million Orthodox Christians. Its role in Czech society, although less so in eastern Slovakia, has been one of a largely alien institution with very limited relevance for the majority community. It has not been able to rely on a fitting past for Czech national myth-making, with the sole exception of Saints Cyril and Methodius, who came to Greater Moravia two centuries before the Great Schism of 1054 in the Christian Church. The Church's historical role during the century since the creation of an independent Czechoslovak state has only once manifested heroism and martyrdom: In the face of the Nazi German repression after the assassination of Reinhard Heydrich, while during the forty years of the communist rule the Orthodox Church engaged in active collaboration with secular authorities. This was probably unavoidable, given its ties to the politically compliant Russian Orthodox Church in Moscow, but it was also shameful in the eyes of much of Czechoslovakia's general population. The tenuous anchor of the Orthodox Church in the Czech and Slovak societies would always have to be connected to the ideals of Slav unity and Russophilism. These ideals were, however, greatly damaged by the August 1968 Soviet-led invasion and occupation which ended the Prague Spring reform movement. There were two historical opportunities for the Orthodox Church to significantly strengthen its status within Czechoslovak society: one during the early 1920s when the newly formed Czechoslovak Hussite Church considered adopting the Orthodox faith and the other, soon after World War Two, when strong sympathies for the Soviet Union coincided with, but did not cause, a rapidly increasing membership base of the Orthodox Church. In both cases, the Church authorities were unable to take advantage of the situation due to factors such as the annexation of Carpathian Ruthenia by Stalin in 1945. The recent widespread reports of corruption and persistent internal infighting within the Czech and Slovak Orthodox Church have further constrained its ability to engage in missionary work in the two states. Its leadership remains strongly oriented toward Russia and the Ukraine and its churches are filled mainly with foreign nationals. For this reason, during the past thirty years, the local Orthodox Church has displayed an impressive ability to maintain its core membership believers, at least in comparison with the Roman Catholic Church which has been so badly hurt by the rise of secular values and atheization, especially in the Czech Republic. The future survival and status of the Orthodox Church in both states are secure and it will continue its marginal presence in the Czech and Slovak societies in the twenty-first century.

NOTES

1. *Aktuálně.cz* (17 November 2014), "Pravoslavná církev," at https://www.aktuálně.cz/wiki/domaci/pravoslavna-cirkev/r~89b15b626e4911e-49bec0025900fea04/ [accessed 2 May 2018].
2. Derek Sayer, *Coasts of Bohemia, A Czech History* (Princeton, NJ: Princeton University Press, 1998), p. 112.
3. Ibid., p. 153.
4. Ferdinand Peroutka, *Budováni státu* (Prague: Lidové noviny, 1991, originally published 1920), p. 885
5. Pavel Marek a Volodymyr Bureha, *Pravoslavní v Československu v letech 1918–1953* (Praha: Centrum pro Studium Demokracie a Kultury, 2007), p. 81
6. Ibid., p. 28.
7. Ibid., p. 188.
8. Ludvík Němec, "The Czechoslovak Orthodox Church," in Pedro Ramet (ed.), *Eastern Christianity and Politics in the Twentieth Century* (Durham, NC and London: Duke University Press, 1988), p. 255.
9. Ibid., p. 257
10. Ibid., p. 258
11. Ibid., p. 263
12. Marek and Bureha, *Pravoslavní v Československu v letech 1918–1953*, p. 424 (own translation from Czech)
13. Ibid., p. 415.
14. Ibid.
15. *Česka televize* (25 May 2013), "Pravoslavný patriarcha uctil v Praze památku Cyrila a Metodeje," at https://cz24.ceskatelevize.cz/domaci/1096719-pravoslavny-patriarcha-uctil-v-praze-pamatky-cylia-a-metodeje [accessed 20 May 2019].
16. Infokurýr.cz (30 May 2017), "PravoslavnííUkrajinci Mají v Česke Republice Své Duchovní Vedení," at http://m.infokuryr.c/news.php?item.18262.2 [accessed 20 March 2019].
17. CNEWA. A papal agency for humanitarian and pastoral support (24 February 2015), "The Orthodox Church in the Czech and Slovak Republics," at www.cnewa.org/default.aspx?ID=26&pagetypeID=9&sitecode=hq&pageno=2 [accessed 28 April 2019].
18. Parlamentní Listy.cz (28 June 2013), "Duchovní pravoslavné církve se bojí o svá místa. Jejich nadřízení je drží v šachu," at https://www.parlamentnilisty.cz/zpravy/kauzy/Duchovni-pravoslavne-cirkve-se-boji-o-sva-mista-Jejich-nadrizeni-je-drzi-v-sachu-277154 [accessed 25 March 2019].
19. *iDnes.cz* (4 June 2003), "Jsem pravoslavný křestan,přiznal Jágr," at https://www.dnes.cz/hokej/nhl/jsem-pravoslavny-krestan-priznal-jagr.A030604_08513_nhl_ot [accessed 28 May 2018].

20. Život.sk (15 February 2014), "Iny Jaromír Jágr: Prečo prestupil na pravoslavnú vieru?" at https://zivot.pluska.sk/clanok/16099/iny-jaromir-jagr-preco-prestupil-na-pravoslavnu-vieru [accessed 28 May 2018], author's own translation from Slovak.
21. Metropolitan Rastislav, whose secular name is Ondrej Gont, was born on 25 January 1978 in the small town of Snina in eastern Slovakia, in an area with strong Orthodox concentration. He was named the Archbishop of Presov in 2012 and in January 2014 was elected as the Metropolitan of the Church. He was just short of his 36th birthday and there has been a significant criticism of the fact that many of the newly elected bishops of the Church have risen to their high posts with limited theological preparation and erudition. They stand in contrast with the former Metropolitan and Archbishop of Prague and of the Czech Lands Krystof (Radim Pulec) and the 93-year-old Archbishop of the Diocese of Olomouc and Brno, Simeon (Radivoj Jakovlevic), both of whom have impressive scholarly credentials.
22. *Prešovska pravoslavná eparchia* (2014), Ustava, clanok 2, at www.eparchiapo.sk/sk/dokumenty/pravoslavna-cirkev/ustava [accessed 24 February 2019].
23. Pavel Marek, e-mail communication with the author, 12 April 2019.
24. Pew Research Center (2 January 2019), "Once the Same Nation, the Czech Republic and Slovakia Look Very Different Religiously," at https://www.pewresearch.org/fact-tank/2019/01/02/once-the-same-nation-theczech-republic-and-slovakia-look-very-different-religiously/ [accessed 7 April 2019].
25. Rene Matlovič, "Geographical Aspects of Religious Diversity in Slovakia at the Beginning of the Third Millenium," in *Peregrinus Cracoviensis* (Zeszyt 13, 2002), at https://www.unipo.sk/public/media14066/peregrinus%20cracoviensis%2013.pdf, pp. 5–51 [accessed 14 April 2019].
26. Pražska Pravoslavná Eparchie (29 January 2019), "Setkáni J.V. Michala arcibiskupa pražskeho a českych zemí s velvyslanci," at http://pp-eparchie.cz/setkani-j-v-michala-arcibiskupa-prazskeho-a-ceskych-zemi-s-velvyslanci/ [accessed 2 May 2019].
27. Pražska Pravoslavná Eparchie (26 October 2018), "J.V. Michael se zcastnil oslav Rakouskeho narodniho svatku," at http://pp-eparchie.cz/j-v-michal-se-zucastnil-oslav-rakouskeho-narodniho-svatku/ [accessed 2 May 2019].
28. Radim Pulec was born on 29 June 1953 in Prague into an Old Catholic Church (Starokatolicke cirkve) family.
29. Mystagogy Resource Center (24 September 2011), Aimilios Polygenis, "Orthodox Christianity in Czech and Slovakia Is Growing," at https://johnsanidopoulos.com/2011/09/orthodox-christianity-inczech-and.html [accessed 25 March 2019].
30. Ibid.

31. European Values. Kremlin Watch Report (4 October 2018), Stanislav Matveev, "Contemporary Influence of the Russian Orthodox Church Within the 'Autocephalous' Orthodox Church of the Czech Lands and Slovakia," p. 11, at https://www.kremlinwatch.eu/userfiles/congtemporary-influence-of-the-russian-orthodox-chuch-within-the-autocephalous-orthodox-church-of-the-cz... [accessed 1 May 2019].
32. Parlamentní Listy.cz (1 October 2016), "Vladimír Wolf: O tragikomedii v česke a slovenské pravoslavné církvi, kdy skončí?" at https://www.parlamentnilistycz./arena/nazory-a-petice/Vladimir-Wolf-)-tragikomedii-v-ceske-a-slovenske-pravoslavne-cirkvi-kdy-skonci-456225 [accessed 5 May 2018].
33. European Values, Kremlin Watch Report (4 October 2018), Stanislav Matveev, "Contemporary Influence of the Russian Orthodox Church Within the 'Autocephalous' Orthodox Church of the Czech Lands and Slovakia," p. 12.
34. Echo24.cz (14 October 2014), Vladimir Ševela, "České restituce tunelují Rusove, ozyva se z Pravoslavné církve," at http://echo24.cz/a/5wnc/ceske-restituce-tuneluji-rusove-ozyva-se-z-pravoslavne-cirkve [accessed 15 May 2018].
35. *IDnes.cz* (14 October 2013), "Restitučni miliony rozkmotřily česke popy, musí zasáhnout Istanbul," at https://www.idnes.cz/zpravy/domaci/restituce-a-pravoslavna-cirkev.A131013_202709_domaci_ert [accessed 16 May 2018].
36. *IDnes.cz* (20 November 2014), "Ministerstvo zastavilo pravoslavné církvi kvuli sporům vypláceni náhrad," at https://www.idnes.cz/zpravy/domaci/pozastavei-penez-pro-pravoslavnou-cirkev.A141120_070630_domaci_jj [accessed 15 May 2018].
37. Ibid.
38. Parlamentní Listy.cz (27 October 2014), "Pravoslavná církev v českych zemích: Důrazne se distancujeme od jednáni ThDr. Martina Marka Krupici," at https://parlamentnilisty.cz/arena/nazory-a-petice/Pravoslavna-cirkev-v-ceskych-zemich-Durazne-se-distancujeme-od-jednani-ThDr-Martina-Marka-Krupici-343403 [accessed 20 April 2019].
39. Pavla Bendová, in an e-mail interview with the author, dated 11 April 2019 from Prague, in which she provided written answers for submitted questions. She wrote in Czech: "Není mi známo, že by ministr Herman pozastavil výplatu Pravoslavné církvi. Všem církvím, včetne Pravoslavné, byla vyplacena finanční náhrada ve stejném termínu, přesne dle ustaveni zákona" (author's own translation into English).
40. Echo24.cz (14 October 2014), Vladimir Ševela, "České restituce tunelujÍ Rusové. Ozýva se z pravoslavné církve," at https://echo24,cz/a/i5wnc/ceske-restituce-tuneluji-rusove-ozyva-se-z-pravoslavne-cirkve [accessed 1 May 2019].
41. Ibid.

42. DeníkN.cz. (9 February 2019), Stanislav Matvejev, "Kreml má v Česku trojského koně-pravoslavnou církev. Její místní hodnostáři se tím ani moc netají," at http://denikn.cz/69878/kreml-ma-v-cesku-trojskeho-kone-pravoslavnou-cirke-jeji-mistni-hodnostari-s-tim-ani-moc-netaji/ [accessed 1 May 2019].
43. Orthodox Christianity (13 January 2016), "Reconciliation in the Orthodox Church of the Czech Lands and Slovakia," at https://orthochristian.com/89666.html [accessed 1 June 2018].
44. *Christianity Today* (10 May 2016). "Pope to Meet Head of Czech and Slovak Orthodox Church for the First Time," at http://www.christianitytoday.com/article/pop-to-meet-head-of-the-czech-and-slovak-orthodox-church-for-the-first-time/129091.htm [accessed 1 June 2018].
45. *Prešovska pravoslavná eparchia* (2014), Ústava, článok 29, at http://www.eparchia.sk/sk/dokumenty/pravoslavna-cirkev/ustava [accessed 24 February 2019], author's own translation from Slovak. The reference to "Declaration of Human Rights and Freedoms" most likely refers to the Czech and Slovak constitutional document entitled The Charter of Fundamental Rights and Basic Freedoms, rather than to the Universal Declaration of Human Rights.
46. Aoiusa. American Orthodox Institute (9 September 2013), FR. Johannes Jacobse, "Pat.Bartholomew: No to Homosexual Marriage," at www.aoi-usa.org/pat-bartholomew-no-to-homosexual-marriage [accessed 2 May 2019].
47. Pravoslaví.cz., "Bůh miluje hříšníka ale nenávidí hřích. Prohlášení biskupů Pravoslavné církve v Českých zemích k problematice homosexualních svazků a k některým v současné době rozšířeným hříchům," at http://pravoslavi.cz./info/prohlaseni-k-homosex.htm [accessed 19 April 2019].
48. Ibid.
49. iSITA (Slovenská tlačová agentůra) Web Noviny (30 January 2013), "Pravoslavná církev vyzývá na trojité ano v referendě," at https://www.webnoviny.sk/pravoslavna-cirkev-vyzyva-na-trojite-ano-v-referende [accessed 2 May 2019].
50. Ibid.
51. Konzervativný Denník Postoj (7 February 2015), "Referendum je neplatné. Prišiel necelý million voličov," at https://www.postoj.sk/4184/referendum-je-neplatne-prisiel-necely-milion-volicov [accessed 1 May 2019].
52. Pražská Pravoslavná Eparchie, "Pravoslavná církev v Českých zemích k tzv.Istanbulské úmluve," http://pp-eparchie.cz/pravoslavna-cirkev-v-ceskych-zemich-k-tzv-istanbulske-umluve/ [accessed 1 May 2019].

53. Cz.Sputnik.news (5 February 2019), "Český pravoslavný arcibiskup okomentoval konflikt Ruska a Konstantinopolu kvůli Ukrajině," at https://cz/sputnik.news.com/ceskarepublika/201809118052724-ceske-pravoslavie-arcibiskup-rusko-konstantinopol-ukrajina-konflikt/ [accessed 2 May 2019].
54. Orthodox Christianity (1 February 2019), "Church of the Czech Lands and Slovakia Calls on Primates to Hold Pan-Orthodox Meeting on Ukraine," at http://orthochristian.com/119083.html [accessed 2 May 2019].
55. Ibid.
56. Cz.Sputnik.news (27 February 2019), "Arcibiskup pražský nařídil, že nová pravoslavná církev Ukrajiny nebude uznána kanonickou," at https://cz.sputninews.com/ceskarepublika/201902279326558-arcibiskup-prazsky-naridil-ze-nova-pravoslavna-cirkev-ukrajiny-nebude-povazovana-za-kanonickou/ [accessed 2 May 2019].

Afterword: Why Are Orthodox Churches Prone to Political Mobilization Today?

Throughout the 1980s and 1990s, Sabrina P. Ramet was at the forefront of the study of religion and politics in the communist and post-communist world. Her many publications, pioneering in their high level of detail and policy insights, have continued to be extensively referenced since then. In her 1989 publication *Religion and Nationalism in Soviet and East European Politics*,[1] she summarized the communist engagement with religion as follows:

> Communist religious policy is determined by at least six factors: (1) The size of a religious organization in question; (2) the organization's disposition to subordinate itself to political authority and its amenability to infiltration and control by the secret police; (3) the question of allegiance to a foreign authority; (4) the loyalty or disloyalty of the particular body during World War Two; (5) the ethnic configuration of the respective country; and (6) the dominant political culture of the country.[2]

Ramet's typology remained valid during the early post-1989 political realities. Religious communities increased in size; predominantly, Orthodox churches in the region became more politicized; the process of lustration, namely removing clergy associated with the communist authorities, was largely non-existent; most religious leaders looked back to the interwar period in attempting to reinstate legislation; religious and political leaders regularly scrutinized the role of religion in shaping the ethnic composition of their country; and religion/church-state relations continued to be defined by the political culture. One particular area remained controversial, namely 'allegiance to a foreign authority.' While, during the Cold War period, allegiance to a religious community based in the West was likely to be subject to persecution, after 1989, freedom of religion and religious competition became the norm. The Greek Catholic Churches were re-established, Church leaders in exile returned to their country, and religious communities multiplied. Issues related to property disputes and the national status of predominant confessions shaped debates on implementing religious legislation. In many cases, contact with high clergy, particularly from the West, was perceived with the fear of proselytism and the inevitable loss of religious influence in society. A number of Orthodox Churches (the Bulgarian, Georgian and Russian) even revoked (or suspended) their membership of international ecumenical bodies.[3] At the same time, religious affiliation increased across the region to the extent that the 2017 Pew Research Forum survey showed that, as a whole, predominantly Orthodox countries in Eastern and Southeastern Europe constituted one of the most religious regions in Europe.[4] The upsurge of religious and national identification across the Eastern Orthodox world has resulted not only in societal transformation but also in the politicization of religion.

Why are Orthodox Churches prone to political engagement today? Is it due to the structure and nature of Orthodox Churches or to the ways in which societies emerged from the Cold War period? Ramet's present volume, *Orthodox Churches and Politics in Southeastern Europe*, builds on the legacy of religious policy behind the Iron Curtain and adds new insights into these questions. The concepts of power, agency and authority, at the regional, national and geopolitical levels, have been present in both the religious and political spheres. After the fall of communism, the Orthodox world has witnessed an exacerbation of religious and political symbols in the public domain. Religion was present in the dissolution of former Yugoslavia and continues to be present in the corridors of power in national parliaments, in mobilizing the masses in the name of traditional values and in electoral processes.

As Ramet wrote in the Introduction to this volume, while religious and national identification exist in other religious confessions, three key elements have characterized the political mobilization of Orthodox Churches in Southeastern Europe, namely nationalism, conservatism and intolerance. The association of these words is not intended to imply that every single member of the Orthodox community is inherently 'intolerant,' a 'right-wing nationalist' or 'supporting conservatism.' On the contrary, each Orthodox Church has been defined by a multitude of voices from local clergy, bishops, top hierarchs and the lay movements. As an institution, the Church is not summed up by public statements from clergy but by the wider mobilization of the faithful sharing the same doctrinal and liturgical practices. Orthodox Churches are both institutional structures and communities of the faithful as an expression of local culture and communities of beliefs. The distinction between the institutional character of the Church and the everyday lived experience of the faithful is fundamental to understanding how political messages are conveyed and received. Political messages are expressed through the following means of communication, all of which are deeply rooted in state building processes.

First of all, political messages from ecclesiastical circles, either at the local or at the national level, emerge in light of the institutional structure of the particular Church. Reaching a position in a Church hierarchy entails engagement with social and political actors. As a general rule, it is impossible to become a dean, bishop or patriarch without the political realm exerting pressure on the most appropriate candidate alongside national and party politics at the local or central levels. Close relations between religious and political authorities are most symbolically suggested by the location of buildings. In Romania, during the communist period, the Patriarchal Cathedral was only a few meters away from the Grand National Assembly, the legislative body. In recent years, a Cathedral of National Salvation was built near the House of the People, the democratic legislator of the country, with both buildings among the largest administrative complexes in the world. In Bulgaria, the location of St. Alexander Nevsky Cathedral is comparably sited, only a few meters from the National Parliament. In Kyiv, the Ministry of Foreign Affairs is facing St Sofia Cathedral, a symbol of national unity and the newly rebuilt St. Michael's Golden-Domed Monastery, which also houses the Theological Academy of the Ukrainian Orthodox Church (previously known as the Kyiv Patriarchate).

Second, from the nineteenth century, the nation-state building processes in Southeastern Europe brought Orthodox churches close to government and political authorities. The 'invention' of states and nations in the region was achieved through taking into account the religious substratum, ethnic competition and political cultures. Contact between religious and political leaders has characterized various patterns of church-state relations, ranging from 'entangled authorities' to the concepts of the (in)compatibility between modernity and *symphonia*.[5] Orthodox Churches stood out in the religious composition of each country by having a prime role in shaping their political cultures. The canon law of the Orthodox Church was applied at times together with that of the state authorities. Issues related to divorce, marriages and social mores were perceived through religious lenses before the secular state imposed its own norms. In the clash between the Church and state norms, the Church was not an easy opponent. The secularization of monasteries in Southeastern Europe in the nineteenth century, the expulsion of Greek-speaking clergy and favoring of nativist authorities are examples of this long legacy. It is therefore no surprise that the Orthodox Church of Greece and the Romanian Orthodox Church have constantly claimed over the last two decades that they would like to acquire the privileged position as landowners in order to be able to administer the faithful successfully.

Third, Orthodox Churches have become politically stronger when states have failed to provide social support for a population in need. The concept of state failure is crucial to understanding the ways in which Orthodox Churches respond at times of crisis. When faced with external challenges, across Southeastern Europe, the Orthodox Churches took on state functions in supporting populations affected by violence and conflict mainly because the state did not have the resources and capabilities. The social mobilization of Orthodox churches has taken different forms across the region. In Greece, at the peak of the 2015 crisis of refugees arriving from Syria and across the Aegean Sea, parishes worked with nongovernmental organizations; similarly, the Serbian Orthodox Church drew on its experience of reaching people affected by flooding and mobilized in support of the refugees crossing the Balkan route.[6] However, in Bulgaria, the Church has remained passive and even condemned the arrival of refugees as an 'invasion' of their country. In all of these countries, when states failed to provide support to refugees, the Church entered the public space. The Church responds to crises in the name of protecting the 'nation' (thus the very close link to nationalism) and searches for the most appropriate means to take on state functions by looking back into history as an example of reaching mutual and beneficial collaboration with the state.

Fourth, and perhaps most important, as a 'lived religion,' Orthodox Christianity provides a fascinating journey into social expressions. For the faithful living in towns and villages, the ritual practices of Eastern Orthodoxy give meaning and sense to life to the extent that no state bodies would be able to achieve. Religious gatherings marking birth, marriage and death strengthen social cohesion by drawing on local traditions which date back centuries. Many clergy do not engage with political issues and focus solely on administering the faithful. During the communist period, the private character of Orthodoxy ensured the survival of religion during atheist persecution. That the 'lived religion' remains an important factor today has been evident in the state and Church mobilization in relation to the 2018 referendum on family in Romania. Despite institutional calls from top hierarchs and politicians that the population should vote for changes to the Constitution which define marriage as the unity between man and woman, the Orthodox faithful refused to endorse the vote. Believers in ordinary churches leaving the Sunday liturgy where in his sermon the priest encouraged people to go to vote for the referendum stated their dissatisfaction with the political involvement of the Church. The refusal of ordinary believers to follow institutional structures was a reminder of an old saying that 'do what the priest tells you to do not what he does,' namely to follow the Christian teaching and not the clergy's example. In other words, the private character of Orthodoxy was more important than the institutional mobilization from both religious and political authorities.

In conclusion, the political mobilization of Orthodox Churches remains embedded in both the structure of Eastern Orthodoxy and the ways in which societies in Southeastern Europe engage with religion. As Sabrina P. Ramet's study has eloquently explored, this mobilization takes different forms not only according to historical patterns of the political culture in each country but also due to the ways in which religious communities adapt to political regimes. The adaptation of Orthodox Churches, at the institutional level, relates to the legacy of religion-state relations during the Cold War period and to the ways in which religious communities have been included in the process of nation-state building.

Notes

1. Pedro Ramet (ed.), *Eastern Christianity and Politics in the Twentieth Century* (Durham and London: Duke University Press, 1988); and Pedro Ramet (ed.), *Religion and Nationalism in Soviet and East European Politics*, 2nd ed. (Durham and London: Duke University Press, 1989). See also Pedro Ramet, *Cross and Commissar: The Politics of Religion in Eastern Europe and the USSR* (Bloomington: Indiana University Press, 1987); Pedro Ramet (ed.), *Catholicism and Politics in Communist Societies* (Durham and London: Duke University Press, 1990); Sabrina Petra Ramet (ed.), *Protestantism and Politics in Eastern Europe and Russia* (Durham and London: Duke University Press, 1992); and Sabrina P. Ramet, *Nihil Obstat. Religion, Politics, and Social Change in East-Central Europe and Russia* (Durham and London: Duke University Press, 1998).
2. Pedro Ramet, "The Interplay of Religious Policy and Nationalities Policy in the Soviet Union and Eastern Europe," pp. 3–41 in Pedro Ramet (ed.), *Religion and Nationalism*, p. 9
3. See the following volumes, by other authors, on religion, politics and society in Southeastern Europe published after 1989: Vasilios N. Makrides (ed.), *Religion, Staat und Konfliktkonstellationen im orthodoxen Ost- und Südosteuropa: vergleichende Perspektiven* (Bern: Lang, 2005); Michael Angold (ed.), *Eastern Christianity: The Cambridge History of Christianity*, vol. 5 (Cambridge: Cambridge University Press, 2006); Ines A. Murzaku, *Quo Vadis Eastern Europe? Religion, State and Society After Communism*, Series on Balkan and East European Studies, University of Bologna (Ravenna: Longo Editore, 2009); Lucian N. Leustean (ed.), *Eastern Christianity and the Cold War, 1945–91* (London: Routledge, 2010); and Lucian N. Leustean (ed.), *Eastern Christianity and Politics in the Twenty-First Century* (London: Routledge, 2014).
4. Pew Research Centre, "Religious Belief and National Belonging in Central and Eastern Europe," 10 May 2017, at https://www.pewforum.org/2017/05/10/religious-belief-and-national-belonging-in-central-and-eastern-europe/ [accessed on 1 April 2019].
5. Tobias Köllner, "Introduction," in Tobias Köllner (ed.), *Orthodox Religion and Politics in Contemporary Eastern Europe: On Multiple Secularisms and Entanglements* (London: Routledge, 2019), pp. 3–16; and Vasilios N. Makrides, "Orthodox Christianity and State/Politics Today: Factors to Take Into Account," in Köllner (ed.), *Orthodox Religion*, pp. 235–254.
6. See examples of case studies in Lucian N. Leustean, *Forced Migration and Human Security in the Eastern Orthodox World* (London: Routledge, forthcoming in 2019).

Lucian N. Leustean (Ph.D., London School of Economics and Political Science, 2007) is Reader in Politics and International Relations at Aston University, Birmingham, UK. His publications include, as author, *The Ecumenical Movement and the Making of the European Community* (Oxford University Press, 2014) and *Orthodoxy and the Cold War. Religion and Political Power in Romania, 1947–1965* (Palgrave, 2009) and, as editor, *Forced Migration and Human Security in the Eastern Orthodox World* (Routledge, 2019), *Eastern Christianity and Politics in the Twenty-First Century* (Routledge, 2014), and *Eastern Christianity and the Cold War, 1945–91* (Routledge, 2010).

Further Reading

General

Billington, James H. "Orthodoxy and Democracy", in *Journal of Church and State*, Vol. 49, No. 1 (January 2007).
Koellner, Tobias. *Orthodox Religion and Politics in Contemporary Eastern Europe* (London: Routledge, 2018).
Leustean, Lucian N. (ed.). *Eastern Christianity and the Cold War, 1945–91* (London: Routledge, 2011).
Leustean, Lucian N. (ed.). *Eastern Christianity and Politics in the Twenty-First Century* (London: Routledge, 2017).
Naletova, Inna. "Other-Worldly Europe? Religion and the Church in the Orthodox Area of Eastern Europe", in *Religion, State, and Society*, Vol. 37, No. 4 (2009).
Parry, Ken et al. (eds.). *The Blackwell Dictionary of Eastern Christianity* (Hoboken, NJ: Wiley-Blackwell, 2001).
Ramet, Pedro (ed.). *Eastern Christianity and Politics in the Twentieth Century* (Durham, NC: Duke University Press, 1988).
Ramet, Sabrina P. "The Way We Were—And Should Be Again? European Orthodox Churches and the 'Idyllic Past'", in Timothy A. Byrnes and Peter J. Katzenstein (eds.), *Religion in an Expanding Europe* (Cambridge: Cambridge University Press, 2006).

Ramet, Sabrina P. (ed.). *Religion and Politics in Post-Socialist Central and Southeastern Europe: Challenges Since 1989* (Basingstoke: Palgrave Macmillan, 2014): Chapters 8 (Serbia, by Radmila Radić and Milan Vukomanović), 10 (Macedonia and Montenegro, by Aleksander Zdravkovski and Kenneth Morrison), and 11 (Romania and Bulgaria, by Lavinia Stan and Lucian Turcescu).

Siecienski, A. Edward. *Orthodox Christianity: A Very Short Introduction* (Oxford: Oxford University Press, 2019).

Spina, Nicholas. "The Religious Authority of the Orthodox Church and Tolerance Toward Homosexuality", in *Problems of Post-Communism*, Vol. 63 (2016).

Stan, Lavinia, and Lucian Turcescu. *Church, State, and Democracy in Expanding Europe* (Oxford: Oxford University Press, 2011).

Ware, Timothy. *The Orthodox Church: An Introduction to Eastern Christianity*, new ed. (Milton Keynes: Penguin Books, 2015).

Albania

"Albania, Orthodox Church Of", in John Anthony McGuckin (ed.), *The Concise Encyclopedia of Eastern Orthodox Christianity* (Hoboken, NJ: Wiley-Blackwell, 2014).

Bowers, Stephen R. "Church and State in Albania", in *Religion in Communist Lands*, Vol. 6, No. 3 (1978).

Endresen, Cecilie. *Is the Albanian's Religion Really 'Albanianism'? Religion and Nation According to Muslim and Christian Leaders in Albania* (Wiesbaden: Otto Harrassowitz Verlag, 2013).

Tönnes, Bernhard. "Albania: An Atheist State", in *Religion in Communist Lands*, Vol. 3, No. 1/3 (1975).

Tönnes, Bernhard. "Religious Persecution in Albania", in *Religion in Communist Lands*, Vol. 6, No. 3 (1978).

Bulgaria

Broun, Janice. "The Bulgarian Orthodox Church: The Continuing Schism and the Religious, Social and Political Environment", in *Religion, State and Society*, Vol. 32, No. 3 (September 2004).

Broun, Janice. "The Schism in the Bulgarian Orthodox Church", in *Religion, State and Society*, Vol. 21, No. 2 (1993).

"Bulgaria, Patriarchal Orthodox Church Of", in John Anthony McGuckin (ed.), *The Encyclopedia of Eastern Orthodox Christianity* (Hoboken, NJ: Wiley-Blackwell, 2011).

Hopkins, James Lindsay. *The Bulgarian Orthodox Church: A Socio-Historical Analysis of the Evolving Relationship Between Church, Nation, and State in Bulgaria* (Boulder, CO: East European Monographs, 2009).

Raikin, Spas T. "The Communists and the Bulgarian Orthodox Church, 1944–48: The Rise and Fall of Exarch Stefan", in *Religion in Communist Lands*, Vol. 12, No. 3 (1984).

Czech and Slovak Republics

"Czech Lands and Slovakia, Orthodox Church Of", in John Anthony McGuckin (ed.), *The Encyclopedia of Eastern Orthodox Christianity* (Hoboken, NJ: Wiley-Blackwell, 2011).

Navrat, Milan. *Religion in Czechoslovakia* (Prague: Orbis, 1984).

Sorokowski, Andrew. "The Orthodox Theological Seminary in Prešov, Czechoslovakia", in *Religion in Communist Lands*, Vol. 14, No. 1 (1986).

Sorokowski, Andrew. "Ukrainian Catholics and Orthodox in Czechoslovakia", in *Religion in Communist Lands*, Vol. 16, No. 1 (1987).

Greece

"Greece, Orthodox Church Of", in John Anthony McGuckin (ed.), *The Encyclopedia of Eastern Orthodox Christianity* (Hoboken, NJ: Wiley-Blackwell, 2011).

Halikiopoulou, Daphne. "Patterns of Secularization: Church, State and Nation in Greece and the Republic of Ireland", in *Journal of Church and State*, Vol. 54, No. 2 (June 2012).

Laitila, Teuvo. *New Voices in Greek Orthodox Thought: Untying the Bond Between Nation and Religion* (Farnham and Burlington: Ashgate, 2014).

Makris, Gerasimos, and Vasilios Meichanetsidis. "The Church of Greece in Critical Times: Reflections Through Philanthropy", in *Journal of Contemporary Religion*, Vol. 33, No. 2 (2018).

Molokotos-Liederman, Lina. "Identity Crisis: Greece, Orthodoxy, and the European Union", in *Journal of Contemporary Religion*, Vol. 18, No. 3 (2003).

Papastathis, Konstantinos. "Religious Discourse and Radical Right Politics in Contemporary Greece, 2010–2014", in *Politics, Religion & Ideology*, Vol. 16, Nos. 2–3 (2015).

Patrikios, Stratos. "Religious Deprivatisation in Modern Greece", in *Journal of Contemporary Religion*, Vol. 24, No. 3 (October 2009).

Macedonia

Gjorgjevski, Gjoko. "Macedonian Orthodox Church in the Context of Balkan and European Orthodoxy", *Occasional Papers on Religion in Eastern Europe*, Vol. 37, No. 4 (July 2017), at http://pbf.edu.mk/wp-content/uploads/2017/07/Macedonian-Orthodox-Church-in-the-Context-of-Balkan-and-European.pdf.

Ilievski, Doné. *The Macedonian Orthodox Church: The Road to Independence*, translated by James M. Leech (Skopje: Macedonian Review, 1973).

Pavlowitch, Stevan K. "The Orthodox Church in Yugoslavia: The Problem of the Macedonian Orthodox Church", in *Eastern Churches Review*, Vol. 1, No. 4 (1967–1968).

Velkov, Pance. "Preserving Historic Churches and Monasteries in the Republic of Macedonia", in *Journal of Architectural Conservation*, Vol. 13, No. 3 (November 2007).

Romania

Andreescu, Liviu. "Romania's New Law on Religious Freedom and Religious Denominations", in *Religion, State & Society*, Vol. 36, No. 2 (June 2008).

Leustean, Lucian N. *Orthodoxy and the Cold War: Religion and Political Power in Romania, 1947–65* (Basingstoke: Palgrave, 2008).

"Romania, Patriarchal Orthodox Church Of", in John Anthony McGuckin (ed.), *The Encyclopedia of Eastern Orthodox Christianity* (Hoboken, NJ: Wiley-Blackwell, 2011).

Romocea, Cristian G. *Church and State: Religious Nationalism and State Identification in Post-Communist Romania* (London: Continuum, 2011).

Stan, Lavinia, and Lucian Turcescu. *Religion and Politics in Post-communist Romania* (Oxford: Oxford University Press, 2007).

Serbia

Alexander, Stella. *Church and State in Yugoslavia Since 1945* (Cambridge: Cambridge University Press, 1979).

Buchenau, Klaus. "Orthodox Values and Modern Necessities: Serbian Orthodox Clergy and Laypeople on Democracy, Human Rights, Transition, and Globalization", in Ola Listhaug, Sabrina P. Ramet, and Dragana Dulić (eds.), *Civic and Uncivic Values: Serbia in the Post-Milošević Era* (Budapest and New York: Central European University Press, 2011).

Drezgić, Rada. "Orthodox Christianity and Gender Equality in Serbia: On Reproductive and Sexual Rights", in Christine M. Hassenstab and Sabrina P. Ramet (eds.), *Gender (In)Equality and Gender Politics in Southeastern Europe: A Question of Justice* (Basingstoke: Palgrave Macmillan, 2015).

"Serbia, Patriarchal Orthodox Church Of", in John Anthony McGuckin (ed.), *The Concise Encyclopedia of Eastern Orthodox Christianity* (Hoboken, NJ: Wiley-Blackwell, 2014).

Vukomanović, Milan. "The Serbian Orthodox Church as a Political Actor in the Aftermath of October 5, 2000", in *Politics and Religion*, Vol. 1, No. 2 (August 2008).

Vukomanović, Milan. "The Serbian Orthodox Church Between Traditionalism, Conservatism and Fundamentalism", in Ulrika Mårtensson, Jennifer Bailey, Priscilla Ringrose, and Åsbjørn Dyrendal (eds.), *Fundamentalism in the Modern World, Vol. 1—Fundamentalism, Politics and History: The State, Globalization and Political Ideologies* (London: I.B. Tauris, 2011).

Index

A
Abbot of Novo Hopovo monastery Ilarion Mišić, 98
Abrami, Thoma, 199
Alojzije Stepinac, Archbishop, 26
Ambrose of Kalvrta, Metropolitan, 9
Amfilohije Radović, Archbishop, 96, 99, 116
Anastasios Yannoulatos, Archbishop, 197, 200, 219, 221
Andrei Saguna of Transylvania, Metropolitan, 43
Archimandrite Nicodemus Barknias of Macedonia, 32
Arkan, Željko Ražnatović, 89
Arsenalului, Dealul, 44

B
Balcı, Zeynep Selin, 9
Baleva, Martina, 64
Bartholomew, Ecumenical Patriarch, 100, 109, 235, 237, 240, 241, 246
Bauman, Zygmunt, 125, 126, 129
Bendová, Pavla, 235, 245
Benito, Odio, 148
Bergholz, Max, 24, 38
Berisha, Sali, 206, 210
Bigović, Radovan, 6
Bishop Ambrosios, Metropolitan of Kalavryta and Aigialeia, 151
Bishop Anthony Merdani of Kruja, 211
Bishop Artemije of Raška-Prizren, 90
Bishop Atanasije Jevtić, 87, 116
Bishop Cornel Onila of Husi, 49
Bishop Georgi Naumov, 175
Bishop Gorazd (Matěj Pavlík), 227
Bishop Illarion, head of the International Relations department of the Russian Orthodox Church, 178
Bishop Irinej of Bačka, 89
Bishop Jovan Vraniškovski, 10, 100, 167, 168, 174–178
Bishop Kozma Qirjo of Apollonia, 211
Bishop Nicholas Hyka of Apollonia, 211

264 INDEX

Bishop Nikolaj Velimirović, 9, 95, 106, 112, 115–117, 122, 127, 128
Bishop Pahomie of Vranje, 174
Bishop Pahomije Gačić of Vranje, 98
Bishop Petar of the Pelagonija-Prespa Diocese, 184
Bishop Simeon of the Olomouc-Brno diocese, 238
Bishop Timotej, Metropolitan of the Diocese of Debar and Kichevo, 185
Bishop Vasilije Kačavenda of Zvornik-Tuzla, 98
Blumi, Isa, 10, 198, 217, 221
Bojarovski, Zoran, 176, 190
Boris III of Bulgaria, Tsar, 60, 78
Boris of Nevrokop, Metropolitan, 57, 76
Brnabić, Ana, 36, 98
Byford, Jovan, 105, 106, 120, 121, 127–129

C
Cacanoska, Ružica, 181, 189, 193
Cannadine, David, 18, 37
Ceaușescu, Nicolae, 25
Christodoulos of Athens and All Greece, Archbishop, 132, 155
Chrysoloras, Nikolaos, 136, 156, 157, 159
Chrysostom, St. John, 113
Cibulka, Frank, 10, 224
Cicero, 3
Constantinescu, Emil, 48
Crvenkovski, Branko, 179, 180

D
Daniel Ciobotea of Romania, Patriarch, 44
Daskalovski, Zhidas, 179, 192

Diamantopoulou, Elisabeth A., 135, 157, 161, 162
Dimitrov, Georgi, 25
Dimitrov, Slavcho, 13, 184
Đinđić, Zoran, 92
Djujić, Momčilo, 24
Djukanović, Milo, 33
Đorđević, Mirko, 4
Dositelj of the Macedonian Church, Metropolitan, 171
Dragostinova, Theodora, 22, 37–39
Duçi, Milo, 199, 200
Đurđević, Ratibor, 121, 122

F
Farský, Karel, 226
Francis, Pope, 60, 78, 237
Frčkovski, Ljubomir, 174
Friedman, Francine, 9, 98, 111

G
Gavrilo Dozić of Serbia, Patriarch, 115
Gavroglou, Konstantinos, 151
German II of Serbia, Patriarch, 30
Gligorov, Kiro, 173
Glock, Charles J., 111
Gruevski, Nikola, 177, 178, 180–182, 184–186, 188
Günal, Altuğ, 9, 132, 165

H
Habsburg Emperor Ferdinand II, 225
Herman, Daniel, 235, 245
Heydrich, Reinhard, 227, 242
Hieronymos II, Archbishop, 150, 153
Hilarion of Volokolamsk, Metropolitan, 58, 234
Hitler, Adolf, 60, 115
Hoxha, Enver, 198, 200, 202

INDEX 265

Huntington, Samuel P., 133
Hus, Jan, 224, 225

I
Irinej of Serbia, Patriarch, 109
Irwin, Zachary T., 10, 168, 193, 194
Ivan of Rila, 61

J
Jáchym (Roman Hrdý) of Prague and of the Czech Lands, Archbishop (later:Archbishop of Beroun), 236
Jágr, Jaromir, 229, 244
Janković, Ivan, 9, 14
Jirásek, Alois, 225
Joan Pelushi of Korça, Metropolitan, 211
John Paul II, Pope, 60, 148
John VII of Byzantium, Emperor, 34
Jovan (Vraniškovski) of Ohrid, Archbishop, 68, 191
Jovan (Vranishkovski) of Ohrid, Metropolitan, 66
Juergensmeyer, Mark, 16, 37

K
Kadelburg, Lavoslav, 118
Kalkandjieva, Daniela, 8, 11, 14, 75, 77, 81
Kanin, David, 7
Karadžić, Radovan, 30, 31
Karamihaleva, Aleksandra, 71
Karavangjelis of Kastoria, 199
King Juan Carlos of Spain, 28
Kirill of Moscow and Primate of the Russian Orthodox Church, Patriarch, 241
Kollettis, Ioannis, 136
Komenský, Jan Amos, 225
Kostryukov, Andrey, 58, 76

Koštunica, Vojislav, 31, 92
Koumandaraki, Anna, 134, 136, 156–160
Kramař, Karel, 227
Krupica, Martin Marek, 234, 235
Kryštof (Radim Pulec), Archbishop of Prague and the Czech Lands and Slovakia, Metropolitan, 232
Kunchev, Vasil, 17

L
Laitila, Teuvo, 135, 157
Lasswell, Harold, 183, 194
Leustean, Lucian, 11, 249
Levsky, Ivan, 17
Ljotić, Dimitrije, 115
Luarasi, Petro Nini, 199, 200, 217

M
Makrides, Apostolos, 137
Marek, Pavel, 228, 230, 243, 244
Maxim of Lovech, Patriarch of Bulgaria, Metropolitan, 56
Methodius, Saint, 60, 66, 80, 224, 225, 227, 242
Michael III of Byzantium, Emperor, 225
Michal Dandár of Prague and of the Czech Lands, Archbishop, 236
Mihailo, Archbishop, 32
Mihailović, Draža, 86, 122
Milošević, Slobodan, 29, 31, 33, 91, 92, 118, 120–123, 126
Milovanović, Milija, 120
Misirkov, Petkov, 169
Mucha, Alfons, 225, 226

N
Năstase, Adrian, 46
Naum of Strumica, Metropolitan, 175

Nedić, Milan, 116, 122, 127
Negovani, Papa Kristo, 199
Neofit of Bulgaria, Patriarch, 76
Neubacher, Hermann, 116
Niebuhr, Richard, 188, 196
Nifon of Targoviste, Archbishop, 48
Nikolay of Plovdiv, Metropolitan, 62, 64, 78
Nikolić, Tomislav, 178

P
Pajaziti, Ali, 186, 195
Papandreou, George, 144, 145, 150
Pavle of Serbia, Patriarch, 88, 117, 118
Pejchinovich, Kiril, 169, 189
Perica, Vjekoslav, 172
Petar of Australia, Metropolitan, 175
Pomohaci, Cristian, 48
Popović, Justin, 4, 11
Pulevski, Georgi, 169
Putin, Vladimir, 33, 67, 71, 241

R
Radić, Radmila, 13, 94, 102–106
Radosavljević, Artemije, 104, 116
Rady, Martyn, 42, 50
Raikin, Spas T., 4, 12, 22, 37–39
Ramet, Sabrina P., 12–14, 37–39, 102–106, 109, 168, 182, 189, 190, 193, 194, 202, 209, 215, 243, 249, 250, 253, 254
Ranković, Aleksandar, 171
Rastislav (Ondřej Gent) of the Prešov and Slovakia Archdiocese, Archbishop, 230
Reshetnikov, Leonid, 58
Reshetnikova, Olga, 58, 76
Rexhepi, Sulejman, 186
Rockefeller, David, 121

Rosen, Rabbi David, 124
Rousseau, Jean-Jacques, 3
Rrok Mirdita, Archbishop, 203

S
Said, Edward, 18, 37
Samuel of Bulgaria, Tsar, 34
Sayer, Derek, 225, 243
Sebastianos, Greek Priest, 200
Sekelj, Laslo, 112, 126, 128, 129
Serafim (Sobolev), a Russian émigré hierarch, Archbishop, 57
Simeon Saxe-Coburg-Gotha, 62, 78
Simits, Costas, 145
Sinadinovski, Branislav, 185
Smith, Anthony D., 134, 156
Solov'ev, Vladimir, 4, 12
Sonnichsen, Albert, 21, 38
Spasenovski, Alexandar, 181, 193
Stalin, Joseph, 43, 59, 227, 242
Stamboliski, Aleksandar, 22
Stan, Lavinia, 7, 13, 14, 50, 51
Stark, Rodney, 111, 126
Stathopoulos, Michalis, 145
Stefan, Archbishop, 66, 67, 167, 172, 184, 188
Stephanopolous, Constantine, 146
Stephen the Great of Moldova, Prince, 43
Subotić, Jelena, 9, 102, 104
Sultan Mustafa III, 171
Svatopluk, Prince, 225

T
Tadić, Boris, 180
Taguieff, Pierre-André, 125, 129
Teoctist Arapasu of Romania, Patriarch, 44
Teodosij (Theodosius) (Vasil) Gologanov, 170

Theofan (Fan) Noli, Metropolitan, 200
Timotej of Debar and Kicevo, Metropolitan, 175
Tito, Josip Broz, 20, 25–28, 31
Todorova, Maria, 17, 37
Trajkovski, Boris, 172, 178
Tritsis, Antonis, 143
Tsipras, Alexis, 151
Turcescu, Lucian, 7, 11, 13, 14, 50, 51

V
Vajgl, Ivo, 186, 195
Venizelos, Eleftherios, 22, 141
Vukomanović, Milan, 13, 94, 103–106, 109

W
Ware, Timothy, 6, 11, 12, 14

Y
Yıldırım, Münir, 135, 157
Yoan of Varna, Metropolitan, 58

Z
Zaev, Zoran, 172, 182
Zaplatin, Viktor, 34
Zarevska, Radmila, 187
Zhivkov, Todor, 25

Printed by Printforce, the Netherlands